PLAYS AND PLAYERS.

BY

LAURENCE HUTTON.

Good my lord, will you see the players well bestowed? Do you hear, let them be well used; for they are the abstracts and brief chronicles of the time!

NEW YORK:
PUBLISHED BY HURD AND HOUGHTON.
1875.

RIVERSIDE, CAMBRIDGE:
PRINTED BY H. O. HOUGHTON AND COMPANY.

TO

JAMES S. WHITE,

AN OLDER VETERAN,

TO WHOM THE YOUNG VETERAN, IN HIS RECOLLECTIONS OF THE STAGE, OWES SO MUCH, THESE MEMORIES OF PLAYS AND PLAYERS IN NEW YORK ARE

AFFECTIONATELY INSCRIBED.

CONTENTS.

PLAYS AND PLAYERS.

CHAPTER I.

THE PROSE AND THE POETRY OF PLAY-BILLS. — THE PALMY DAYS OF THE DRAMATIC PAST.

"And tell old tales and laugh."
King Lear, Act V. Sc. 3.

POETS have never rhymed of old play bills, nor do minstrels sing of them. While the muse has been invoked, and often, on the subject of Old Times, Old Songs, Old Oaken Buckets, Old Folks at Home, and Old English Gentlemen all of the Olden School, eyes never seem to have rolled in frenzy over play-bills, nor have minstrels ever seemed to think them worthy of their song. There is music and poetry in old play-bills to us, however, and we handle them very tenderly, these faded, silent records of old friends and of old times; records of old friends with whom we have never exchanged a sentence in our lives, who have never even known of our existence or the good they have done us, but still old friends who were very real and very near to us in their day, who have afforded us much harmless pleasure and enjoyment, and who are still very pleasantly remembered.

No doubt it is but human nature, but blessings *do*

seem to brighten as they take their flight, and things and times, and plays and players, do seem better to us as we look back at them. Ten or twenty years ago, so it appears to us now, *prime donne* sang better than they do to-day, dramatists wrote better, players played better, society was purer, taxes were lower, and summers were not so hot. Men are always talking of the "palmy days" of the drama, always have talked of them, and always will; are always praising past excellence, preaching present degeneracy, and prophesying future demoralization.

In our "palmy days" long ago, which were not "palmy days" to us then, there were, we remember, plenty of old play-goers lamenting that theatres and the drama had declined since the "palmy days" of the "Park" years before; and ten or twenty years from this no doubt we will mourn, or those of us who live will mourn, for the "palmy days" of '74 and '75, and longing for a repetition of "The Shaughraun" and "The Sphinx;" will sigh as we think that there is no "old man" like John Gilbert left, nobody so funny as Harry Beckett, nobody so strong as Clara Morris, nobody so pretty as Sara Jewett on the stage. We trust, however, that Gilbert and Wallack, and Beckett and Jewett and Morris, and the many favorites of the present, may go with us into the future and sigh with us in '90 for the "palmy days" of to-day.

But those old play-bills of ours, we will take them from the traditional old desk and spread them out, and moralize over them. It may be a pleasure to us, and it certainly cannot do the player of the period any harm. How old-fashioned they look, and how yellow and time-stained they are; the very scent of the gallery hangs round them still, and we instinctively put our hand in our pocket for a peanut, as we read the familiar large type in which Burton and *Toodles* were announced. Was n't it *Grimaldi*, in the "Life of an Actress," who said, "Dere is no talent dat is talent, if it shall not be in big letters ?" We remember the twinkle in his eye as he hung up the poster, and added, "but dere is very little talent dat is as big as its letters!" No letters were ever too big to express the talent of Burton!

They only date back a score or so of years these old play-bills, but what happy, "palmy" scenes they recall!

BURTON'S CHAMBERS STREET, FRIDAY EVENING.
March 5, 1852.

Dress Circle, 50c.; Second Tier, 25c.; Private Boxes, Five Dollars ($5); Orchestra Chairs, with cushioned seats, 75c. each. Doors open at half-past 6; to begin at 7 o'clock.

All that sounds "palmy" enough!

Mr. Burton as *Sleek* and the *Mummy*. This evening will be played the never-tiring comedy, in three acts, of the "Serious Family."

Captain Murphy Maguire	J. W. Lester.
Charles Torrens	Bland.
Frank Vincent	Levere.
Aminadab Sleek	Burton.
Servant	Lawson.
Lady Sowerby Creamly	Mrs. Hughes.
The Widow Delmaine (first time) . . .	Miss Weston.
Mrs. Charles Torrens	Miss Mary Taylor.
Emma Torrens	Miss E. Taylor.

In the piece the celebrated "Serious Family Polka," the most popular dance of the day, will be performed by sixteen ladies and gentlemen.

This was followed by the "J. J.'s," "second Time," with Blake, Lester, Fisk, Mrs. Holman, Mrs. Rea, and Miss Fisher in the cast; then a "Pas de Deux Provençal" by Mr. Frederic and Miss Malvina; the whole to conclude with the very laughable farce of "The Mummy." "*Toby Tramp*, a travelling tragedian, afterwards the *Mummy*, Mr. Burton."

They gave us a good deal for our fifty cents in those days.

We find Mr. Burton, in July of the same year, 1852, playing in "Toodles," and "The Mummy," at Niblo's Garden. "*Toodles*, originally played by him at the various theatres in America over four hundred nights, Mr. Burton." We might as well try to paint the rainbow as describe Burton's *Toodles*. No one who ever saw it will ever forget it, and no one who never saw it can ever conceive it! In this cast were Mr. Howard, Russel, Gourley, and Levere; Parsloe played *Lawyer Glib*, Mrs. Skerrett was *Mary Acorn*, and Mrs. Dyott played *Mrs. Toodles*. Signor La Manna was leader of the orchestra, that "man in the middle," whom John Brougham a few years later, in his famous "Pocahontas," at Wallack's Theatre, addressed as "that harmonious Italian, La Manna, come rosin your bow!" John Sefton was stage manager. Mr. Burton played Tuesdays and Thursdays, always to crowded houses. The other nights were called "ballet nights," — Señorita Soto in Spanish dances, Mlle. Pougaud, and other Sangallis and Bonfantis of that day, no doubt capering and pirouetting into public favor, whose very names now are almost forgotten. Such is stage fame. And all the world 's a stage!

The Roussett sisters, who danced on Niblo's stage this season (we find them playing alternate nights with Mme. Anna Thillon in June, 1852), were deservedly popular. Adelaide Roussett's benefit is underlined on the bill of Mme. Thillon's "Enchantress" for Thursday, June 3, and also "Positively the last nights of the Wonderful Caroline and her Three Sisters." Madame Thillon, if we remember rightly, was new to the New York stage at that time. Her *Stella* was charming, and her engagement a success. She was supported by a Mr. Hudson — in "big letters" — of whom we have no recollection, unless he be the good-looking Irish Hudson so popular in his day in Hibernian parts.

Here is another old bill of that same season at Niblo's, — a bill calling itself "a great bill:" —

MONDAY, JULY 5, 1852.
THE DAY WE CELEBRATE!
NATIONAL ANTHEM AT EIGHT O'CLOCK.
To be followed by the "Eaton Boy."

Captain Popham	J. Wallack Lester.
The Eaton Boy	Mrs. John Drew.
Dabster	John Drew.
Sally	Mr. Conover.

Then followed a ballet. After which "Sketches in India," with Lester, Blake, Howard, Rea, Mrs. Drew, Mrs. Blake, and Miss Hosmer in the cast. Then still more ballet, and "the whole to conclude with a Great Spanish Pas de Deux by Soto and Mons. Mege.

On the 15th of June of the same year, at the Lyceum Theatre, Broadway, near Broome Street, is announced, for the benefit of M. Robert Kemp, "Elle est Folle," in which "Mrs. Catherine Sinclair, formerly Mrs. Forrest, will give her first performance in the French language, and make her last appearance before her departure for Europe." "The orchestra chairs and private boxes will be sold at auction at the theatre on the morning of the performance!" This was the last time, we think, that Mrs. Forrest appeared on the New York stage. Her career here was short. She made her *debut* early in 1852, just after the settlement of the famous Forrest divorce suit in her favor. She was very successful, drawing great houses, but perhaps more on account of the interest in her domestic troubles than of any decided histrionic talent she may have possessed. The particulars of this French essay of hers we cannot recall at the present writing, nor have we any recollection of the M. Robert Kemp, for whose benefit the essay was made.

We have kept until the last the bill of an entertainment which, not even excepting "Toodles" and the "Serious Family," is the most agreeable on which we now look back. Of all the scenes of our childhood sweet to our heart, by far the sweetest were the scenes enacted by the Ravels on the stage at Niblo's and at Castle Garden. Castle Garden for their sakes was one of the loved spots that our infancy knew, and even yet for their sakes do we hold the emigrant sheds in the tenderest regard. "Castle Garden. Extra Grand Gala Night. September 2d, 1852. Benefit of the Ravel Family, forty in number, and positively their last appearance. Admission to all parts of the house, fifty cents! To begin at 7.30."

We were on hand with our silver quarter, saved for the occasion, children half price, long before the doors opened! There was "The Soldier for Love," and the "Coopers," with François, Antoine, Gabriel, and Jerome Ravel, the Marzettis, Martinettis, and Paul Brillant in capers and "conductions," exploits and "feats," the like of which we will never see again. The days of the Ravels were "palmy days." There are no more Ravels nor Marzettis nor Martinettis nor Brillants left, and none to fill their places. Blondin, we notice, was one of the "family" then, and the entertainments began with wonderful achievements on the tight rope by M. Blondin and François Ravel. Now Blondin is "starring" it alone through the world, over Niagaras, and with no "support" but the cable under him, and his own magnificent nerve.

The changes that death and time have made in the "profession" since the days of which we write are many. Of the great cast of the "Serious Family," given above, only one actor is now left to the New York stage, Lester Wallack. Bland, the best *Jacques* of his day, Burton, and Emma Taylor, are dead. Mary Taylor retired the following year, and Mrs. Hughes, like whom there has been seen no "old lady" since, took her farewell of the stage some time ago full of years and honor. We have never heard of her death. If still living she must be more than eighty years of age. The Miss Weston, afterwards Mrs. "Dolly" Davenport, is the present Mrs. Charles Mathews. She made her first appearance here in thirteen years on the 29th of May, 1871, at the Fifth Avenue Theatre, in the "Comical Countess," for the benefit of her husband, and played but one week. The Miss Malvina, who danced at Burton's in 1852, was Miss Malvina Pray, now Mrs. William J. Florence. Of the other artists of whom we have spoken, Mrs. Drew is now lessee of the Arch Street Theatre in Philadelphia, and is much respected in the city of brotherly love. Madame Thillon, at last accounts, was teaching music in England. The Ravels, if still living, are in retirement in France, and Blake, John Drew, John Sefton, La Manna, Paul Brillant, and Marzetti have each "finished his mortal act."

CHAPTER II.

A FORMER GENERATION OF ACTORS. — "THE SCHOOL FOR SCANDAL." — SOMETHING OF ITS HISTORY IN NEW YORK. — ITS STRONG CASTS.

"Our old acquaintance of this isle."
Othello, Act II., Sc. 1.

THE Poet at the Breakfast Table, whose happy faculty of saying the happiest things in the happiest way has become proverbial, remarks that the graveyard and the stage are the only places where we can expect to find our friends as we left them, five-and-twenty years ago; and adds that old theatre-goers bring back the past with their stories more vividly than men with any other experiences. Of the truth of this latter statement it is for our readers to judge. We only hope that our recollections bring back the past half as vividly and agreeably to you in reading, as they do to us in writing them.

That among living people, however, none remain so long unchanged as the actors, the presence on our boards to-day of players of both sexes who, five-and-twenty and even more years ago, pleased our fathers and our younger selves in the same parts in which they please us now, is proof undeniable. John Brougham played *O' Callaghan* in "His Last Legs" in New York in 1842, with the same rich brogue and in the same rollicking, happy, devil-may-care Irish way that is peculiarly his to-day. Jo. Jefferson is said to have played juvenile parts thirty-five years ago, and his first appearance on the stage as a young man was made in 1849. E. L. Davenport played *Romeo* in 1846. Where is there to-day a better or more artistic Romeo than his? Mr. Davidge played *Sir Peter Teazle* at the Broadway Theatre in 1850.

Miss Jean Margaret Davenport Lander, still one of the most acceptable and thoroughly artistic of our actresses, was playing in New York so long ago as 1838 in child's parts, and ten years later was recognized on our boards as a star of great promise in the same leading characters, which she fills to-day with more excellence than many of her younger rivals. Miss Charlotte Cushman played *Lady Macbeth* and *Meg Merrilies* here, in 1837, thirty-seven years ago. Madame Anna Bishop, in 1847, first sang in New York, and sings here still. Lester Wallack, the freshest, most dashing, youngest of young men of the present, played *Charles Surface* in the "School for Scandal" twenty-eight years ago, probably the best *Charles Surface* then in America, as he is, without question, now. Mrs. E. L. Davenport played *Margaret Elmore* in 1854; she is now almost as young as her daughter. Mrs. John Wood, in 1856, was as charming in *Hiawatha*, as she is in *Pocahontas* to-day. How many changes have these players seen in men and things; how little changed are they themselves!

The Autocrat might have said, and truly, that dramatic literature, like dramatic people, is longer lived, longer retains the flavor of its youth, than any other. Even the comedies and tragedies of the divine William himself, are certainly better known, more familiar in our mouths as household words, because they *are* comedies and tragedies, than if the same grand thoughts, sentiments, and ideas had been given to the world in any other form. The fact that the acting plays are most familiar to us is proof of this. And so it is with writers of later days. Goldsmith's "Vicar of Wakefield" is perhaps the work to which his name is most frequently attached, but his "She Stoops to Conquer" is certainly to-day the better known, and on the comedy will his fame in after years rest. We read or pretend to read the book because we think it is "the thing" to do, but how many of us have read it through, or more than once, while how often do we see and enjoy the play, — the satisfaction it gives when well played being as great the tenth time as the first or second! *Tony Lumpkin* is destined to live long after Moses is forgotten.

No work of fiction, no literary work of any kind of its day, has retained its place in popular favor, not only among the comparatively uneducated, but among students of the literature of the last century themselves, so decidedly as Sheridan's "School for Scandal." It has outlived its contemporary novels of Smollett and Fielding, and even the solid works of Johnson, and will, no doubt, outlive the more pretentious works, dramatic or otherwise, of these our later times. The best of comedies, a standard play wherever the English language is spoken and played, it has been on the stage for a hundred years, and is as fresh and sparkling, as full of wit, wisdom, satire, and human nature now as when first produced.

Written by Sheridan when a young man, not more than twenty-six years of age, "The School for Scandal," and "The Rivals," are almost the only works that attest his greatness; although he was at one period of his existence the most gifted genius of his time. Of surpassing eloquence, the rival of Pitt and Burke and Fox, more famous as an orator, a statesman, and a wit, than as a playwright in his own day, almost wholly by his plays is he known in ours. *Sir Peter*, *Mrs. Sneerwell*, *Joseph Surface*, were his greatest creations, however, and it was jestingly said of him, after this comedy had established his reputation, that he was always afraid of the author of the "School for Scandal." He certainly wrote nothing later that equalled it.

The "School for Scandal" was first produced at Drury Lane Theatre, London, in 1777, although not printed for some time after, and at once achieved the popularity it has since maintained.

Its prologue was written by Garrick, who had then retired from the stage. The epilogue usually spoken by *Lady Teazle* was from the pen of Colman; but prologue and epilogue, both of considerable merit, are rarely spoken now. It is said that we possess no printed copy of this play authenticated by its author. The copy usually followed was printed in Ireland in 1788, and although said to be incorrect, has, doubtless, greater pretensions to "authority" than any other.

The "School for Scandal" was first played in New York, and probably for the first time in America, at the John Street Theatre, 16th December, 1785. The cast, as preserved to us, contains, of course, no names familiar to the play-goers of to-day. It has been represented here undoubtedly more frequently than any other play, and on many occasions with the very best talent this country has ever seen in its cast. A history of the "School for Scandal" on the New York stage, is almost a complete history of the New York stage itself, so thoroughly is it identified with the drama here. Among the most famous of its casts, to come down to a "period within the memory of men still living," was the following at Brougham's Lyceum, February 7, 1852, when the principal parts were thus filled: —

Sir Peter Teazle	W. H. Chippendale.
Crabtree	Skerrett.
Joseph Surface	C. Mason.
Charles Surface	Walcot.
Sir Benjamin Backbite	Brougham.
Trip	Florence.
Lady Teazle	Mrs. Catherine N. Sinclair.
Mrs. Candour	Mrs. Maeder.
Maria	Mrs. Conover.

Mr. Chippendale was at that time the manager of the Lyceum, the best and most effective actor of old men's emotional parts in his day, dividing always the honors with the leading "juvenile parts." The year following the *début* of Miss Sinclair (Mrs. Edwin Forrest) was the worst ever known financially to New York managers, the Lyceum often playing to less than two hundred dollar "houses." Mr. Chippendale shortly after went to London, to assume the duties of manager of the Haymarket, a position which we believe he still holds. There has never been a better *Crabtree* on this stage than Mr. Skerrett's. The part seemed to have been made for him, and he for the part. Mrs. Skerrett (his wife), the most youthful of the "old school" of actresses left to us, survives him, and still essays "juvenile business." Charles Kemble Mason, the *Joseph*, was good in most parts, not great in any; he was the strong point, however, during Mrs. Forrest's engagement, which was about his own last really successful engagement in New York. Charles Walcot, the elder Walcot, was an excellent *Charles Surface*, as he was excellent in everything. The *Trip* was the William J. Florence so well known to us of the present, who in those days had not attained anything better than second or third "walking gentleman." Mrs. Maeder and Mrs. Conover were to the stage at that time, what Mrs. Gilbert and Mrs. Chanfrau are in this: "most excellent accomplished ladies."

"The School for Scandal" with an unusually strong cast, was given for the benefit of the family of Manager Simpson, of the Park Theatre, at that famous old house on the 7th December, 1848, just one week before its total destruction by fire. The following great artists played in the principal parts: —

Sir Peter Teazle	Mr. Henry Placide.
Sir Oliver Surface	Mr. Wm. E. Burton.
Joseph Surface	Mr. Thomas Barry.
Charles Surface	Mr. George Barrett.
Crabtree	Mr. W. R. Blake.
Sir Benjamin Backbite	Mr. Peter Ritchings.
Careless	Mr. C. M. Walcot.
Sir Harry	Mr. H. Hunt.
Moses	Mr. John Povey.
Trip	Mr. Dawson.
Lady Teazle	Mrs. Shaw.
Lady Sneerwell	Mrs. John Gilbert.
Mrs. Candour	Mrs. Winstanley.
Maria	Miss Mary Taylor.

Of this company, so far as we can remember now, only Mr. Thomas Barry, who is still living in Boston, and Mrs. Winstanley, of whose death we have never heard, are left to us.

We give below a cast of the "School for Scandal," as played at Laura Keene's in the fall of 1858, which will be remembered by many of our readers, and which was uncommonly strong: —

Sir Peter	W. R. Blake.
Sir Oliver	J. G. Burnett.
Joseph Surface	Couldock.
Charles Surface	E. A. Sothern.
Crabtree	Joseph Jefferson.
Sir Benjamin Backbite	Chas. Peters.
Lady Teazle	Laura Keene.
Lady Sneerwell	Mary Wells.
Mrs. Candour	Mrs. Wm. R. Blake.
Maria	Sara Stevens.

Mr. Blake was probably the best *Sir Peter* we ever had in America. Mr. Burnett, who will be better remembered by the present generation of theatre-goers as the original *Von Puffengruntz* of the "Black Crook," was a very good *Sir Oliver*. Sothern and Jefferson, as *Charles* and *Crabtree*, were very satisfactory, although their most decided hits were still to be made, and in this season and at this theatre, in the original "Our American Cousin." Sara Stevens made a very pretty *Maria*, and Laura Keene as *Lady Teazle*, appeared to much better advantage than when we last saw her play one scene, in this part, to the *Sir Peter* of Mr. John Jack at Niblo's Garden, on the occasion of a benefit to Matilda Heron, given in January, 1872.

Mrs. D. P. Bowers is one of the best living *Lady Teazles*, although no finer perhaps than her sister, Mrs. Conway of Brooklyn, who has played it on more than one occasion, if we remember rightly, to the *Sir Peter* of Blake. Miss Henriques enacted the part very prettily, and Mrs. Hoey — in her time — excellently well. She played it at Burton's Theatre in 1850 (she was then known as Mrs. Russell) to Blake's *Sir Peter*. Burton was *Sir Oliver;* Bland, *Joseph;* Lester Wallack, *Charles;* Johnstone, *Crabtree*, and George Jordan,

Sir Benjamin. Mr. Harry Placide was very happy in the part of *Sir Peter*, but take him for all in all, we do not recall now a better than John Gilbert; his personation of the testy, disappointed, uxorious, but high-minded and forgiving old Baronet, is almost faultless. John Brougham is the best living *Sir Oliver*, we think; Chas. Fisher the best "*Moshes;*" Wallack, as we have said, the best *Charles Surface;* Miss Fanny Morant the best *Mrs. Candour.*

This comedy at the Prince of Wales' Theatre in London, during the seasons of '72, '73, and '74, enjoyed a run of many hundreds of nights, the house presenting nothing else in the London "season," and out of it, for two years. Such a success of the work of a man who belonged to a past century and who was not a theatrical manager in this, is without parallel in the history of the stage in any country, which speaks well for England's appreciation of the standard drama, and which is another laurel in Sheridan's crown.

A version of this comedy, called the "Prince of Wales' version," and the same as played at the Prince of Wales' Theatre in London (differing from other versions in but few respects and these unimportant), was presented by Mr. Daly at his Fifth Avenue Theatre in New York in the fall of 1874, and was very successful. Mr. Davidge was the *Sir Oliver;* Mr. Fisher for the first time played *Sir Peter* and Miss Fanny Davenport made a decided hit as *Lady Teazle.*

The "School for Scandal" has been put upon our stage so often, so handsomely and so strongly cast, that we might almost fill a book the size of this with an account of it. No other play, probably, has ever seen so many remarkable representations, no other play certainly has seen stronger combinations of talent in its cast. One of the finest of the later performances of this comedy was given at the Academy of Music here for the poor of New York, on the 19th of March, 1874, when Mr. Gilbert played *Sir Peter*, Mr. Brougham *Sir Oliver*, Mr. Fisher *Joseph*, Mr. Lester Wallack *Charles*, Mr. Davidge *Crabtree*, Mr. Harry Beckett *Moses*, Mr. E. Arnott *Careless*, Mr. Whiting *Rowley*, Mr. George L. Fox *Trip*, Mr. Louis James *Sir Benjamin*, Miss Fanny Morant *Lady Candour*, Mme. Ponisi *Lady Sneerwell*, Miss Dora Goldthwaite *Maria*, and Miss Madeline Henriques, who came out of a long retirement for the purpose, *Lady Teazle*.

Five years previous, for the benefit of John Brougham, May 19th, 1869, the "School for Scandal" was given at Niblo's Garden, with a cast so immensely strong that we cannot resist giving it in full, not stronger perhaps than some of the others we have mentioned above, but so it seemed to us at the time and so it is remembered as we look back at it now, taking it all in all, the finest and most perfect dramatic entertainment which it has ever been our good fortune to witness.

Sir Peter Teazle	Mr. John Gilbert.
Charles Surface	Mr. Edwin Adams.
Joseph Surface	Mr. Neil Warner.
Sir Oliver Surface	Mr. John Brougham.
Sir Benjamin Backbite	Mr. Owen Marlowe.
Crabtree	Mr. A. W. Young.
Moses	Mr. Harry Beckett.
Snake	Mr. F. Rea.
Careless	Mr. J. W. Collier.
Rowley	Mr. T. Hind.
Trip	Mr. J. C. Williamson.
Sir Harry Bumper (with song)	Mr. R. Green.

Joseph's servant	Mr. J. W. Leonard.
Lady Sneerwell's servant	Mr. G. F. Maeder.
Lady Teazle	Mrs. D. P. Bowers.
Mrs. Candour	Miss Fanny Morant.
Lady Sneerwell	Mrs. John Sefton.
Maria	Miss Pauline Markham.

Niblo's was crowded at this matinee performance with the most brilliantly critical and intellectual audience it has ever seen; and the 19th of May, 1869, we will always recall as *the* "palmy day" *par excellence* of all of the palmy days in our recollections of the stage.

2

CHAPTER III.

THE OLD OLYMPIC. — WILLIAM MITCHELL. — HIS SUCCESSES. — HIS STRONG COMPANIES. — HIS MANY NEW PLAYS.

"The thunder-darter of Olympus."
Troilus and Cressida, Act II. Sc. 3.

THE Old Olympic is but a dream in these days, and even its once familiar "whereabouts" is now almost forgotten. Very few of the play-goers of the present can tell where the Old Olympic stood. On Broadway, of course, and down Broadway, of course; but how far down, and where? And yet even a young veteran can remember when the Olympic — a spot synonymous with all that is bright and sparkling and merry and tender and good in the drama — was as well known in New York as is Niblo's or Booth's to-day.

Many modern play-goers confound the present with the original Olympic, and refer to the glorious seasons of Laura Keene, when the "American Cousin," the "Seven Sisters," and other *kindred* plays were first produced, as *the* palmy days of *the* Olympic. Strange as it may seem, we venture the assertion that not one in a thousand of our readers, not even those claiming a thorough knowledge of New York's development, can answer the question as to its locality, or give even a faint idea of its history. And yet from the time of the rise and progress of the Olympic we date so many of the happiest memories of plays and players, so many of the best and most finished of our old actors, of both sexes, and of every branch of the profession, owe their first success to the Olympic, so many of the most popular and most meritorious of our dramas, comedies, and burlesques were first produced on its boards, that we deem it essential that they should at least receive a passing word from us here, serving, as they do, as a prologue to our entire reminiscences.

Early in the year 1837, on the east side of Broadway near Howard Street, was laid the foundation-stone of the original Olympic; and early in the fall of the same year was opened to the public this perfect little gem of a theatre, the equal of which for coziness, compactness, and completeness, had never before been seen in New York, — and, we may add, as we remember it in its later years, has hardly been seen here since. Small, snug, bright, comfortable, it was all that a theatre should be; its interior presenting more the appearance of the home of an elegant lady in its refined and tasteful surroundings, than of the mere regulation tinsel-ornamented "home of the drama."

Mr. Blake we believe, was the originator of the proposition to build the Olympic, while Henry E. Willard and his friends were the financial authors of its existence. The fittings and furnishings of the house introduced for the first time in America all that was new in the London theatres, and some fine stage effects were produced. The narrowness of the building prevented the use of "flats," and confined the entire scenic display to "drops," a fashion that has been adopted from choice by the builders of some of our modern and more pretentious houses.

The first season of the new house was not a successful

one, although in the stock company were George Barrett, — "Gentleman George," — Mr. Blake himself, as the stage manager, Mrs. Blake, Mr. Nickinson, Mrs. Hughes, and Mr. Kirby, afterwards the great Kirby, — the wrap-me-up-in-the-American-flag Kirby, the East Side favorite, the Kirby whose very name has become proverbial for all that is decidedly blood-and-thundery in the melo-dramatic school in this country, the-wake-me-up-when-Kirby-dies Kirby, the news-boys' idol, the beloved hero of the pit. We may mention also, in passing, that during the first season of this house was for the first time produced in New York the drama of the "Last Man," with Mr. Blake as *Geoffrey Dale.*

In all our experiences of theatre-going, we do not remember any other piece of character-acting so terribly earnest and powerful as this. *Geoffrey Dale* became in Blake's hands an intensified reality; and so completely were actor and audience in unison, that heart-beatings were almost audible in the house during the last scene of the play. Mr. Blake played the "Last Man" for the last time in New York, at Laura Keene's Theatre in 1863, an occasion we remember well, and only a few days before we heard of his own untimely death. No actor, so far as we know, has had the courage to assume the part of *Geoffrey Dale* since Mr. Blake made it so entirely his own in this country, either during his lifetime or since his decease.

As an interesting reminiscence of Mr. Blake's career, and for the purpose, too, of showing the strength of the company of the Olympic this first winter of its existence, we transcribe here the original cast in New York, of

"THE LAST MAN."

OCT. 9, 1837.

Geoffrey Dale (the Miser)	Mr. Wm. R. Blake.
Henry Wentworth (a City Blade)	Mr. Corey.
Major Battergate (of The Brothers' Club) .	Mr. W. Jones.
Lawyer Weaver (from London)	Mr. Weston.
Jacob Codling (the Miser's Man)	Mr. Nickinson.
Henry Dare } (Ruffians. Alice Gurton's	{ Mr. Thoman.
David Dare } Nephews)	{ J. H. Kirby.
Lucy Dale (the Miser's Niece)	Mrs. Conway.
Alice Gurton (Old Maid of Eltham) . .	Mrs. W. Jones.
Barbara Gay (Pretty Maid of Kent)	Mrs. Blake.

Mr. Blake left the concern about the 1st of January, 1838, and the house soon passed out of the hands of Mr. Willard. It was opened successively by Mr. D. D. Kinney, and by Elder Addams, the actor, lecturer, poet, tailor, and Mormon preacher, but never with anything like success until it came into the hands of Mr. Wm. Mitchell in 1839.

We find on reference to the play-bills of that date — to an old collection of which we are indebted for many of our facts and hints of time and place in the early drama in New York, — that this house was doing business as a low-price theatre, with admission to boxes fifty and twenty-five cents, and to the pit a shilling. It will be remembered by the oldest of our inhabitants that, following the financial crash of 1837–38, the dramatic business, like every other business, was dismally bad; a black cloud seemed to hang over the theatres which no "Star" could successfully shine through, and there seemed to be no bow promising future prosperity. Realities were stern indeed with the people, and all entertainments depending upon popular support were affected by the general gloom. The Olympic opened with burlettas and musical travesties, to which the despondent came, and at which the despondent laughed, and continued to come and to laugh, until the Olympic became the fashion. During this and the following season were introduced at this house some of the most intense jokes that are recorded in dramatic history.

It was here that Dr. Northall perpetrated his erratic travesty "Macbeth," and here the "Magic Arrow," "Virginius Travestie," "King Cole," "The Roof Scrambler," "Sam Parr," "The Humpback," "Cats in the Larder," "Mrs. Normer," "Mephistophiles," "Richard No. Three," "The Revolt of the Poor-house," "Cinderella," and scores of other burlesque attractions were first produced, and with a company which was regarded in those days as being wonderfully strong. On the bills of the Olympic, during the ten or twelve years of Mitchell's connection with it, we find the names of Mrs. Watts (now Mrs. John Sefton), of Miss Singleton, of Mr. Edwin, who died in 1842; of James Henry Horncastle, who died in England in 1869; of John Nickinson, who died in Cincinnati in 1864; of George Graham, who died in Boston in 1847; of Mrs. Timm, who died in New York in 1854; of Henry Russell, the original *Savage* in the "Savage and the Maiden;" of Miss Clara Roberts; of George Loder, leader of the orchestra, who died in Australia in 1867; of Mrs. Loder, his wife, who died in San Francisco in 1855; of Mr. James Dunn; of Mr. Charles Walcot, who died in Philadelphia in 1868; of Miss Mary Taylor, who died in New York in 1866; of Miss Constantia Clarke, who died in New York in 1853; of George Holland, who died here in 1870; of Mr. Conover, who died in 1851; of Mr. Chanfrau, who at this house first played *Mose;* of Wm. Reynolds, who was drowned at Keyport in 1863; of Miss Gannon, who died in New York in 1868; of Miss Fanny Herring; and of Mitchell himself, who died in New York May 12, 1856.

Mr. Mitchell first opened the Olympic on the 9th December, 1839, and retired abruptly from its management on the 9th of March, 1850. Mr. Mitchell's career was eventful and "checkered." He was born in England toward the close of the last century. He was brought to this country by Mr. Willard, then manager of the National Theatre, Leonard Street, corner of Church, in 1836, and made his American *debut* there on the 29th August as *Jem Baggs*, in "The Wandering Minstrel." His last days were not prosperous or happy; his friends were preparing a "Complimentary Testimonial" for him in the spring of 1856, in order to give him the pecuniary aid which he absolutely needed, but he passed out of the reach of benefits before the arrangements were completed.

Personally as a manager he was popular, his bearing was manly and courteous to all with whom, in a business and social way, he came in contact; he was straightforward in his dealings with men, was possessed of tact and a seeming innate knowledge of everything that was promising of success in a player or a play.

As an actor himself, Mr. Mitchell was in his line almost inimitable, at all events so say old play-goers who remember him and his representations of such parts as *Jem Baggs* and *Crummles;* he could "make up" the most irresistibly funny faces ever seen on the New York or any other stage, and he was the only manager who ever dared to make his entire audience members, so to speak, of his stock company. To the pit he was never known to appeal without meeting with its entire approbation; were his auditors there uproarious he would chide; did they appreciate a "point" he would make manifest his own appreciation of their applause. He would stop suddenly in the midst of a scene from "Macbeth," and marching down to the foot-lights would say, with the utmost seriousness, that "If any boy in the pit thought he could do that any better he might come on to the stage and try!" The effect upon the boys in the pit can be imagined. Not only the pit but the whole house "came down" at this, although no boy was ever known to go on the stage to try.

There seemed to be a perfect sympathy between Mitchell and his audiences, and the habitual visitor to the Olympic cannot remember an occasion when the desire to please on the part of the performer did not meet with the ready and cordial approval of the house, or when any shortcoming or disability was not as cordially and as readily overlooked or forbearingly borne. To this sympathy and fellow feeling may be ascribed much of Mitchell's success, for prosper at that time he and the Olympic did, and to the eight or nine years of his management do the old play-goers refer when they speak of "the palmy days of the Olympic."

During Mitchell's management the theatre was noted for the number of successful new plays produced. It was here that the town first laughed over the "Savage and the Maiden," a sketch founded on Nicholas Nickleby's dramatic experiences, when Mr. Mitchell's *Crummles* was regarded as "side-splitting" as Burton's *Toodles*, while his burlesque *Hamlet* had as many amused admirers as Fox's *Hamlet*, so heartily enjoyed at the present Olympic a season or two ago. Wherever the "legitimate" was struggling with any show of success, Mr. Mitchell seems to have been immediately at its heels with a burlesque performance that attracted as much attention as the original, and not infrequently appears to have added to the success of the travestied as well as of the travesty itself. Mr. Mitchell placed novelty, genteel and low comedy, so rapidly before the public, new play followed new play so quickly at his house, that his company was probably the hardest worked that the stage has ever known.

That our readers may fully comprehend how prominent a place in dramatic history this same old Olympic occupies, we will say that old note-books record the first representations here, under Mitchell's management, of two hundred and thirty dramatic productions, classified as nearly as possible as follows: Farces, one hundred and nineteen; burlettas, eleven; comediettas, four; operas, seven; burlesques, fifteen; sketches, thirty; extravaganzas, sixteen; comedies, thirteen; ballets, seven; and travesties, eight; these being entirely new plays, that were first produced on any stage at this house.

The names of many of these last we have given above. The cast of a few plays at the Olympic, during the several seasons, we reproduce here as likely to interest the rising generation, and as subjects of pleasant reminiscence to the generation that is passing away.

Dr. Northall's "Macbeth" was first produced on the 16th October, 1843; it met with decided success at once, and drew great houses for almost a month, and this too in times of novelty and of short "runs." Mr. Mitchell's *Macbeth*, semi-comic, semi-tragic, semi-

Mitchell and semi-Macready, "took" amazingly, and is said to have been very funny.

The principal parts of the "Tragedy" were thus filled: —

Macbeth	Mr. Mitchell.
Macduff	George Graham.
Banquo	Mr. Clarke.
Duncan	Mr. Everard.
Fleance	Master Taylor.
Hecate	Miss Mary Taylor.
First Witch	Mr. Nickinson.
Second Witch	Mrs. Watts.
Third Witch	Miss Clarke.
Lady Macbeth	Mrs. J. B. Booth, Jr.
Gentlewoman	Mrs. Everard.

The Mrs. J. B. Booth, Jr., *née* Miss de Bar, was a clever actress with a sweet voice, and a great favorite with Olympic audiences. Her *Lady Macbeth* was considered as a fit companion picture to Mr. Mitchell's *Thane.*

Mr. Planché's "Captain of the Watch" was first produced on the 26th December, 1842, cast as follows: —

Viscount de Ligny	Mr. C. M. Walcot.
Baron Vanderpotter	Mr. Nickinson.
Adolf de Courtray	Mr. Clarke.
Officer of the Watch	Mr. Barnett.
Kristina	Mrs. Mossop.
Katryn	Mrs. Timm.

Mr. Walcot as the *Viscount* made a great hit; it was an exceedingly natural and effective performance, but has since been rivalled by the representation of the same part by Mr. Lester Wallack, who first played it in 1847, at the Old Broadway, his second part in this country.

"The Devil in Paris" was presented on the 3d of February, 1845, cast as follows: —

Count Vanille	Mr. Walcot.
Count Beausoliel	Fenno.
De Plumet	Mr. Nickinson.
Crequet	Mr. Holland.
Chicore	Mr. De Bar.
* * * * * (The Devil in Paris)	Miss Mary Taylor.
Mlle. de Nantelle	Miss Clarke.
Mme. de Luceval	Mrs. Hardwick.
Madeline	Miss Roberts.
Mme. de Sericourt	Mrs.Barnett.

In this play Miss Taylor made one of her first successes. It was almost as popular as her *Lize*, a few seasons later, in the now famous "Glance at New York," first presented in 1848. We give its cast: —

Mose	Mr. Frank Chanfrau.
Jake	Mr. W. Conover.
Morton	Mr. Henry.
Harry Gordon	Mr. Arnold.
Charles Parselle	Mr. Clarke.
Sykesy	Mr. James Seymour.
Mrs. Morton	Mrs. Henry.
Mary	Miss Matilda Phillips.
Jane	Miss Roberts.
Lize	Miss Mary Taylor.
Jenny Bogert	Miss Barber.

With the cast of one more play we close this chapter on the Olympic and its career. Of the many names we have mentioned as figuring on the bills of the Olympic, Mr. Chanfrau's and Mrs. Sefton's are almost the only ones that are seen on New York bills to-day. We find the former in this same year, 1848, playing *Jerry Clip* in the "Widow's Victim," with the following support: —

Mr. Twitter (a married gentleman, extremely irritable, extremely imaginative, and extremely jealous)	Mr. Arnold.
Mr. Byron Tremaine (a single gentleman, extremely polite, extremely fashionable, and extremely nervous)	Mr. Geo. Holland.
Jeremiah Clip (a barber's clerk, and amateur actor, extremely imitative, extremely useful, and extremely impudent) . . .	Mr. Chanfrau.
Tinsel John (a livery servant, extremely intrusive, extremely familiar, and extremely annoying)	Mr. Chanfrau.
Moustache Strappado (a mysterious foreigner, extremely ferocious, extremely melo-dramatic, and extremely pantomimical)	Mr. Chanfrau.
Mrs. Rattleton (a young widow, extremely handsome, extremely accomplished, and extremely irresistible)	Mrs. Sherwood.
Mrs. Twitter (a married lady, extremely amiable, extremely forgiving, and extremely affectionate)	Miss Roberts.
Jane Chatterley (a lady's maid and companion, extremely sensitive, extremely literary, and extremely affectionate) . .	Mrs. Timm.

A glance at the cast of characters in the "Widow's Victim," and the "extremely" strong descriptive adjectives employed, will give one a very fair idea of the nature of the farce. *Jeremiah Clip* was a stage-struck barber. The part was a favorite part with Mr. Burton, and being what in these days is termed on the bills a "protean part," it gave its representatives full scope for the indulgence of versatile powers, and of caricaturish imitations of the prominent actors of the time. As *Jerry Clip* and as *Mose*, Mr. Chanfrau made his first successes. They drew him out of the comparative obscurity of his satelituous course round the planets of the Olympic and other stock companies, and sent him careering about in an orbit of his own, as a full-fledged "Star." Always popular in New York, Mr. Chanfrau added greatly to his popularity and his brightness when he became a double star, and for no "transit" does New York look forward more eagerly and pleasantly than for that of Chanfrau and his wife.

As to how much Mr. Chanfrau is indebted to Mr. Mitchell for his present prosperity as an actor we will not say. It was quite a common sentiment in the days of Mitchell that Mitchell *made* the brilliant people who first became prominent at his theatre. We hold ourself that actors are not made at all, but are born; and if anybody did make Chanfrau we are inclined to think he made himself, as did Miss Mary Taylor, Miss Clarke, and other shining lights who first shone at the Olympic. Nevertheless if Mitchell was not the "Father of Genius," he was its nurse, while the Olympic was its cradle, and on this account should the memory of the Old Olympic and of Mitchell be kindly cherished in New York.

CHAPTER IV.

MISS MARY TAYLOR. — MISS EMMA TAYLOR.

"'T was a goodly lady, 't was a goodly lady."
All's Well, Act IV. Sc. 5

AMONG the so many artists most excellent and commendable in their nature whom the records and reminiscences of the Old Olympic note and recall, it is difficult indeed to particularize individual merit. Among so many choice and master spirits of that age, who are so fondly and so kindly remembered in this, it is by no means an easy task to select any one spirit, or any few spirits, whom we can call the choicest. There is however one name which of all others seems to be the sweetest in the remembrance of old play-goers of this city, a name for many years past unknown to the stage, and now only a pleasant memory, but a name once as familiar in the mouths of Olympic audiences as a household word, and one which Olympian audiences have never forgotten for the charm it bore, — the name of "Our Mary."

Miss Mary Taylor, "brightest of stars" and best of women, whose many graces of mind and of person endeared her to all who came in contact with her in her professional and private capacities, was one of the most deservedly popular actresses who ever appeared upon the stage, one of the most estimable ladies who ever shone in any sphere. By the magnetism of her presence and the charm of her voice she seems to have carried everything before her, to have won the love and esteem of old and young, male and female, and to have made herself a veritable power in the land. The boxes were nightly filled with her adorers, and she seems to have had as many worshippers as the pit would hold. The whole town seems to have wept with delight when she gave them a smile, and to have gone almost mad over "Our Mary." This was not a mere passing fancy, the passion of an hour, but a lasting, sincere affection that existed as long as the object of it remained upon the stage, and is still remembered by the many theatre-goers of other days, who even now confess —

> "With rapture smitten frame,
> The power of her grace, the magic of her name."

What was the real cause of this enthusiastic popularity which is almost without precedent in the annals of the stage; what was the real secret of "Our Mary's" power, it would be difficult to determine. We have seen many better actresses, have heard many better singers, have upon the stage now many more beautiful women, and many women as good and sweet and womanly and true; but we have not now, and have never had, any popular favorite who was so universally loved, and known, and respected, and petted as was "Our Mary" in her day. We know of no lady on the stage now with whom we can compare her. Many there are, who, in certain parts, are her equal, or her superior, while many are, by the few who know them, as highly regarded and as cordially esteemed; but there are none who have won that fond and affectionate admiration which she inspired, and so long retained, in the hearts of the whole theatre-going town.

Mary Gannon, who was a contemporary of "Our Mary's," although her survivor on the stage for some years, succeeded in some measure, but in a limited degree, to the popular favor in which "Our Mary" was held. Mrs. Hoey was regarded by a comparatively small circle of play-going people with affection and respect approaching that of Miss Taylor's; Miss Henriques, during her too short career, experienced some of this "popular petting," but not in so marked a degree; Mrs. John Wood when she belonged to us, and before she had made her local habitation over the ocean, was one of our established and popular favorites; Miss Clara Morris of the present, perhaps the most universally liked of this generation of stars, holds a place in the affection of the public, which although by no means so marked is more like the position of popular idol so long held by "Our Mary;" but not one of these is so absolutely beloved as was "Our Mary" during her reign, and for no actress on our boards has this devoted personal attachment been felt since she made her last bow to the public, more than twenty years ago.

Miss Taylor was entirely a New Yorker. She was born in Stanton Street in this city, on the 3d March, 1827. Her father was William Taylor, a celebrated musician. She made her first public appearance as a child in New York at a concert given by the Euterpean Society, sang alto in the choruses at the National Theatre in Church Street, under the management of the elder Wallack, as early as 1838, and when still almost a child joined the Olympic Company in 1842, playing at this house and at other establishments here until her marriage and retirement, but never, so far as we have heard or can remember, appearing in any other city; being altogether *Our* Mary, — New York's own.

During the eight years of Miss Taylor's connection with the Old Olympic she became so thoroughly identified with it, so many of its historical and traditional associations are connected with her presence on its stage, and she figures so largely in so many of its sunny memories, that any account of the Olympic, no matter how imperfect the account may be, while under the famous management of Mr. Mitchell, without making particular and honorable mention of "Our Mary," would not be placing the credit of Mr. Mitchell's and the Olympic's success where very much of that credit is due.

Her special forte was light comedy, and she seldom played any other than light comedy and burlesque parts, in which she had few equals and no superiors. She had decided talent, fine address, a sweet voice, and great personal charms. She soon became the marked favorite that we have shown her to have been, and her reputation once established she industriously strove to maintain it, never neglecting her art or forgetting herself or her duties as an artist and a lady, in which respect she was such a woman as well might be a copy to these our younger times.

Miss Taylor has been accused of not putting feeling or expression into her parts, and of having retained in all of her characters too much of the "pert sauciness" of the petted *soubrette;* but it must be remembered that this was her *line*, and that educated in and essaying only broad farce, operetta, burlesque, burletta, light comedy, and only occasionally, serious comedy parts, she could hardly have been expected to have reached the sublime or the "immensely high toned." She was never vulgar or unrefined, never lost her self-respect or the respect of those who played with her; is said by those who knew her well, both on and off the stage, to have been a whole-souled, true-hearted woman, whose better nature shone through her speaking countenance, who charmed her fellow actors, as well as the boxes and the pit; sustaining through life an unblemished character; a lady so far above the reach of scandal and gossip, that there never seems to have been even hinted the faintest shadow of suspicion as to her rectitude.

That our readers may have some idea of the amount of labor Miss Taylor's professional connection with the Olympic caused her, and some comprehension of her talent and versatility, we may say that the parts assigned her in the following productions she made exclusively her own, and these are only a few selected at random to show how much she accomplished, her position in the company, and with what well-known names in the profession her own was associated in those days.

She was the original *Marton* in this country in Planché's "Pride of the Market." Mr. Chanfrau and Mr. Holland being in the cast.

In the "Magic Arrow" she played *Prince Ahmed*, Mr. Walcot playing *Bonnyclabber*.

In "Open Sesame" she played *Morgiana*, Mr. Nickinson playing *Ali Baba*, and Mr. Holland *Hassarac*.

She was the first *Marie* in any English version of the "Child of the Regiment" on the American stage, either in opera or drama, making in this opera one of her first and most decided hits. She was also a charming *Zerlina* in "Fra Diavolo," and equally as charming as *Amina* in "La Sonnambula." In the burlesque of "Cinderella" she played the titular part. She was *Susanna* in the "Marriage of Figaro," *Venus* in the "Paphian Bower," *Gisselle* in "The Night Dancers," *Percinet* in "Graciosa and Percinet," and *Diana* in the burletta of "Diana's Revenge," winning golden opinions in these and other productions of the extravaganza school, from pit and boxes, critics and town.

In "Don Cæsar de Bazan" she was the original *Lazarilla* in this country, playing that part to the *Don Cæsar* of Mr. Walcot and the *Don Jose* of Mr. Fenno.

In "The Devil in Paris" she played the part of the gentleman, who in the play-bills was thus delicately designated, "*****." Mr. Fenno, Mr. De Bar, Mr. Nickinson, Mr. Walcot, Mr. Holland, and the whole strength of the Olympic Company being in the cast. "The '*****' in Paris" made a great hit, and was frequently repeated for many seasons.

Miss Taylor's most absolute success, perhaps, was her *Lize* in "A Glance at New York," which took the town by very storm, and for the year or more that the piece held the stage, she almost lost her own identity in that of *Mose's Lize*. Mr. Chanfrau, as we have shown, was the original *Mose*, a piece of character acting that is still well known on the stage to-day. Retiring from the Olympic Company, to renew on other boards the successes she had gained there, we find her during the season of 1850-51 at Brougham's Lyceum, enacting the original *Miss Georgiana Primitive*, "a girl of inexpressible assumption," in a "new local peculiarity" called the "Bloomers, or Pets in Pants." We find her cast also as *Princess Carissima*, "in the new imported Geological, Quizzical and Hopperatical Extravaganza," "The Queen of the Frogs." We find her playing in the "Home Book of Beauty," with Mr. and Mrs.

Brougham, Mrs. Blake, and Mrs. Vernon; a piece very strongly cast, and having "descriptive *scena*" by George Loder. We find her cast as *Victoire* in "The Invincibles," as *Toots* in "Dombey and Son," and as *Mrs. Charles Torrens* in "The Serious Family," her sister, Emma Taylor, then fast gaining a favorable place in the public estimation, appearing as *Emma Torrens* in the same play.

Her best engagement was played at Burton's during the "cholera season," when she made a decided hit in the part of *Toots*, and received a clear half benefit once a fortnight during the entire season.

At this house, Burton's, at Brougham's Lyceum, and elsewhere, Miss Taylor was the acknowledged favorite of the town, retaining the admiration and respect of the public as an actress, until her marriage to Mr. Ewen, and her final farewell of the stage, which took place on the 3d of May, 1852, at Burton's Theatre, when the following bill was produced: —

"DELICATE GROUND."

Citizen Sangfroid . . . . . Mr. Lester (Wallack).
Pauline . . . . Miss Mary Taylor.

After which

"THE HAPPIEST DAY OF MY LIFE."

Gilman . . . . Mr. Burton.
Mrs. Dudley . . . . Mrs. Hughes.
Sophia . . . . Miss Mary Taylor.

To be followed by the Second Act of

"THE CHILD OF THE REGIMENT."

Tonio . . . . Mr. Holman.
Marie . . . . Miss Marie Taylor.

The whole to conclude with the Farce of
"The Fire Eater."

Jeremia Gosling . . . . Mr. Johnstone.
Grace . . . . Miss Emma Taylor.

The announcement that this was to be the last appearance of Miss Taylor was received with deep sorrow; and notwithstanding the great attractions at other houses, — Lola Montez dancing the Andalusian dance at the Broadway Theatre, and Miss Cushman playing *Rosalind*, Mr. Conway playing *Orlando*, and Mr. Davidge *Touchstone* in "As You Like It," — Burton's was crowded to overflowing, although prices of admission were doubled, and thousands of her friends and admirers were turned from the doors unable even to gain an entrance. Her first manager, Mr. Wallack, occupied a prominent box; many of the best known faces in the city among the dramatic profession, among "society people," and among literary and artistic circles, were seen in the galleries and in the pit; and her last manager, Mr. Burton, in making for her an address to the audience, said, in the so well-known Burtonian way, that although she was never more to represent the "Child of the Regiment" on the stage, it was seriously hoped that she would be represented on the stage by a regiment of children!

"Our Mary," the Child of New York, and of a whole brigade and division of New York regiments and troops of friends, made her last bow, and on no artist has the green curtain dropped forever who was so sadly missed, so universally regretted, and so fondly remembered as "Our Mary." In all of her career, the only act that met with public disapproval while she was upon the stage was her leaving it.

It is to be regretted that we have no satisfactory portraits of Miss Taylor; there are but three engravings of her in existence — one in character — so far as we have ever heard or seen, none of which are considered reliable or correct; and there are no photographs, except such as may be in the possession of her family and personal friends. How many of the pictures of blondes, balladists, ballet-dancers, contortionists, and "posturists" which crowd the show cases and show windows of our photographers, we would gladly exchange for one carte of "Our Mary!"

Miss Taylor (Mrs. W. Ogilvie Ewen) died suddenly of disease of the heart, in this city, on the 10th of November, 1866, leaving behind her an unsullied name as wife, mother, and friend. The news of her death cast a gloom over the whole theatre-going community, and her funeral from St. Mark's Church was very largely attended, — thousands mourning sincerely who had never known her except in her professional capacity, and who had never seen her during the fifteen years of her retirement from the stage.

Miss Emma Taylor, by some years her sister's junior, and hardly her sister's equal in beauty, ability, or public favor, was, nevertheless, a very charming artist, greatly esteemed by the members of the profession to which she belonged, and greatly liked upon the stage of Boston, Philadelphia, and New York. She made her *debut* upon the New York stage only a short time before her sister's farewell to it, and is said to have been introduced to the Olympic audiences by "Our Mary" in the simple words, "My Sister Emma."

She was attached to the Boston Theatre Company for the first two or three seasons of that establishment, and was afterwards for a short time engaged at the Boston "Howard," under the management of Mr. Davenport. Miss Taylor then went to Philadelphia, where she remained some seasons, and, joining what was then called the "Wheatley, Davenport, & Jarrett Combination," she visited Boston and other cities during the summer preceding her death. At the Arch Street Theatre, Philadelphia, she was very popular, not only on account of her intelligence and ability as an actress, but on account of her charming *personelle*, and winning, lady-like manners. It was said of her at the time of her death, that "she was young, not unhandsome, and, best of all, she was good."

Her first part on the New York stage, and on any stage, was that of *Miss Totts* in the "Milliner's Holiday," at the Olympic Theatre, November 8, 1849; her last part in New York, we believe, was that of *Prince Merlin*, in an extravaganza play called "Blondette; or, the Naughty Prince and Pretty Peasant," at Laura Keene's, in February, 1863. She went with a portion of Laura Keene's Company a few days later to New Haven, where she met with an accident, while running off the stage, that produced convulsions and caused her death in New York on the 24th of February. She was buried in a vault beneath St. Mark's, on Second Avenue; Miss Mary Taylor rests in Mr. Ewen's family vault in the yard adjoining the same church.

CHAPTER V.

TWO MEMORABLE BILLS. — DICKENS AS AN ACTOR. — "OUR AMERICAN COUSIN" AS HE FIRST APPEARED. — MR. SOTHERN'S LORD DUNDREARY. — HIS DAVID GARRICK.

"Many things of worthy memory."
Taming of the Shrew, Act IV. Sc. 2.

AMONG our play-bills highly prized and carefully preserved are two, which of all others are most valuable to us for their associations' sake, and which are now almost historical, the first and earlier, being the bill of a dramatic performance perhaps the finest and most remarkable we have ever seen, the other of an awful tragedy, the witnessing of which we were happily spared.

The talent displayed by Charles Dickens as an actor is well known, although probably few of us on this side of the Atlantic can say from actual knowledge how great a comedian the world lost when Dickens chose literature as a profession. It was our good fortune to witness in Liverpool, many years ago, an amateur dramatic entertainment, from the bill of which, framed and hanging among the treasures of our sanctum, we now quote: —

The Amateur Company
Of the Guild of Literature and Art.
To encourage Life Assurance and other Provident Habits among Authors and Artists; to render such assistance to both as shall never compromise their independence: and to found a new Institu-

tion where honorable rest from arduous labors shall be associated with the discharge of congenial duties:

Will have the honor of presenting the petite Comedy in two acts of

"USED UP."

Sir Charles Coldstream, Bart. . .	Mr. Charles Dickens.
Sir Adonis Leech	Mr. Coe.
The Honorable Tom Saville	Mr. John Tenniel.
Wurzel (a farmer)	Mr. F. W. Topham.
John Ironbrace (a Blacksmith) . .	Mr. Mark Lemon.
Mr. Fennel (a Lawyer) .	Mr. Augustus Egg, A. R. A.
James	Mr. Wilkie Collins.
May	Mrs. Compton.
Lady Clutterbuck	Mrs. Coe.

This was followed by Planché's "Charles XII.," with Frank Stone, A. R. A., Peter Cunningham, Coe, Tenniel, Egg, Topham, Wilkie Collins, Miss Fanny Young, and Mrs. Henry Compton in the cast.

To conclude with the original Farce in one act, by Mr. Charles Dickens and Mr. Mark Lemon, entitled

"MR. NIGHTINGALE'S DIARY."

Mr. Nightingale	Mr. Frank Stone, A. R. A.
Mr. Gabblewig (of the Middle Temple)	Mr. Charles Dickens.
Charley Bit (a Boots)	
Mr. Poulter (a Pedestrian and Cold Water Drinker)	
Captain Blower (an Invalid) . .	
A Respectable Female	
A Deaf Sexton	
Tip (Mr. Gabblewig's Tiger)	Mr. Augustus Egg, A. R. A.
Christopher (a Charity Boy)	
Slap (a Country Actor)	Mr. Mark Lemon.
Mr. Fickle (Inventor of the Compounds)	
A Virtuous Young Person in the Confidence of "Maria"	

Lithers (Landlord of the "Water Lily")	Mr. Wilkie Collins.
Rosina	Miss Fanny Young.
Susan	Mrs. Coe.

The scene was by Mr. Pitt, Mr. Stanfield, R. A., Mr. Telbin, Grieve and Louis Haghe.

"The whole production under the direction of Mr. Charles Dickens."

This is an evening we will never forget, and never on the best professional stage do we think we have seen a better, brighter, smoother, more enjoyable performance, although the artists were, as Mrs. Gamp assured Mrs. Harris, "hammertoors." "'Mrs. Harris,' I says to her, 'be not alarmed, not reg'lar play-actors, hammertoors.' 'Thank 'evens,' says Mrs. Harris, and bustiges into a flood of tears!'"

These theatrical representations, of which Dickens was master spirit, and in which he took so prominent a part, have been too often and too well described by John Forster, by Hans Christian Andersen, in his "Story of His Life," and by other eminent literary people who were not only witnesses but performers, to bear further description from our pen. In the "company," besides those famous amateurs named above, were, at different times and on different occasions, John Leech, George Cruikshank, John Forster, Douglas Jerrold, and Mrs. Cowden Clarke,—each in his own profession a "star" of the first magnitude, and taken collectively a galaxy of wit, wisdom, pathos, humor, and artistic excellence never seen together on any boards, amateur or professional, before or since. With "Used Up," and Charles Mathews' own *Coldstream*, a part written by himself and for himself, and a part which he acted in his younger days and still acts, and long may he act, to the "very life," old New York play-goers are of course familiar. It was in this part of *Sir Charles Coldstream*, by the way, that Lester Wallack made his first appearance in America at the Broadway Theatre, in September, 1847. But "Charles XII." and "Mr. Nightingale's Diary" are not so well known on our boards;" the latter, we think, has never been played here. It was the most farcical of farces and well calculated to exhibit the versatility of the principal actor, Mr. Dickens. As *Mr. Gabblewig* he assumed four or five different disguises, changing his look, voice, and dress with a completeness and rapidity that no Lingard or Maccabe on the regular boards has ever excelled. His "make up" as *The Respectable Female*, was particularly good. She was a Mrs. Gamp sort of "party," who, if we remember rightly, could never remember *Mr. Nightingale's* name, but called him all the birds imaginable, *Mr. Robin Redbreast* being the favorite. Her principal distress, however, was the loss of a "hinfant," her boy, for the abduction of whom she seemed to consider Mr. Frank Stone, as *Mr. Nightingale*, in some way accountable; and between Dickens as the *Respectable Female*, and Mark Lemon as the *Virtuous Young Person in "Maria's" Confidence*, *Mr. Nightingale's* stage existence was made a burden to him. How much of the dialogue was what is technically called "gag" we cannot of course say, but it all seemed to flow so naturally and rapidly and spontaneously, to be so much a matter of surprise and enjoyment to the actors themselves, that we felt at the time as if we were listening to a bit of unpremeditated but immensely clever nonsense, gotten up on the spur of the moment by Lemon, Dickens, Collins, and Egg, for our amusement and their own.

Of that other play-bill to which we have alluded above we will say but little here; with the players or the occasion we have nothing to do now. Of the play itself, we would give some short account. The bill we prize as a sad memento of the saddest scene in our history as a nation. "Ford's Theatre, Washington." "Benefit and Last Appearance of Miss Laura Keene in 'Our American Cousin.'" The announcement this bill contained, as follows, will tell its story: "This evening, Friday, April 14, 1865, the performance will be honored by the presence of President Lincoln." That evening the players, "come to play a pleasant comedy," were themselves witnesses of that awful tragedy which stunned the civilized world and orphaned us as a people!

Miss Keene had at that time played *Florence Trenchard*, her original part, upwards of one thousand nights in different parts of the country. "Our American Cousin," not the Dundreary monologue that was produced at Wallack's Theatre and at Niblo's during the season of 1871–72 arranged by Mr. Sothern for Mr. Sothern himself, and to inaugurate Mr. Sothern's return to the American stage, but Tom Taylor's original "American Cousin," was played for "the first time on any stage" at Laura Keene's Theatre in this city on the 18th October, 1858, with the following cast: —

Asa Trenchard	Mr. Jefferson.
Lord Dundreary	Mr. Sothern.
Sir Edward Trenchard	Mr. E. Varrey.
Lieutenant Vernon	Mr. M. Levick.
Captain de Boots	Mr. Clinton.
Coyle	Mr. J. G. Burnett.
Abel Murcott	Mr. C. Couldock.
Binney	Mr. Peters.
Buddicombe	Mr. McDougal.

Florence Trenchard	Miss Keene.
Mrs. Mountchessington	Miss Mary Wells.
Augusta	Miss Effie Gormon.
Georgiana	Mrs. Sothern.
Mary Meredith	Miss Sara Stevens.
Sharp	Miss Flynn.
Skillett	Mrs. Levick.

This comedy was remarkably successful, was played one hundred and forty consecutive nights, and was frequently repeated until the end of the season, achieving a popularity that no play, excepting "Uncle Tom's Cabin," had known up to that time in New York; for this was before the days of long "runs," when no manager dreamed of one hundred nights of "Hamlet," or of the one thousand and one nights of "Humpty Dumpty" or "Black Crook," that have since been attained. It was revived at the same theatre in May, 1859, under the management of Mr. Jefferson himself, with Sothern, Couldock, and Jefferson in their original parts, and Mrs. John Wood as *Florence.*

As *Asa Trenchard*, Mr. Jefferson, then a young man, although not new to the New York stage, made his first great success, — "a very palpable hit." He seemed to be made to fit the part of the long, simple, uncouth, but shrewd "Vermonter;" it was in his hands a most truthful picture, quaint, easy, natural, and never overdrawn, — quite as admirable in its way as the merry care-for-nought young *Rip* and the broken-hearted old sleeper of the Catskills, in the portrayal of whom he has since become so well known. It is a matter of regret to more than one of Mr. Jefferson's admirers that, except on the single occasion of the Holland Benefit in 1871, he has played nothing on the New York stage for many years but *Rip Van Winkle.* He has an extensive range of characters; in comedy, farce, burlesque even, he is equally at home and equally admirable. His *Bob Acres*, *Trenchard*, *Newman Noggs*, and *Dr. Panglos*, are among the best we have in America, and his *Caleb Plummer*, of which we will perhaps speak in another chapter, is simply perfection.

In the original representation of "Our American Cousin," Couldock's *Abel Murcott*, Burnett's *Coyle*, and poor Peter's *Binney*, were exceedingly well played, particularly Mr. Couldock's delineation of the fallen but faithful attorney's clerk. It was a painfully real bit of character acting that was one of the features of the play. Mr. Stoddart, in the same part at Wallack's during the revival of the piece of which we write, was equally effective, and made as much as possible, and that was a great deal, of the little the scissors had left *Abel Murcott* to do. The play was very much "cut." The archery "business," the scenes in the wine cellar and in *Coyle's* office, which were among the best in the piece, were then entirely unknown to it; and in their stead were other acts and scenes of *Dundrearyism*, which, though amusing in their way, did not add to the merit of the comedy. So much was "Our American Cousin" changed, and so little improved, that the management, probably out of respect to the feelings of the author, left his name from the bills. Mr. Polk, laboring under all the disadvantages of playing a part so well known as the specialty of so excellent a comedian as Mr. Jefferson, made a very good *Asa*, but the weight of the play of course fell on the shoulders of Mr. Sothern, whose *Lord Dundreary* is no doubt better known in England and America than any other character on the stage or in fiction.

Dundreary is almost a creation of Mr. Sothern's own, an original conception of which Mr. Taylor had no idea; exaggerated, of course, but very clever. As written by Mr. Taylor the part is very short, of but a few "lengths" and very insignificant, a part so small that Mr. Sothern, although then only a "walking gentleman," objected very strongly to it, and only assumed it at the earnest request of the manageress Miss Keene, to oblige her and "for a few nights." His "few nights," have been many hundreds of nights (he is said to have played the part five thousand times), and in pleasing Miss Keene he pleased the theatre-going population of almost half the world, and has made his own fortune. His drawl, his lisp, his excellent "make up," his peculiar *skip*, his many absurdities "took" at once, were laughed at, were copied, and were talked of in every corner of the town. How great a surprise all this was to Mr. Sothern himself, he has often told his friends. *Dundrearyism* as a synonym for the languid swell has become an accepted word in the language, and will be found no doubt in the universal and unabridged dictionaries of the next generation. Laura Keene's Theatre, and New York itself, became too small a field for his Dundrearian lordship; he went abroad and was as successful and popular in England as here. Mr. Sothern was a member of the London Haymarket Company for several years, and played *Dundreary*, it is said, on the Haymarket stage over four hundred and fifty times in one season, becoming almost a "one part actor" by reason of the repeated demands of the public for the representation of that one part. That Mr. Sothern is capable of better things than *Dundreary*, or his equally absurd *Brother Sam*, is very clear; his *David Garrick*,

— first played by him in this city at Wallack's Theatre February 8, 1873, — proved his decided fitness for the higher walks of the drama. The original cast of "David Garrick" at Wallack's is worthy of preservation.

David Garrick (his original character) .	Mr. Sothern.
Simon Ingot	John Gilbert.
Squire Chivey	J. B. Polk.
Mr. Smith	G. F. Browne.
Mr. Brown	W. J. Leonard.
Mr. Jones	E. M. Holland.
Miss Ada Ingot	Miss Katherine Rogers.
Mrs. Smith	Mme. Ponisi.
Miss Araminta Brown	Mrs. John Sefton.

This comedy of Robertson's enjoyed a run of two hundred nights on its first production in London, but was not so decidedly popular here as was "Our American Cousin." Mr. Sothern's *David Garrick* was a very polished artistic performance. His affectation of drunkenness in the second act was particularly fine, a roaring obstrepulous but always gentlemanly drunk, and the feeling shown in his sober asides, when he began to realize the effect of his condition upon the woman he loved, was very touching; nevertheless the critical public cried for more Dundreary, and proved by this preference how much better the ridiculous is apt to "draw" than the sublime. *Lord Dundreary*, as he himself says of his brother, "is wather an ass, but you like him;" his asking the object of his affections if she can "wag her left ear" is certainly original, but why the "good public" should prefer this to the standard comedy parts that Mr. Sothern is so capable of filling, "is one of those things that no fellow can find out."

CHAPTER VI.

JOHN BROUGHAM. — HIS CAREER AS ACTOR, AUTHOR, AND MANAGER. — HIS "DOMBEY AND SON."

> "The Poet and the Player."
>
> *Hamlet*, Act II. Sc. 1.

ONE of the brightest of our dramatic critics said, at the time of its first production here, that Mr. Sothern played "David Garrick" almost as well as David Garrick could have played it himself. This, like the famous approbation from Sir Hubert Stanley, is praise indeed. David Garrick himself, however, never played the romance of his own life in that way. He would, no doubt, have been very much amused, or perhaps quite the reverse, could he have foreseen the disposition made of him matrimonially, by Robertson, and Sothern, and their French original. Mrs. Garrick, although a most estimable lady, was not the daughter of a wealthy self-made London merchant; she sprang from the ballet, not from the severely respectable parlors of worthy Simon Ingot, and she first made Davy's acquaintance behind the footlights, not before them.

Very likely in the year 1970 somebody will write a comedy and call it "John Brougham," and very likely the Nym Crinkle, or the Whoppers of the period, will claim for the star who plays the titular part that he out-Broughams even Brougham himself. The "Squire Polk-Chivey" of the company, in purple velvet shooting-jacket and check trowsers, will conduct himself as

4

the members of the Lotos and Arcadian clubs are supposed to conduct themselves now; the leading old man will present a perfect picture of our merchant princes of the nineteenth century, and they will marry Brougham to somebody of whom he never heard. There will be a little pathos in the play, some farce, and a good deal of rich Irish brogue. Our great grandchildren's grandchildren will flock to see it, and will crowd the orchestra on to the stage. There will be a run of a hundred or more nights, and Brougham will not mind it any more than Garrick minds it now!

John Brougham is not a David Garrick, by any means, but he is, in his own way, a genius almost as remarkable, not only as a player, but as a writer and an adapter of plays. He is personally, and in his profession, undoubtedly the most popular man on the American stage to-day, a popularity he achieved on his first appearance, and which he has steadily maintained during the thirty or more years of his residence among us. Brougham and his Broughamisms are so familiar to us of this generation, however (we see him so often, so easily, and in so many parts; he is so much a matter of course) that possibly he is not so much appreciated as he should be, or as much appreciated and praised as he will be in a generation or two to come, when his plays have become classic (perhaps) and his playing has that halo of perfection about it that only tradition, retrospection, and a sense of loss, can lend; when Brougham's *Pow-Ha-Tan*, in his own "Pocahontas," and his *Bunsby*, in his own dramatization of "Dombey & Son," itself only a recollection even now, will be ranked (perhaps) with Garrick's *Hamlet*, or with Kean's *Richard III.*

His version of Dickens's masterwork was, as a play, immensely popular, and was one of the happiest and most successful adaptations of a popular novel ever put upon the stage. It was for many years almost unequalled in its repetitions and the length of its "runs." It was first produced in the summer of 1848, at Burton's Chambers Street Theatre, the "genial John" playing both *Bunsby* and *Joey Bagstock*, and winning golden opinions from all sorts of people. This was Burton's first season as manager here, and financially, for a time, it was far from a prosperous one. John Brougham was stage manager, and the company was strong. It was not until "Dombey & Son," however, took the town by storm, that Burton's fortune as an actor and manager was made, and the reputation of many of the gentlemen and ladies of his troupe established. It developed many fine bits of character acting, which, although widely copied, have never been improved upon. It was Oliver B. Raymond who individualized the part of *Toots;* Tom Johnston, his successor, while very happy in his interpretation of the part, owing much of his success in it to his imitations of the manner and style of poor Raymond. We say "poor Raymond," for he was in very feeble health this season, and died of consumption shortly afterwards. His humor was infectious; his hat, and cane, and gloves, were seemingly everybody's property but his own, and his utterance of the well-known "It 's of no consequence, thank you," was so palpably plain that *Toots'* secret was shared by his audience at once, and so plaintive and suggestive of good natured simplicity that *Toots* at once won the smiles and sympathy of everybody before the curtain. Raymond's *Toots* was so thoroughly *Toots*, we had learned to know and to think of *Toots* so decidedly, as Raymond, and subsequently as Johnston had shown him to us, that the *Toots* of Dickens himself, when the novelist read "Dombey" to us here, was a woful disappointment. Neither in tone nor look was he our *Toots*, and *Toots* has never been *Toots* to us since. Dickens, who created *Toots*, ought to have known him, but we could not give up the friend of our youth for the *Toots* Dickens introduced to us that night at Steinway Hall, and between the two *Toots* we are *Tootsless*. Dickens's *Toots* may have been the real *Toots*, but we felt when we saw him that even "Diogenes" himself would not have recognized him.

To return to the comedy and to Chambers Street. In the cast were Mr. Nickinson and his daughter, whom we remember as the best *Haversack* and *Melanie* (in the "Old Guard") of their day. Lately from Mitchell's "Olympic," they added strength to Burton's company, and their *Dombey* and *Florence* were perfect gems of acting. *Mrs. Skewton* had in Mrs. Vernon's hands an artist's help to make her prominent. She was one of the strongest and most effective characters in the play, a very careful study, and so near perfection that we can never conceive of "Cleopatra" otherwise than as Mrs. Vernon, that always excellent "old lady," represented her. Burton was *Captain Cuttle*, with his hook and tarpaulin hat, and his "cheery" voice crying, "A friend in need's a friend indeed;" "Time and tide wait for no man;" "Overhaul your Walker's Dictionary, and when found make a note," receiving, when he first "comes on," an uproarious reception; the whole house, from the twenty-five cent family circle and its democratic occupants, to the aristocratic holders of seventy-five cent cushioned and comfortable chairs, going into convulsions of laughter over Burton, the only *Cuttle*. Brougham, as *Bunsby*, uttering his wisdom in solid chunks, giving in his ponderous way an occasional "opinion as is an opinion," was rich and rare; and his *Bagstock* left not the least doubt in the minds of his audience that Joey B. was not only "rough and tough, sir," but "de-vilish sly." Mrs. Brougham's *Susan Nipper* deserves a kindly mention, as being a gleeful specimen of character-acting that kept her on the stage when physical infirmities suggested her retirement. The part of *Edith* was played by Mrs. A. Knight, but did not attract particular attention, nor was it worthy of particular note. The cast of the piece, on the whole, however, was a very strong one, and "Dombey and Son" ran throughout the season.

The fall of 1849 saw some changes in the company: the Nickinsons having seceded, we find, in the bills of that date, Harry Lynn playing the part of *Dombey*, Miss Jane Hill (afterwards Mrs. Burton) playing *Florence*, and Mrs. Russell, *Edith*. Mrs. Josephine Russell, the present Mrs. John Hoey, joined Burton's company, and made her first appearance here on the 3d of September, 1849, in the play of "Faint Heart Never Won Fair Lady," her *Duchess* being a lady-like, pleasing personation. That Mrs. Russell should have full credit for her decided dramatic success in this part of *Edith*, however, we must review the situation. Up to the time of her assumption of the *role*, *Edith*, in Brougham's version of the story, was comparatively a secondary part, and one to which but little attention had been paid either by performer or audience. Mrs. Russell, however, by her splendid acting, and by her refined and elegant manner, brought *Edith* and herself into favor and prominence. She made of *Edith* more than Brougham himself ever imagined could be made, and *Edith* made her a reputation and success on the New York stage, which, until her honorable and much to be regretted retirement, she ever sustained. It was a masterly creation, by which Mrs. Shaw's *Edith*, at the Park Theatre, the season before, in Walcot's version of "Dombey and Son," although careful and meritorious, was almost eclipsed. Walcot's adaptation was finely written, beautifully mounted at the Park, and cast with the following strength :—

Captain Cuttle	Placide.
Dombey	John Gilbert.
Carker	Corson W. Clarke.
Major Bagstock	George Barrett ("Gentleman George").
Toots	Charles Walcot.
Edith	Mrs. Shaw.
Mrs. Skewton	Mrs. John Gilbert.
Florence	Mrs. Chas. Walcot.
Susan Nipper	Mary Taylor.

Notwithstanding this array of talent, the piece ran but little over a week, and Mrs. Shaw was compelled to go back to the legitimate. The management alternated between ballet and tragedy, until the establishment was destroyed by fire on the evening of the 15th December, 1848, happily before the opening of the doors. This ended the season and the Park; Brougham's "Dombey and Son," meanwhile, at the rival house, continuing its successful career, making the fortunes, or, at all events, the reputation, of everybody concerned.

To "Dombey and Son," as we have seen, Burton

owed much of his success as manager and actor; Brougham his first success as writer or adapter of plays; and Mrs. Hoey her great success as artist and public favorite; and, above all, we, the public, are indebted to "Dombey and Son" for Mrs. Hoey, for Burton, for Brougham, and for the lesser stars it developed and presented to us. Let us, therefore, thank our "stars" for "Dombey and Son," and "Dombey and Son" for our "stars."

CHAPTER VII.

BROUGHAM'S LYCEUM. — ITS BRILLIANT COMPANY. — ITS OPENING BILL. — JOHN E. OWENS. — "WHAT SHALL WE DO FOR SOMETHING NEW?"

"Altogether conducted by an Irishman; a very valiant gentleman, i' faith."
King Henry V., Act III. Sc. 2.

Ask the play-goer of the present how much he remembers of Brougham's Lyceum, if he remembers it at all, and the probability is that you will find this house, under this particular management and name, as vague and indistinct in the memory of an ungrateful town as we tried to prove in another chapter Mitchell's Olympic to have been. And yet the brief career of Brougham's Lyceum (two short seasons of only partial pecuniary success) was very full of bright and charming incidents, and very happy are the reminiscences of its "palmy days" to veterans, young and old.

It shall be our object here to show how the "genial John" devoted two years of his existence, two years of his "most golden prime," to the endeavoring to initiate an unsympathetic and *porco-cephalic* public into the mysteries of the richest and rarest wit and humor, and to show how unappreciative the public was, and how thankless was the task.

His managerial success at Burton's Theatre had not unnaturally raised in his ever-sanguine breast fond hopes of like prosperity as manager of a theatre of his own, and encouraged by this success, the Lyceum, built by the architect Trimble, on Broadway, next door to the southwest corner of Broome Street, subsequently Wallack's old theatre, later the "Broadway," now demolished and its site given to business purposes, was opened to the public for the first time on the evening of the 23d of December, 1850, "Brougham & Co.," in a farce of that name, written for the occasion, hanging out their banners on the outer wall. The initial performance included "Crimson Crimes," in which Mr. Brougham introduced for the first time to a New York audience the now so favorite comedian, Mr. John Owens, in the character of *Mr. Fright.* From the opening bill of Mr. Brougham we copy the following announcements: —

An Address introducing the principal artists, called

"BROUGHAM & CO.,"

Followed by a Musical Intermezzio composed by Geo. Loder, after which Grand Pas de deux, Mlle. Dacy-Barre and Mr. Smith, then an Interlude entitled, —

"DEEDS OF DREADFUL NOTE."

Mr. Fright	Mr. John Owens.
Mr. Tremour	Mr. H. B. Phillips.
Mr. Stuffem	Mr. Thompson.
Mr. Grabbem	Mr. Fletcher.
Susan Fright	Mrs. Brougham.

Concluding with the "Light Guard, or Woman's Rights," with Mr. and Mrs. Brougham, Mr. Lynne, Mr. Palmer, Mr. Florence, Mrs. W. R. Blake, Miss Mary Taylor, and others in the cast.

Mr. Owens remained in Mr. Brougham's company for a few weeks, playing the low comedy parts, such as *Paul Pry* and *Selim Pettibone*, for which he was already famous in Philadelphia and Baltimore, and in which he had many admirers here. As we look back now upon the careers of these two Johns, both so popular as actors and as men, both contributing so much in their professional capacities to the public amusement and enjoyment, both so genial, and in their ways so good, is it not a little curious that the one John, who owes in a measure so much of his early and original popularity in this city to the management and introduction of the other John, should on this same stage in later years, in the summer of 1864, and again in the winter of 1866, have won such decided and deserved success in his incomparable rendering of the part of *Solon Shingle*, while that other John, the "*createur dramatique*," has, during his entire career, benefited only at his own expense. An artist who has always held and retained the respect of the public, who has catered to the public theatrical taste under the management of others always so successfully and so satisfactorily, Mr. Brougham seems, whenever he has ventured to assume the management himself, to have had empty benches and a bankrupt treasury as his reward.

Mr. Brougham engaged for the Lyceum this season, a company that should have filled it nightly as long as it remained open, and should have insured him undoubted prosperity while his reign lasted. We find on his bills of 1851 and 1852, among others, such names as Mrs. William Rufus Blake (Caroline Placide), Miss Mary Taylor, Miss Emma Taylor, Miss Kate Horn, Julia Gould, Mrs. Vernon, Mrs. George Loder, Mrs. Maeder (Clara Fisher), Mrs. Conover, and Mrs. Skerrett, — surely an array of female talent and beauty that should have brought profit and fame to any management, and that no house of the present can pretend to surpass.

Prominent in his stock (his was entirely a stock company, composed of not a few brilliant stars) we find the following gentlemen engaged for the leading business: John Brougham himself, John Owens, as we have seen, W. H. Chippendale, George Jordan, said to have been one of the handsomest men of his day, Oliver B. Raymond, Corson W. Clarke, Stephen Leach, Tom Johnston, Henry B. Phillips, Harry Lynne, David Palmer, and others. All of these were favorites, or had been, with the public, and were as well known as John Gilbert, Stoddart, Charles Fisher, James Lewis, Mrs. G. H. Gilbert, Miss Morant, Miss Dyas, and Miss Morris, are to-day; but after the opening, business was bad and uncertain at the Lyceum, and full houses became the exception; only some unusually brilliant production, or some new and erratic absurdity from the pen of the master spirit himself, throwing anything like life or enthusiasm into the audiences, or filling the benches or the exchequer.

As one of the objects of this particular chapter is to give our readers some faint idea as to what straits a conscientious and painstaking management may be reduced in its efforts to entertain and divert a public, that seemed absolutely to refuse to be comforted or pleased, we will here reproduce some of the play-bills of the period of which we write, believing that they will best speak for themselves and for the attractions of the Lyceum, and best show how hard the "Jolly John" worked to amuse the town, to add to the pleasure of the people, and to his own profits.

One evening during the summer of 1852, the long white bill read as follows: —

A New Local Operatical Colloquiality, on the high pressure principle, to be called,

"WHAT SHALL WE DO FOR SOMETHING NEW,"

in which will be indistinctly recognized glimpses of "La Sonnambula."

The Libretto and music by Brougham & Bellini.

CHARACTERS IN THE COLLOQUY.

Mr. Chippendale, an anxious Manager . . . Mr. Chippendale.
Mr. Dombey, on this occasion only . . . . Mr. Lynne.
The Ghost of Wilkins Micawber, most sincerely hoping something may turn up . . . . . Mr. Brougham.
Mr. Panels, the Van Amburg of the Tigers . Mr. Tom Johnston.
Tom Crop — A valuable acquisition . . . . . Mrs. Skerrett.
Mercury — A contribution from the World's Fair . . . . Miss Julia Gould.
Mrs. Buzzard — Generally in a Row at the Lyceum . . . . Mrs. Brougham.
Prompter — With foreign innovations . . Mr. H. B. Phillips.

CHARACTERS IN THE OPERA.

Elvino — An enthusiastic and melodious young peasant, the tenor of whose thoughts usually finds vent in songs; the violence of his love for Amina receiving a temporary check from the circumstance of his having had the misfortune to discover her in a peculiar position . . . . Mrs. Skerrett.
Rudolpho — A travelled young nobleman, on the best of terms with everybody, himself included . . . . Mrs. Brougham.
Amina — A psychological phenomenon, being strongly addicted to walking in her sleep, and singing at the same time . . . . . . Tom Johnston.
Teresa — The prima donna's shadow, a most useful addendum to all operas . . . . Mr. Bristol.
Liza — Whose cue is to be jealous, but who in consequence of the shameful inattention of the original author has no opportunity to develop the passion . . . . Mr. Skerrett.

This entire performance was a huge joke; "Sonnambula," indeed, but such a "Sonnambula" as only a John Brougham could have written or conceived; and sung and acted by a company with which none of the burlesque troups of the present can compare. The sex of the whole *dramatis personæ* was reversed in the "opera," the *Tom Crop* of the "Colloquy," Mrs. Skerrett, proving himself, or herself, a most "valuable acquisition" as *Elvino*, while Tom Johnston as *Amina*, stepping gingerly along a narrow plank labelled "This is a Bridge," seemed to have reached the very summit of burlesque absurdity. The flat behind him that was to represent the town, was simply a blank, lead-colored surface, with the announcement in straggling black letters printed conspicuously upon it, "This is a Village." Scenery, other than this, there was none; a labelled substitute informing the audience what each "wing," "property," or "flat" was supposed to be, as "This is a Tree," or "This is a Pump," being the only attempt at scenic display.

For a time "Sonnambula" drew, the public appearing to be pleased with the novelty of the idea; but as soon as it ceased to be a novelty the management was once more met with small receipts and thin houses, and tormented again with the old, old question, "What *Shall* We Do for Something New?" something new being weekly, almost nightly, demanded. The craving on the part of the public for a change of bill, for something new, seems to have been intense during the seasons of Brougham's management of the Lyceum, and the tax upon his imagination and invention was such as only his fertile brain could have borne so long.

When the public showed its unwillingness or inability

to appreciate his untiring and expensive efforts at elegant settings and dresses, he endeavored to gratify its tastes by going to the other extreme, and produced the entirely unadorned "Sonnambula," certainly "something new" enough to have satisfied the most exacting audiences, but with the unpaying results that we have shown.

Undaunted, however, by many failures to please and to draw, he perpetrated this season his "Row at the Lyceum," the most remarkable of all of his remarkable productions, and one of the most original plays ever put upon any stage, unique, original and important enough to have devoted to it a chapter of its own.

CHAPTER VIII.

"THE ROW AT THE LYCEUM."

"O what a scene of foolery I have seen."
Love's Labor Lost, Act IV. Sc. 3.

ON the evening of the 22d of April, 1851, Mr. Brougham perpetrated quietly, and without warning, the most Broughamesque of his Broughamisms, produced with the following remarkable cast, copied *verbatim* from the bills of the day: —

A ROW AT THE LYCEUM;

OR, GREEN ROOM SECRETS.

Characters in the Green Room.

The Manager, wishing to progress with the times	Mr. Brougham.
The Stage Manager, with a slight hankering after the legitimate	Mr. Lynne.
The Prompter, in the proper exercise of his arduous duties	Mr. H. B. Phillips.
The Costumer, likewise attending to his business	Mr. Taylor.
The Call Boy, also pursuing his calling . .	Tom.
Mr. Dunn, not supposed to be on the stage at present	Mr. Dunn.
Mr. Thompson, a little discontented . . .	Mr. Thompson.
Mr. Arnold, with a heavy part weighing on his mind	Mr. Arnold.
Mrs. Vernon, with reminiscences of the palmy days	Mrs. Vernon.

Miss Julia Gould, vocal and instrumental to the success of the Lyceum	Miss Julia Gould.
Mrs. Dunn, with recollections of Gummidge.	Mrs. Dunn.
Miss Emma Taylor, with commendable aspirations	Miss E. Taylor.
Mrs. B ——, a victim to an obstinate husband, and to stage fright	Mrs. Brougham.

Characters in the unfinished fragment of an exceedingly blank-verse Tragedy by Carlyle, called

HORROR ON HORROR'S HEAD;

OR, THE LIAR AND SLAVE.

Beaudinaris, the Baron, a Tragedy Father.	Mr. Lynne.
Ferdinando, the Count, a light comedian .	Mr. Dunn.
Rulaldo the Red, the Mysterious Marquis, a heavy villain	Mr. Arnold.
Grufus, the Seneschal, utility	Mr. Bristol.
Ildefensa, the Baroness, high tragedy . .	Mrs. Vernon.
Preciosa, the Princess, very much distressed	Mrs. Buzzard.
Kuneyonda, the Young Damsel	Miss E. Taylor.

This was the old idea of a play within a play revived; but the tragedy contained in "Hamlet," or the comedy of "Pyramus and Thisbe" in the "Midsummer Night's Dream," were as naught to the "Horror on Horror's Head," performed in "Green Room Secrets," at Brougham's Lyceum those April nights.

The curtain rose to a crowded house on a scene at rehearsal, after the manner of Sheridan's "Critic," the actors and actresses in their ordinary street dresses, looking in every respect like the not more than ordinary men and women they really were, when paint and tinsel, sock and buskin, were discarded, dropping in casually like other ordinary mortals on business bent, to read and discuss Carlyle's new and wonderful production.

It was the green-room proper of a theatre, with all the green-room accessories and surroundings, the scenes and incidents, concords and discords of a green-room gathering; and was as heartily enjoyed by the Lyceum audience as would one of Wallack's famous Saturday night "houses" of the present, enjoy being invited to visit *en masse* that unknown and mysterious land contained "behind the scenes," and to assist at Mr. Boucicault's reading of "The Shaughran" to the assembled company for the first time.

Mr. Dunn as *Mr. Dunn*, Tom the Call Boy as *Tom*, and Mrs. Vernon as *Mrs. Vernon*, were very natural of course and very funny. As it was Tom's first appearance before the curtain in any *role*, he was not a little excited, and his very evident consciousness, was as amusing and refreshing as was the *sang-froid* of the rest of the *dramatis personæ*.

The audience was thoroughly interested and amused at the *realism* of the performance, when, "Enter Mrs. B.," the scene changes, and the "Row at the Lyceum" begins. While she greets her friends, looks over her part, objects to her "business," and lays her claims to something "more in her line," a stout, middle-aged gentleman, seated in the middle of the pit, clothed in a Quakerish garb, who had hitherto quietly listened and laughed with the rest, rises suddenly in his place, with umbrella clasped firmly in both hands, and held up on a line with his nose, to the astonishment of the house, calmly and sedately addresses the stage and the house, in words to this effect: "That woman looks for all the world like Clementina! Her voice is very like — the form the same." And then, with emphasis: "It is! it is! my wife!" at the same time leaving his seat in great excitement, he rushes toward the foot-lights, and cries wildly and loudly, "Come off that stage, thou miserable woman!"

The utmost confusion quickly reigned in the theatre. The audience, at first amused at the interruption, seeing that the Quaker gentleman was in earnest, soon took sides for or against him, and saluted him with all sorts of encouraging and discouraging cries as he fought his way toward the orchestra. "Who is he?" "Who is she?" "Shame! shame!" "Put him out!" "Go it, Broadbrim!" "Sit down!" "Police!" Hootings, hissings, cat-calls, making the scene as tumultuous as can be well imagined. The boys in the gallery, delighted at the "Row," in which, from their distance, they could only participate vocally, —

"Hailed him from out their youthful lore,
With scraps of a slangy *repertoire*:
'How are you, White Hat?' 'Put her through!'
'Your head 's level!' and 'Bully for you!'
Called him 'Daddy!' — begged he 'd disclose
The name of the tailor who made his clothes," —

and did all that boys in a gallery could do, to "worse confound the confusion."

Up in the third tier, in a corner near the stage, in prominent position, visible to all, was one particularly gallery and "gallus" boy, — a fireman, red-shirted, soap-locked, with tilted tile, a pure specimen of the now obsolete b'hoy, — Mose himself. He added greatly to the excitement of the scene, by the loud and personal interest he seemed to take in the proceedings, and promised, in a vernacular now happily almost as obsolete as is the *genus* itself, to give the indignant husband a sound lamming if he ventured to lay a hand on that young 'oman; volunteering, if the indignant husband would wait for him, to go down and do it then and there; proceeding then and there to go down to do it!

At this stage of the proceedings, the dramatic performances of "Green-Room Secrets" were entirely stopped. The artists were utterly unable to proceed on account of the uproar in front. The ladies were frightened; the gentlemen, addressing the house, and striving vainly to restore order, were quite powerless to proceed; while *Mrs. B*——, the innocent cause of all the trouble, evidently preparing for flight, was agitated and very nervous. All this time the irate husband was struggling to reach his wife, and fighting his way toward her. He finally climbed over the orchestra, the red-shirted defender of the young 'oman close behind him, when both were collared by a policeman or two, dragged upon the stage, made to face the house, the regulation stage semicircle was formed before the foot-lights, and the epilogue was spoken, — the audience beginning to recognize in the efficient policemen, the supes of the establishment; in the fire-laddie of the soap-locks and tilted tile, Mr. W. J. Florence, a member of the company; in the indignant husband, Mr. Brougham himself; in the recovered wife, Mrs. Brougham; and to realize that the "Row at the Lyceum" was a premeditated and magnificent "sell."

We may mention here in passing, that this peculiar part of the "rough," played by Mr. Florence, was his first decided success on the New York boards; it brought him much notoriety and applause, and encouraged his adoption of the eccentric comedy and sensational parts he has made his *forte*, and in which he is so well known at present. Previous to this *hit*, we find him doing a general utility business, as second or third walking gentleman, chiefly in Brooklyn and the provinces, — playing such parts as *Witherton* in "Paul Pry," *Valare* in "The Secret," *Langford* in "My Precious Betsey," *Brockett* in "The King and the Mimic," *Mr. Wickfield* in "David Copperfield," *Brandt* in "The Soldier's Return," *Captain Cannon* in "The Dead Shot," *Frampton* in the "Nabob for an Hour," and in other parts of similar kind. Among the bills of the Broadway (the old Broadway) for 1852, we find his first appearance on that stage recorded in the character of *Lord Tinsel* in "The Hunchback," with the following well-known artists cast for the leading parts: —

Master Walter . . . . Mr. F. B. Conway
Julia . . . . Miss Julia Dean.
Clifford . . . . Mr. Humphrey Bland.

To return to the "Row at the Lyceum." The deception was very cleverly managed, only those in the secret having any idea that all of this uproarious disturbance in the auditorium was part of the play, and the *denouement* was received with shouts of laughter and applause. The piece ran for some time, amused the town, and brought profit and fame to the manager. The original victims to the hoax, eager to see the effects upon other unsuspecting people, went again and again; took their friends to be sold; these friends in their turn taking their friends; everybody who had "bitten" having that anxiety to see somebody else "bite," — that desire to relieve themselves at the expense of others, that is natural to "poor humanity," and filling the house as long as anybody was left to "nibble," when more novelty was demanded, and the "Row at the Lyceum" was withdrawn.

CHAPTER IX.

BROUGHAM'S LYCEUM. — HIS LAST SEASON. — SOME OF HIS NEW PLAYS. — "THE CHRISTMAS CAROL."

"And Don John is the author of all."
Much Ado about Nothing, Act V. Sc. 2.

IN the two preceding chapters upon Mr. Brougham's brief but brilliant career at the Lyceum, a career in which the public benefited if the management did not, we have called especial attention to two pieces, the "Row at the Lyceum" and "What Shall We Do for Something New," as perhaps best calculated to show the extremes to which a conscientious and novelty-seeking management may resort, in its efforts to please the public and to increase receipts. Comedy, farce, burlesque, operetta, drama, legitimate and otherwise, — everything but high tragedy was produced in quick succession, with fine mountings and excellent casts, during Mr. Brougham's two seasons at the Lyceum; but neither season was profitable, although no fault of the management, and the house soon passed into other hands. Space will not permit our giving here a full list of the plays, standard or sensational, old or new, originals or reproductions, of a season's business at the Lyceum; but, to give our readers some idea of the infinite variety of its attractions, we select, at random, from old play-bills lying before us, the following plays, with the casts of some of the principal parts, as they were produced at this house: —

"Romance and Reality," a comedy in five acts, by John Brougham. "Lady of Lyons," with Mr. George Vandenhoff as *Claude Melnotte*, and Mrs. Sinclair as *Pauline*.

Mr. Vandenhoff, the present popular reader, was equally popular as an actor twenty or thirty years ago; and Mrs. Sinclair was Mrs. Edwin Forrest, who studied for the stage under Mr. Vandenhoff's instruction. Mr. Vandenhoff remained a member of Mr. Brougham's company a few weeks only. Mrs. Forrest made her first appearance on any stage under Mr. Brougham's management in 1852.

"Captain Charlotte," a farce popular at the Olympic, was produced, with Miss Annie Lonsdale as *Captain Charlotte Clapier*, a lady who will be pleasantly remembered by many old play-goers. This was her American *début*. She had many admirers, and was very happy in all the parts she undertook. She was, we believe, the original *Nan-the-Good-for-Nothing* in this country, playing the part very successfully at Brougham's Lyceum in 1852, and at the Metropolitan Theatre some years later. She retired from the stage some years ago.

Mr. Brougham produced "The Irish Widow," with Miss Kate Horn (afterwards Mrs. Buckland) as the *Widow Brady*.

He introduced Miss Julia Gould to the American stage as *Captain Phœbus*, in a version of "Notre Dame." He played his own inimitable *Micawber* and *Captain Cuttle*. He gave us "The Military Drama of the Invincibles," "The Row at the Lyceum," "Money Market: a Romance of Wall Street," by Mr. Brougham; "Queen of the Frogs," introducing the whole strength of the company.

The bill for Monday evening, January 5, 1852, contains the following announcement: "The entertainment will commence with a new comic farce in one act, first time in America, called 'The Two Bonnycastles.'"

The 14th of May, 1851, — we are not taking these plays in the order of their production, but as they occur to us — was "the first night of an absolutely new and original drama in three acts, written by J. W. Lester, Esq. (Lester Wallack), called 'The Fortunes of War; or, a Soldier's Honor,'" in the cast of which were Brougham, Dunn, Raymond, Lynne, Mrs. Blake, Miss Julia Gould, and Miss Tayleure. To this bill was attached the following note: "N. B. — The attention of the audience is respectfully directed to the triumph of mechanical skill and scenic effect achieved in the moonlight scene." And yet the croakers are wont to call this an age of scenic display, and to compare our "gorgeous transformations," our "cascades of real water," and all that, with the refined simplicity and absence of "grand spectacular appointments" that distinguished the drama in the "palmy days" of which they think so much! This play of Mr. Wallack has not been put upon the stage, as far as we can remember, in some years; it was the first, we think, of his efforts at dramatic construction, and not so successful as was his "Veteran," and his "Rosedale" in later years, although of the same martial school; — his fondness, as an author, for "the military" being as great as that which distinguished her Offenbachanalian Highness of Gerolstein.

Among the other productions at the Lyceum during these two seasons, we may mention Morton's "Irish

Tiger," with Mr. Brougham as *Paddy Ryan;* "Lola Montez," with Madame Celeste as *Katharine Klosser;* "Jennie Lind," with Miss M. Taylor as *Jennie Leatherlungs;* "Lady of Lyons," *Claude Melnotte*, Mrs. Melinda Jones; *Pauline*, Miss Julia Bennett; "Columbia at Home, or, New Year's Calls for 1852," with forty-two people in the cast; and "The Christmas Carol in Three Staves," with the whole strength of the company.

How much earnest business was contained in the above list of dramatic representations our readers can readily comprehend, and old play-goers will recall with lively and pleasant interest many of the prominent names to which we have called their attention. Here, as we have said, Mr. Brougham originated some of his happiest and most popular productions, while other authors were well represented, many now well known, and many almost forgotten plays, being for the first time brought before the public at this house.

During the Christmas holidays of 1851, was introduced Edward Sterling's version of Dickens's "Christmas Carol" in "Three Staves," with Mr. Chippendale as *Old Scrooge*, and Brougham as *Bob Cratchet.* Good as Mr. Brougham was in this part, and as he always is in all the parts he assumes, his *Cratchet* was quite eclipsed by the *Scrooge* of Mr. Chippendale. Notwithstanding the number of years that have elapsed since the production of this play, and our own youth at the time we saw it, we still vividly remember *Scrooge* on that stage, and can never think of Dickens's *Scrooge* other than as Mr. Chippendale represented him to us. It was a very careful study, a true picture; and Marley's *Ghost* was as real to us as if we had seen it with *Scrooge's* own eyes. "Marley was dead—dead as a door nail," we knew that as well as *Scrooge* did, and yet we saw Marley's face in the knocker as plainly as *Scrooge* saw it, and it had almost the same effect upon us.

We believe that this has been the only representation of the "Christmas Carol" on the stage, in which the entire ghost business has been enacted,—*Scrooge* only giving up his *Scrooginess* by degrees, and as the story of his life was shown him by the three spirits. Even the boyhood of *Scrooge*—cleverly played by a young person called in the play-bills "Master Henry," but who Master Henry was, and what was his subsequent career, we cannot now remember—was as clearly portrayed as Dickens has portrayed it in the book. The piece, as a whole, was a decided success, leaving nothing in the way of scenery, dialogue, or acting to be desired; and yet, as soon as the Christmas holidays were passed, the houses became so thin that barely money enough was taken at the doors to pay for the lighting of the building. It is true, old inhabitants remember that winter as a very inclement one, snow and ice keeping even theatre-goers, to a certain extent, within their own doors; but the withdrawal of the "Christmas Carol" demonstrated conclusively to the management of the Lyceum that dramatic success had for the time but little to do with dramatic merit, and that the true secret of prosperity consisted in novelty, no matter how much at variance with the standard or the legitimate that novelty was.

Before quitting the subject of Brougham's Lyceum, we must recall to the memory of our readers one other of Brougham's clever "whimsicalities," the remarkable bill of which we reproduce. Who ever equalled, or who ever will equal, John Brougham in the eccentric originality of his play-bills? This particular bill reads in part as follows: —

The performance will conclude with a new and wonderful romantic, mysterious, and original production, to be called

WANTED, A WIZARD;
OR, THE RIVAL MAGICIANS.

Mr. Crummles, Manager of the Areopagus, with his own Idea of Legitimacy . . .	Mr. Brougham.
Babble, Stage Manager, going in for the Regular Drama	Mr. Thompson.
Squeak, Prompter, another Stickler for the Old School	Mr. H. B. Phillips.
Roscius Rant, an aspiring Genius	Mr. Tom Johnstone.
Mr. Stall, a Disinterested Friend to Crummles and the Drama	Mr. W. J. Florence.
Wizard No. 1	Mr. Crummles.
Wizard No. 2	Mr. Roscius Rant.

In other words, Mr. Brougham and Mr. Tom Johnstone were the "Rival Wizards," and this announcement was printed at the bottom of the cast: "In the course of the piece will be presented many novel and interesting experiments in Natural and Unnatural Magic, Pneumatics, Dogmatics, and Psychological Phenomena. N. B. — The Experiments will be Varied Slightly! Nightly!"

Recall, O reader, if you can go back with us to the days of the Lyceum, the faces of John and Thomas! The Brougham you all know, for he is with us still; and Tom Johnstone, who was always funny, — was funny here beyond compare. We were reminded of him a season or two ago at Niblo's, by a Mr. Harry Hotto whom we saw there, playing a low comedy part in the spectacular piece called "Azrael." Mr. Hotto was wonderfully like "Poor Tom Johnstone" in face and feature, in walk and action, in this part, although, of course, by no means his equal as an artist. Mr. Johnstone's solemn and unmoved countenance as in the character of *Wizard No.* 2, he presented to the audience some of the stalest and simplest "sleight-of-hand" tricks, as wonderful and original, was irresistibly comic; but the "Rival Wizards" was another play added to the list of those that did not draw or pay, and was sacrificed on the altar of "more novelty."

Mrs. Forrest's engagement was the last of any importance at this house during Mr. Brougham's management. Her second and last season ended abruptly on the 17th March, 1852.

In the fall of the same year, Brougham's Lyceum became Wallack's Lyceum, though better known later as Wallack's Theatre, and entered upon a career of prosperity, to which we shall again have occasion to refer; Brougham, "the genial, jovial John" resigned the perilous position of manager and proprietor, and assumed the more certain and no less honorable position of leading artist under the veteran Wallack.

CHAPTER X.

MR. BROUGHAM'S LAST THEATRE. — THE ORIGINAL FIFTH AVENUE THEATRE. — ITS SHORT BUT BRILLIANT CAREER.

"A Daly beauty."
Othello, Act V. Sc. 1.

"NEW YEAR'S DAY, with a bad beginning for all parties." Such was the somewhat sadly prophetic play-bill announcement of the "table of contents" of the third act of "New Year's Eve, or, False Shame," a comedy, by Mr. Frank Marshall, of London, and underlined for production at Daly's Old Fifth Avenue Theatre, Twenty-fourth Street, near Broadway, on the 1st of January, 1873. A prophecy which neither Mr. Frank Marshall of London, nor the management of the Fifth Avenue Theatre Company ever expected to be so painfully realized. On that New Year's Day, within an hour after its *matinée* performance, the cosy, pleasant little theatre was burned to the ground, a total and complete wreck.

Mr. Daly and his artists had the sympathy of all classes and conditions of people in their misfortune, and universally was the hope expressed that but short would be the "wait" between this act and the next, and that the "Midsummer Night's Dream" of the company would be much happier for all parties than was the terrible reality of the bad beginning of its "New Year's Eve."

The Fifth Avenue Theatre had, in its Augustan age, been the home of so much pleasant comedy, the scene of so many triumphs of many public favorites, that the whole town, which seemed to have an almost personal interest in its welfare, was deeply stirred by the news of its disaster. Next to the weather and the walking, it was the favorite topic that New Year's night in the "gabble-gobbles of society," as our contemporary, Mr. Whoppers, of the *Universe*, so happily terms the receptions of the upper circles. It was noticeable that, while the callers lamented the loss to the city and Mr. Daly of his play-house and his valuable papers, the *callees* were only interested in the loss of the wardrobes of the leading ladies. Even the important discussion of Miss A.'s *gaze de chambrais*, the "loads of flowers" sent to Miss B., and of the blue silk of the young bride over the way, "without a scrap of trimming on the sleeves," were for a time forgotten in the all-absorbing wonder, *Did* Fanny Davenport save that maroon velvet?

The career of the legitimate drama at this house was, unhappily, so short, and just now is so much a thing of the present, that recollections of its stage will hardly interest readers of to-day. All play-goers must have their own recollections of it, which cannot fail to be fresh and pleasant. The Old Fifth Avenue Theatre, as it stands, a charred, melancholy ruin, only its outer wall remaining, absolutely a thing of the past, has, under Mr. Daly's management, played an important part in New York dramatic history. There is so much poetry, although modern poetry, in its play-bills, that we cannot resist speaking of this Theatre somewhat fully, particularly in this connection, it being the last, as the Lyceum was the first, of Mr. Brougham's ventures in the lesseeship and financial management of a theatre.

The house was built about 1865, and was originally used as an evening gold-room at the time of the absurd excitement in New York called the gold-fever. When this subsided, its ground floor was used as a billiard saloon, while its upper stories were occupied by a minstrel troupe, under the management of Geo. Christy. On the 25th of January, 1869, Mr. Brougham opened it as a theatre, — Mr. James Fiske, Jr., its then proprietor, having made it one of the prettiest theatres, small, but bright and brilliant, that New York has ever seen.

Mr. Brougham's opening bill we give here to considerable extent, although not in full, as a curiosity of Broughamism, and as giving a very fair idea of its management, its company, and the style of entertainments Mr. Brougham intended, and did produce : —

BROUGHAM'S THEATRE.

24TH STREET, NEXT DOOR TO 5TH AVENUE HOTEL.

Proprietor . . . . James Fiske, Jr.
Lessee and Manager . . . . John Brougham.
Stage Manager . . . . James Schoonberg.
The Scenery by Messrs. C. J. Hawthorne, L. Duflocq, Marston, and Assistants.
Leader of Orchestra . . . . H. Eckhardt.
Prompter . . . . C. K. Mason.
The Act Drop . . . . Mr. Russell Smith.

The Theatre will open for the Season on Monday, January 25, 1869, with a New and Original Comedy, in two acts, by John Brougham, entitled, —

"BETTER LATE THAN NEVER."

Major Fergus O'Shaughnessy	Mr. John Brougham.
Reginald Wyndham	Mr. Geo. Stoddard.
Sir Malachi Weovyl	Mr. C. Hale.
Squire Fallowfield	Mr. E. Lamb.
Jacob Mullett	Mr. C. Edmunds.
Annabel Wyndham	Miss Eliza Newton.
The Lady Neil Wycherlie	Mrs. W. Winter.
Widow Griffin	Miss Mary Carr.
Tabitha	Miss E. Andrews.

Act I. An Exterior. Act II. An Interior.

After the Comedy Mr. Brougham will make a few Remarks.

Subsequently will be published the First Edition of the *Dramatic Review* for 1868, being a series of somewhat personal, but the compiler hopes not unpardonable, reflections upon the abilities and notabilities of the past season, etc.

TABLE OF CONTENTS.

Plate First. Allegorical Group, New York.

INDIVIDUALITIES.

Manhatta (the favorite daughter of Columbia, by her union with a highly respectable Dutch settler, named New Amsterdam, progenitor of all the other dams, except McComb's, etc.)	Miss Annie Firmin.
Brooklyna (the oldest of her numerous family, a remarkably forward young lady, proud, pious, and independent, holding but ferry little intercourse with her Ma, and that she means to abridge)	Miss E. Lyle.
New Jersia (another offspring, unhappily born out of the Union, and not in complete union with her sisters)	Miss L. Mahon.
North Rivero (a fluent individual, etc.)	Mr. Hurley.
East Rivero (the Janitor of Hell Gate, shallow in spots, but sound in the main)	Mr. C. Hillyard.
Mdlle. Fashion, from Paris (Manhatta's dearest friend, etc.)	Miss Effie Germon.
Public Opinion (the "Great Sir Oracle" of Social Life, whose judgments wise men reverence, fools fear, and knaves deride)	Miss Eliza Newton.

Melpomene (an old and melancholy muse who has seen better days, etc.) . . . . . . Mrs. J. J. Prior.
Captain Jenks (of the Naval Equestrian Service) . . . . Miss Effie Germon.

ILLUSTRATION I.

Subject: "The Emerald Ring."

Didlight the Vyllyan . . . . Mr. C. Edmunds.
Mike the Avenger . . . . Mr. Corrie Crosbie.
Geraldine the Persecuted . . . . Miss Thomas.
Maggie the Resolute . . . . Miss Horne.

ILLUSTRATION II.

Subject: "Barbe Blue. After Dark."

Barbe Blue . . . . Mr. A. Matthison.
Bonlotte . . . . Miss Amy Ames.
The One More Unfortunate . . . . —— ————

ILLUSTRATION III.

Subject: "The Fox's Nest."

Humpty Dumpty the Illimitable . . . . Mr. Corrie Crosbie.
Pantaloon (an excellent pair to wear) . . . . . Mr. Grossie.
Harlequin the Velocipedal . . . . Mr. Alexander.

ILLUSTRATION IV.

Subject: "A Plate of Bouffe-Alemode."

ILLUSTRATION V.

Subject: "The Lancashire Lasses."

ILLUSTRATION VI.

Subject: "The Man at the Wheel."

ILLUSTRATION VII.

Subject: "Pike's Grand Palace."

Grand Duchesse No. 1 . . . . Miss Effie Germon.
Grand Duchesse No. 2 . . . . Miss Lizzie Eckhardt.
Fritz the Embarrassed . . . . Mr. A. Matthison.

ILLUSTRATION VIII. AND LAST.

Subject: "The Deep Sea Depot," etc.

Mr. Brougham's reign here was very brief. As Viceroy to Mr. Fiske he was never comfortable and was not kindly treated. He retired from the management in the course of two months, and has not since in New York conducted any theatrical establishment.

Mr. Fiske then assumed the management himself, and produced *Opera bouffe*, Tostee and her company being the attractions. Subsequently, in the early summer what was called the "Selwyn Boston Combination," a comedy company, played a short engagement at this house, but in August, 1869, it was opened by Mr. Augustin Daly, as the "Fifth Avenue Theatre," with a comedy by Thomas W. Robertson, entitled "Play." The cast of "Play" on this occasion, although we have devoted already too much of this chapter to play-bills, as inaugurating Mr. Daly's management, we must reproduce. The leading parts were thus filled: —

The Hon. Bruce Farquehere . .	Mr. E. L. Davenport.
Chevalier Browne	Mr. Geo. Clarke.
Graf Von Stauffenberg	Mr. W. Beekman.
Hauptmann Stockstadt	Mr. W. Davidge.
Bodmin Todder	Mr. Geo. Holland.
Frank Price	Mr. J. B. Polk.
Rosie Farquehere	Miss Agnes Ethel.
Amanda	Mrs. Clara Jennings.
Mrs. Kinpeck	Mrs. G. H. Gilbert.
Flower Girl	Miss Emily Lewis.

The comedy, the company, and the management were at once pronounced a success, and Mr. Daly entered into a career of popularity and prosperity that lasted as long as his house remained to him. "Play" enjoyed a run of three weeks, during which time Miss Fanny Davenport assumed the part of Miss Agnes Ethel, who was prevented by illness from appearing at the theatre.

During the first season of Mr. Daly at this house, he produced Robertson's "Dreams," and introduced Mr. James Lewis in the cast; he produced "Twelfth Night," "Wives as they Were," "Old Heads and Young Hearts," "London Assurance," "Surf," "Frou Frou," "Fernande," and other old and new plays, always well done, and to the public satisfaction.

His second season opened with "Man and Wife," followed by Bronson Howard's "Saratoga," which ran one hundred nights, as did "Frou Frou" during the previous season. Mr. Charles Mathews played an engagement here in April, 1871, with Mrs. Mathews (Lizzie Weston Davenport), who made her first appearance in New York in thirteen years as the *Countess de Lespalia*, in "The Comical Countess," and as *Media* in "The Golden Fleece," May 29, for the benefit of her husband. "Jezebel," "London Assurance," "No Name," "Delmonico's," and "An Angel" were among the attractions of this season, which closed July 20th.

On the 5th of September, 1871, he opened with "Divorce," which was played without change of bill until the 18th of March, 1872, two hundred nights. On Washington's birthday he took his company to Philadelphia, where they played "Divorce" at a matinee performance, and presented the same comedy at his own theatre with the same people in the evening; an undertaking which was successfully, and with no difficulty accomplished, and which reminds us of a similar frolic of Mr. Brougham's in the winter of 1856 or 1857. Mr. Brougham, who was at that time manager of the Bowery Theatre, played one evening the part of *Tactic* in a farce called "The Stage Struck Irishman," in his house in New York, and made a speech at the close of the performance, which began at seven o'clock. Before half-past seven Mr. Brougham and his party were on their rapid way to the train, made all connections, and at 10.45 he stepped upon the stage of the National Theatre, Philadelphia, fully dressed for his part of *Powhattan* in his own burlesque "Pocahontas." After the close of the performances at the National, Mr. Brougham and his friends were entertained at the Girard House, but returned to New York before day-light the next morning. A much more wonderful specimen of theatrical enterprise and of "magic transformation business," even than Mr. Daly's.

But to return to the Fifth Avenue Theatre. "Divorce" was followed by a revival of old comedies, and by "Article 47," produced April 2, and running until the end of the season, June 15, giving Miss Clara Morris in the part of *Cora*, an opportunity which she did not lose, to make her first decided hit in New York.

Mr. Daly's last season at the old theatre opened on the 3d September, 1872, with Bronson Howard's "Diamonds," when Miss Sara Jewett as *Mabel Wyckoff* made her first appearance on the professional stage. "Diamonds" was repeated nightly for six weeks ; it was followed by "The Road to Ruin," "Belle's Stratagem," "The Inconstant," "Merry Wives of Windsor," "The Baroness," "Bold Stroke for a Husband," and "False Shame," produced December 23, and the last play, as we have seen, ever performed on its stage. On this account we give its cast.

"NEW YEAR'S EVE, OR FALSE SHAME."

Earl of Dashington	Mr. D. Whiting.
Arthur, Lord Clinton, his son	Mr. Geo. Clarke.
Captain Ernest Bragley	Mr. C. H. Rockwell.
Colonel Howard	Mr. Wm. Davidge.
Lieutenant Frank Percy	Mr. B. T. Ringgold.
Hon. Chas. Ewart	Mr. J. H. Burnett.
Philip, Bragley's man	Mr. Owen Fawcett.
Servants, Visitors, Choristers.	
Magdalen Atherleigh, ward of Lord Dashington	Miss Clara Morris.
Mrs. Howard	Mrs. G. H. Gilbert.
Constance Howard	Miss Fanny Davenport.
Mary, maid to Magdalen	Miss Nellie Mortimer.

Act I. Summer Fête. The Turquoise Ring.
Act II. New Year's Eve. Seeing the Old Year out.
Act III. New Year's Day with a bad beginning for all parties.

How melancholy was the New Year's day, and how bad its beginning for all parties, we have already shown.

Mr. Daly, on the 21st January of the same year, opened the establishment now known as the Globe Theatre, at one time called the Broadway, formerly Lucy Rushton's, originally the Church of the Messiah, No. 728 Broadway, as the New Fifth Avenue Theatre, with "Alixe" and a strong cast. His company remained here, playing "Divorce," "False Shame," "Madeline Morel," etc., until the close of his regular summer season, late in the month of June. He opened his present Fifth Avenue Theatre on Twenty-eighth Street, near Broadway, on the 3d December, 1873, with a play by James Alberry of London, entitled "Fortune." With the last Fifth Avenue Theatre and its "Fortune," however, we have not to do here.

To Mr. Daly as a manager and proprietor, in his old

house, we owe very much for his revival of good old comedies, and for his renewing our acquaintance with good old comedians, to say nothing of the new plays and new players he has introduced to us. We have seen on his boards within these few years not only an occasional star, but the best regular talent the country can produce. No house in the history of the New York stage can show so brilliant a record in so short a time as his. Mr. Daly numbers to-day among his company four of the best artists in their respective lines in America: Mr. Davidge, said to be the best Shakespearean actor on the stage; James Lewis, one of the funniest of eccentric comedians; Charles Fisher, "good in everything," unequalled as *Triplet;* and Mrs. Gilbert, undoubtedly the very best "old lady" now remaining on our boards. During these four seasons of Mr. Daly's management we have seen on his stage, E. L. Davenport, George Holland, Davidge, Polk, James Lewis, Harkins, George Browne, George Clarke, Fisher, Whiting, Ringgold, Mr. and Mrs. Charles Mathews, Mrs. Scott Siddons, Agnes Ethel, Mrs. Jennings, Mrs. Gilbert, Miss Davenport, Miss Fanny Morant, Misses Morris, Dietz, Jewett, Amy Ames, Ione Burke, Lizzie Winter, Kate Newton, and Jennie Yeamans, all good, and some of them never before known to this or to any public. Miss Dietz as *Mrs. Glenarm* in "Man and Wife" in 1870, and Miss Jewett as *Mabel Wyckoff* in "Diamonds," in 1872, making their first appearance on any stage.

Miss Morris made her first bow to a New York audience in "Man and Wife," and as *Annie Sylvester*, in that play, made those favorable impressions which in some of the old comedy characters, and in her original parts, as *Cora* in "Article 47" and *Jezebel*, she has so well sustained. Miss Agnes Ethel here also as *Frou Frou* and *Fernande* made her first success as an actress, and James Lewis here first astonished us by his wonderful talent in the invention of wonderful trowsers and waistcoats, and made the town laugh at his wonderful *sit downs*.

If the new comedies and "society plays" that were produced here were not of the highest tone, or of the most brilliant construction, plot, or dialogue, they were at least well acted. The smallest parts were creditably filled. We do not remember a single decided stick in all the casts, every artist was at home in his part, the gentlemen were all gentlemanly, and the ladies were all ladies; and some plays, very indifferent in themselves, were thoroughly enjoyable here, because so satisfactorily performed. It is one of our pet theories in dramatics that a poor play well played is better than a great play badly played, and even Olive Logan's "Surf," produced as it was produced at this house, is better than "Richard III.," played, as we have seen it lately, with but one or two performers, who are *actors*, in its cast.

Among the most satisfactory of the revivals that Mr. Daly has given were "Twelfth Night" and a "New Way to Pay Old Debts." In the former George Clarke's *Malvolio* and Polk's *Sir Andrew* are the best things we think that either of these gentlemen has ever done. Of Mr. Davidge's *Sir Toby* it is only necessary to say that Mr. Davidge played it. Mr. Davenport's *Sir Giles*, in Massinger's celebrated comedy, was unquestionably the finest piece of acting this house has seen. The most important revival here was "The Merry Wives," with Fisher's assumption for the first time of the part of *Falstaff.* Probably the best of the modern plays was the unfortunate "False Shame" of this last season; decidedly the worst was "The Baroness." "The Baroness" had the shortest run, — two nights; 'Divorce" had the longest, — two hundred. "Man and Wife" was, as a whole, one of the most successful dramatizations of a popular novel that we remember; such works being usually stilted and unnatural, except as in the case of "Masks and Faces," when the comedy and the story are prepared by the same pen, and the intention from the first, is to produce a work for the stage as well as for the reading public. It was well dressed and well mounted, and Mrs. Gilbert's *Hester Dethridge* was one of the finest bits of character acting we have ever seen; painfully true and artistic, without being in the slightest overdrawn. Miss Fanny Morant, always an excellent actress, has never appeared to better advantage than as *Clothilde* in "Fernande." Miss Ethel's rendering of the unhappy heroines of "Frou Frou" and "Fernande" will be remembered by all theatre-goers. They were not very healthy or very proper plays these, sensational and French, but they *drew* and *paid;* and while "everybody" condemned, "everybody" went to see them.

Probably the funniest scene ever enacted at this house was a scene not on the bills. When a certain leading lady whose name we will not mention, playing *Celia* to Mrs. Scott Siddons' *Rosalind* in "As You Like It," was tripping lightly through the forest of Arden, she stumbled over a stage rock and fell backwards between it and a stage oak, shutting herself up, involuntarily, of course, like a jack-knife, and leaving only her heels and her head visible to the audience. It was a pose that only the most accomplished of Majiltons could have assumed, and it brought down the house. The oak was firm and the rock would not budge, and *Celia* was utterly unable to extricate herself. The dismayed, startled, serio-comic expression of her face, as seen framed between her own red shoes, was irresistibly ludicrous. The vain efforts of *Rosalind* to restore her sister to her natural position, *Celia's* own complete helplessness, and the final coming on from the wings of the melancholy *Jaques* — in anything but a melancholy mood — to the rescue, was funnier than the funniest scenes Fox or Beckett ever conceived. The audience did not recover during the entire evening. An occasional infectious laugh would start the house; and stage, gallery, and pit would in a moment join, interrupting altogether for the time the business of the play. The leader of the orchestra could hardly wave his *baton*, and the base-viol lost entire control of himself, once disappearing altogether through the little trap-door under the foot-lights in evident hysterics.

No doubt the saddest scene, sadder even than that last scene of all in the little church round the corner, was the farewell benefit and farewell appearance on any stage of George Holland, the veteran actor and universal favorite, after almost half a century's professional labor in this country. He made his *début* before an American audience at the Bowery Theatre in 1826, and played his last part as *Mr. Jenkins connected with the Press* in "Surf," at this house in January, 1870. He joined Mr. Daly's company during its first season of 1869 and '70, and appeared but a few nights, too old and too feeble to act his wonted parts, or to acquire new ones, although, through the kindness and generosity of

Mr. Daly, he remained a member of his company, we believe, until his death in 1870. On this benefit occasion of which we have spoken above he appeared for the last time before the curtain — he was not cast in the play "Frou-Frou" — and, too much affected to respond to the kind plaudits of his audience, he spoke his last lines in public, probably the most touching that he ever uttered, impromptu and from his heart, "God bless you all!"

CHAPTER XI.

WALLACK'S THEATRE. — THE WALLACK FAMILY.

"The house is a respected house."
Measure for Measure, Act II. Sc. 1.

THE dramatic season inaugurated in the opening of the several theatres for the fall and winter campaign of 1852–53 was remarkable for its promise of great things, the several managers having started out with the avowed determination to obtain success, provided mere strength of representation could secure that result. The companies of the Broadway, of Burton's, of Niblo's, and of the East Side theatres were unusually strong. Mr. Forrest, Miss Julia Dean, the Florences and the Williamses, the Bateman children and Sontag, were among the stars of that season here, and Miss Laura Keene, Miss Caroline Richings, Miss Matilda Heron, and Charles Fisher, then made their first bows to the New York public.

The most important event in the history of our local stage was the opening of the theatre on the corner of Broadway and Broome Street (formerly Brougham's Lyceum), as Wallack's Lyceum, by Mr. James W. Wallack, with a number of ladies and gentlemen as his support who have played very important parts in the annals of the American stage. Mr. John Lester Wallack, the present proprietor, was the first stage-manager, and his brother, Charles Wallack, both sons of the manager, was its original treasurer. From the opening play-bill, dated September 8, 1852, we copy and condense the following strong announcements: —

Wallack's Lyceum, Broadway, will open this evening with new decorations, embellishments, etc. [Here comes some eight inches of closely-printed matter, all descriptive of the embellishments.] The following list comprises the officers of the establishment and a company which the lessee confidently asserts cannot be surpassed in talent or popularity.

The company comprised —

Mr. Seguin,	Mr. J. W. Lester,	Mr. Walcott.
Mr. W. R. Blake,	Mr. Brougham,	Mr. C. Mason.
Mr. Hale,	Mr. F. A. Vincent,	Mr. Reynolds.
Mr. H. B. Phillips,	Mr. Lyster,	Mr. Rea.
Mr. Bernard,	Mr. Chippendale, Jr.,	Mr. Baker.
Mr. Trenor,	Mr. Hunt,	Mr. Browne.
Mr. Stuart,	Mr. Burke,	
and	Mr. Wallack.	
Mrs. Buckland,	Mrs. Blake,	Mrs. Brougham.
(Miss Kate Horn)	Mrs. Hale,	Mrs. Stephens.
Miss Julia Gould,	Mrs. Crammer,	Mrs. Rea,
Miss Tayleure,	Miss Malvinia,	Miss Osborne.
Miss Barton,	Miss Dean,	Miss Scott.

The Band, under the direction of Mr. Tyte, will consist of the following gentlemen, each of whom is a first-class musician, perfection in the department being studiously considered by the lessee.

Here are given the names of the "Band." We notice, by the way, that what in the other city theatres is now styled the orchestra is still called on Mr. Wallack's play-bills by the honest hearty Anglo-Saxon name of "Band," and it is only a season or so ago that the "Band," of Wallack's Theatre, under the direction of Mr. Baker, accomplished the great feat of playing a "*New* aria, by Louis XIII.," which was probably "new" when Louis XIII. composed it, some two centuries and a half ago. Nevertheless we must confess a lingering affection for that old-fashioned word, and are obliged to

Mr. Wallack and to Mr. Baker for their "Band." We do wish, however, that Mr. Baker's "Band" did not indulge itself quite so much in "popular melodies" and in sleigh-ride vocal choruses. But this is a digression! Mr. H. Isherwood, the present scenic artist at the present Wallack's Theatre, occupied that by no means unimportant position at the original house.

The performances on this opening night commenced with the "Popular and Brilliant Comedy of 'The Way to Get Married,'" with a cast so strong that we cannot resist giving its principal parts: —

Toby Allspice	Mr. W. R. Blake.
Dashall	Walcot.
Sargent	Lester.
Faulkner	C. Mason.
Caustic	H. B. Phillips.
Julia Faulkner	Mrs. Hale.
Lady Sorrell	Mrs. Crammer.
Fanny	Miss Tayleure.
Clementine	Mrs. Buckland (late Miss Kate Horn).

Previous to the Play

"The Band will perform a Grand Medley Overture."

Mr. Baker, it would seem, has inherited his medleys from Mr. Tyte. "A picturesque *pas-seul* by Miss Malvina" (now Mrs. W. J. Florence), succeeded the comedy. She became Mrs. Florence early in the following year. They were married, we believe, on the 1st of January, 1853, and made their first joint appearance as Mr. and Mrs. Florence at the National Theatre in June. But again we wander! On the bill was the announcement that "during the evening Mr. Wallack would have the honor of addressing the audience."

The whole to conclude with the farce of the "Boarding School," which had an uninterrupted run of one hundred nights in London, and will be presented with the following immense cast : —

Captain Harcourt . . . . Mr. Walcot.
Lieutenant Varley . . . . Mr. Lester.
Count Kavanagh . . . . Mr. Brougham.
James, Mrs. G.'s Page . . . . Mr. Blake.
James Holly . . . . Mr. Chippendale.
Miss Biggs, Teacher . . . . Mrs. Brougham.
Mary Mite . . . . Miss Julia Gould.
Miss Flinter . . . . Mrs. Stephens.
Julia Manvers . . . . Mrs. Hale.
Mrs. Grodenap . . . . Mrs. W. R. Blake.

On Thursday "The Poor Gentleman."
On Friday "John Bull."

Doors open at 7 o'clock. To commence at 7.30.

Prices of Admission.

Parquet and Dress Circle . . . . 50 cents.
Family Circle . . . . 25 cents.
Orchestra Chairs . . . . 75 cents.
Private Boxes, $6 and $7, according to size."

We have given you here, old play-goer, for old time's sake, the first bill of the Wallack management, shorn of course of its fair proportions, and ornamented, if not improved, by certain "asides" of our own. A bill which, in every well-organized play-going mind, we are sure will stir up many pleasant recollections; and a bill which, as the first of almost twenty-five consecutive seasons of bills, or of fifty seasons, including those of its twenty-five summers, deserves all of the prominence and publicity we have given it, and is as well worthy of careful preservation among our dramatic archives, as are the Declaration of Independence or the Civil Rights Bill, among the archives of the State.

Wallack's Theatre and the Wallack family, James W., Henry, James W., Jr., and John Lester, have occupied so important a position and have played such important parts in the history of the New York stage, that any recollections that do not embrace them, would be as incomplete as the proverbial playing of "Hamlet" with the omission of *Hamlet* himself.

The "Elder Wallack," and his brother Henry, crossed the ocean more than fifty years ago, and were ever prominently and honorably before the public of this country as proprietors, actors, and managers; doing everything in their power to educate the popular taste to an appreciation of what was high and moral in their profession, and to elevate the standard of the drama in New York. We can hardly realize how many healthy, pure new plays, how many great and good old plays, and how many of the best stock actors, have been introduced to us by the Wallack family; nor do the public fully appreciate how immense as actors, and how excellent as gentlemen these Wallacks have been. More careful, more highly cultivated, more studious artists our stage has never known. A better *Shylock* or *Benedict* than the elder Wallack's, a better *Squire Broadlands*, so says tradition, than that of his brother Henry, our stage has never seen. A better *Fagin* or *Henry Dunbar*, a better *Man in the Iron Mask* than the late James W. Wallack, Jr., our stage will perhaps never see again, while as *Charles Surface*, *Young Marlowe*, *Alfred Evelyn*, and a host of other comedy characters, Lester Wallack has no equal on our stage to-day.

That dramatic talent is inherent there can be no doubt. The fact is evident in the history of the Keans, the Kembles, the Mathews, and the Davenports; but it is a little remarkable that the members of three families — all of them now represented on our boards — should have furnished many of the best and most eminent comedians and tragedians known to the American stage. We refer to the Booths, the Jeffersons, and the Wallacks. Of the elder Booth and his three sons, Junius, Edwin, and John Wilkes; of the four generations of Jeffersons known to our stage; of Miss Effie Germon, a member of the Jefferson family; and of other descendants of the original Jeffersons, we have not space here to speak.

Of the Wallacks, however, besides those we have mentioned above, there were Miss Fanny and Miss Julia, daughters of Henry Wallack, and George his son, now long since passed away, all popular and commendable in their day, making of that family by birth no less than seven members, whose professional careers during the last half century have been so deservedly popular and successful, who have done so much for the drama and for our enjoyment of it, that the name of Wallack would ever stand most prominent in our dramatic annals, even were there no Wallack's Theatre in our midst to serve as a lasting monument to those who are gone. A brief chronological record of the connection of this family with the stage may be of interest here, and will serve to show of how much importance as a family they have been to the drama, and how varied and honorable have been the positions they have filled.

James W. and Henry Wallack, the sons of an eminent actor and actress of London, many of whose descendants are still on the London boards, were born in that city late in the last century, Henry being the elder of the two. They came to this country when quite young, about the year 1818, the name of James W. being found on the bills of the old Park Theatre in 1818–19, and that of Henry on those of the Anthony Street Theatre in

1820–21. James Wallack made his first appearance in America on the 7th of September, 1818, at the Park as *Macbeth*, and followed in a succession of Shakespearean and other high tragedy characters with much success. As a tragedian, however, he was not in public estimation the equal of Kean, Macready, Cooper, Cooke, or the elder Booth, although his ability and natural qualifications were many, and he was considered an artist of by no means the ordinary stamp; but, as a melodramatic actor, and as a light comedian, in such parts as *Rob Roy*, *Mercutio*, *Charles Surface*, *Benedict*, *Martin Heywood*, *Rover*, and *Master Walter*, he was, even in his early youth, looked upon as one without a rival in America, — a reputation he always retained.

He played in New York and elsewhere in this country for many years, always popular and attractive on any stage. His first efforts as manager and proprietor were at the National Theatre, Leonard Street, corner of Church, which he opened in 1837 with a very strong company, embracing his brother Henry and his nephew James W. Wallack, Jr., Miss Emma Wheatley, Ben de Bar, Mr. Vandenhoff (the elder), Mr. Hackett, Mr. William Mitchell, Miss Mary Gannon, Miss Mary Taylor, Mr. Burton, and many other well-known names.

Mr. Burton's having made his first appearance on the New York stage at the National Theatre, under Mr. Wallack's management, is a fact which is not generally known. The occasion was a benefit performance given for Woodworth, the author of the "Old Oaken Bucket," who was in New York, broken in health, at that time, and who died a year or two later, and Mr. Burton played *Guy Goodluck*, in "John Jones."

Mr. Wallack's connection with the National Theatre

continued until its destruction by fire in 1839. He returned frequently to London, but in 1847 he settled finally in New York.

In 1852 he opened "Wallack's Lyceum," afterwards "Wallack's Theatre," on Broadway and Broome Street, and in the fall of 1861 the present "Wallack's Theatre," Thirteenth Street and Broadway, dying, as many of our readers no doubt remember, on Christmas Day, 1864, deeply regretted and cordially esteemed.

Henry Wallack's position on the New York stage was not so prominent, although he was in his day well and favorably known. He made his New York *début* at the Anthony Street Theatre, under the management of Mr. Simpson, as *Young Norval* in "Douglas," on the 9th of May, 1821.

In 1825 he was manager of the Chatham Theatre, and played at this house and at other of the East side and Broadway houses successful engagements for ten or twelve years. In 1839 he was stage manager of the National Theatre. In 1847 he was leading "old man" at the Broadway, playing such parts as *Sir Anthony Absolute*, *Sir John Vesey*, in "Money," and *Sir Peter Teazle*. He retired forever from the stage fifteen or twenty years ago.

The name of Miss Julia Wallack, his elder daughter, is seen on the old bills of the Park and Niblo's, dated 1839, 1840, and 1841. Her sister, Miss Fanny Wallack, was at the National in 1840, and leading lady at the Broadway on its opening in 1847. She was very happy in such parts as *Volante* in the "Honeymoon," *Margaret Elmore*, *Lydia Languish*, *Clara Douglas*, *Lady Gay Spanker*, *Juliet*, *Ophelia*, and *Julia*. In 1850 she was the *Juliet* to the *Romeo* of Charlotte

Cushman. She took a benefit at the Astor Place Opera House, June 8, of that year, where she played *Hamlet*, and was advertised as "that talented young actress." She played *Julia* to Mr. Eddy in the "Hunchback," *Ophelia* to his *Hamlet*, *Juliet* to his *Romeo*, and *Mrs. Haller* to his *Stranger*, at the Bowery, in February, 1852. We find her later in this same spring supporting Mr. J. R. Scott in "Richelieu" at the National. She appeared there as *Nancy Sykes*, *the Duchess* in "Faint Heart," etc. Her accession to the National Company was considered very valuable, and she filled the house while she remained. On March 12th she played *Don Cæsar de Bazan* for her own benefit, and on the 17th played *Julie* in "Richelieu," her last appearance, we believe, on the New York stage. She died in Scotland in 1856.

Mr. Henry Wallack had two sons on our stage, George Gordon Wallack, who never attained great eminence in the profession; and James W. Wallack, Jr., the most prominent and most popular of his children. He was born in London in the year 1818, brought to this country when an infant, made his first appearance as *Cora's Child*, in Pizarro, at the Chestnut Street Theatre, Philadelphia, in 1822, his *début* in New York at the National in 1838, and since that time until the day of his death in May, 1873, has been ever prominently and honorably connected with dramatic affairs, not only in New York, but throughout the United States. About the year 1860, he began his starring tour with the "Wallack-Davenport Combination," presenting "Oliver Twist," and making his great hit as *Fagin*. No one who saw him in the part at Wallack's Theatre some years ago, supported by

E. L. Davenport and Rose Eytinge as *Mr. and Mrs. William Sykes*, can forget his magnificent rendering of the part, and the great strength of his company. His last theatrical engagement was played at Booth's Theatre in the summer of 1872, when he appeared in one of the finest of his modern parts, that of *Mathias*, in "The Bells." As *Mercutio* and *Jaques* he supported Miss Neilson a little later in the season, and made his last appearance on any stage as *Henry Dunbar*, December 28, 1872. Failing health took him South for the strength he never found; and, on his return home in May of the next year, he died in the sleeping car between Aiken and Richmond. He was buried from Dr. Houghton's Church of the Transfiguration, May 27, 1873.

John Lester Wallack, son of James W. Wallack the elder, was born in New York in 1819. He made his *début* at the old Broadway Theatre in 1847, was at the Bowery in 1849 and 1850, a member of Burton's Company during the seasons of 1850–51, and 1851–52, and became stage manager for his father on the organization of the new company and opening of the new theatre in 1852, where he has since remained; on his father's death becoming proprietor of the establishment. He is now sole representative of his family; professionally, the last of his race.

CHAPTER XII.

WALLACK'S THEATRE. — MISS LAURA KEENE. — MRS. HOEY. — JAMES W. WALLACK. — HIS SHYLOCK. — HIS BENEDICT.

"These are STARS indeed!"
Henry VIII., Act IV. Sc. 1.

MR. WALLACK gathered about him at the old theatre, Broadway and Broome Street, probably the strongest combination of theatrical talent that the New York stage has ever known; if not precisely at the period of which we write, at all events in later seasons, when his already strong company was enriched by the addition of John Dyott, Humphrey Bland, Mrs. Hoey, Mr. Sothern (then Mr. Stewart), Laura Keene, Rosa Bennett, Mrs. Vernon, Mr. Placide, Mr. Holland, Miss Gannon, Sara Stevens, Mrs. Wood, Charles Fisher, John Gilbert, and a host of other well-known and favorite artists. There was hardly a play in the whole range of the drama, tragedy, comedy, history, pastoral, pastoral-comical, historical-pastoral, tragical-comical-historical-pastoral, scene individuable or poem unlimited that this company could not present, and in the highest style of art.

The following cast of

"LONDON ASSURANCE."

Dazzle . . . . Mr. Wallack.
Charles . . . . Mr. Lester.
Sir Harcourt . . . . Mr. Brougham.

Meddle	Mr. Blake.
Dolly Spanker	Mr. F. A. Vincent.
Max Harkaway	Mr. Chippendale.
Cool	Mr. Stewart (Sothern).
Lady Gay Spanker	Miss Rosa Bennett.
Grace	Mrs. John Hoey.
Pert	Mrs. Stephens.

will refresh the memory of our older readers as to the *palminess* of those days; and to our readers, whose recollections of the New York stage do not go back so far, will be some excuse for the enthusiasm with which those palmy days are still remembered.

Miss Laura Keene's name we find on the bill of this house dated September 20, 1852, playing *Albina Mandeville* to the *Sir Solomon* of Blake, in an old comedy by Reynolds, entitled "The Will;" we find her after that date figuring but rarely in our file of Mr. Wallack's bills, and her engagement at that house was brief, although not unsuccessful. This evening, September 20, is recorded as "being her first appearance in America."

Miss Keene's dramatic career, although somewhat erratic, was very eventful, and her subsequent position in New York and influence upon local dramatic affairs, warrant our devoting more than a paragraph to her here. She was born in England in 1820, and first appeared on the London stage, at the Lyceum Theatre, as a pupil of Madame Vestris. She was engaged by Mr. Wallack in London, and brought to this country to play leading parts, was received very kindly, and was highly praised for her grace, "intellectuality," and personal beauty. She was not in 1852 a very young, but she is remembered as being a very attractive woman, with a musical, sympathetic voice, and charming carriage. She played during that first season at Wallack's, such parts as *Beatrice*, to Mr. Wallack's *Benedict; Rosalind* to his *Jaques; Rachel Heywood* to his *Martin* in the "Rent Day;" *Lady Gay Spanker*, *Clara Douglas*, and *Lady Teazle*, giving him throughout most excellent support, and making the great mistake of her life when she left his company. She was succeeded by Mrs. Hoey. After leaving Wallack's she travelled about this country as a star, returning to New York in December, 1855, to open the Metropolitan Theatre as "Laura Keene's Varieties." On the 18th of November, 1856, she opened the present Olympic Theatre, which was built for her and called "Laura Keene's New Theatre." The first play was "As You Like It," Miss Keene playing "*Rosalind*" with G. K. Dickinson as *Jaques*, George Jordan *Orlando*, and Charles Wheatleigh *Touchstone*. She produced, during the four or five years of her management, the "Colleen Bawn," "The Victims" (with Jefferson as *Joshua Butterby*), "The Sea of Ice," "The Seven Sisters," and "Our American Cousin," all of them new to the New York stage, and some of them very popular and very successful. We remember her very pleasantly as *Florence Trenchard*, a part she played over a thousand times in America, as *Effie Deans* in Boucicault's version of the "Heart of Midlothian," as *Ann Chute*, *Rose Fielding*, *Cicely Homespun*, *Clara Douglas*, and *Lady Teazle*.

She was certainly a clever actress while in her prime, and very many of her old comedy parts were admirably and charmingly played. During the last ten years of her life, she was little known to the New York stage. Her last managerial effort here was very unsuccessful. She produced at the Fourteenth Street Theatre, in 1870, a drama called "Nobody's Child," but her engagement came to a sudden termination after a week's performance. She appeared about the same time in "Hunted Down" at Lena Edwin's Theatre, but all her former attractiveness was gone. We saw her last at Niblo's Garden, January 17, 1872, at a complimentary benefit given to Miss Matilda Heron, when she played *Lady Teazle* to the *Sir Peter* of Mr. John Jack, in one scene of "The School for Scandal." The spectacle was a very melancholy one. Superfluous indeed the veteran lagged! She died of consumption, November 5, 1873, at the Hillside House, in Montclair, New Jersey, and was there buried privately in the Roman Catholic Cemetery. At her own request her death was not publicly announced until the last rites were performed. Her beauty, it is said, was entirely gone and not even her oldest and most intimate friends could have recognized her as the brilliant Laura Keene of other days, who on her *début* here was so enthusiastically received, so often recalled, and so loaded with flowers and honors.

The comedy revivals at Wallack's Theatre in 1852 compare favorably with the present commendable efforts of Mr. Lester Wallack, and with the many efforts in past seasons, of father and son, to elevate the standard of the drama. Then as now there was much that was sensational and irregular on the stage, and some determined movement was deemed necessary to restore its healthful tone. Strong casts on old established and approved plays appeared to be the best tonics, and these were administered in careful and not too frequent doses by Mr. Wallack, to a public which acknowledged the efficacy of the medicine and cried for more.

The old comedies were presented and in all their splendor; we will mention the "Heir at Law," "Road to Ruin," "West End," "She Stoops to Conquer," "Speed the Plough," "Money," "London Assurance," "Old Heads and Young Hearts," "Much Ado About Nothing," "Don Cæsar," "Merchant of Venice," and "The Stranger." We refrain from giving casts, but those who are interested with us in these matters, will understand how we are tempted to particularize the parts played in every one of the well-known pieces, by "these our stars." No doubt, in their mind's eye, many of our readers have done this for themselves, and have peopled every one of the above plays with the company we have mentioned, and which they remember so well. They have seen Lester Wallack as *Alfred Evelyn*, as *Charles Courtly*, and as *Littleton Coke*, William Rufus Blake as *Daniel Dowlas*, *Old Dornton*, *Mr. Hardcastle*, *Jesse Rural*, *Sir Harcourt*, *Meddle*, *Col. Damas*, and *Sir Robert Bramble*, George Holland as *Tony Lumpkin*, Mrs. Vernon as *Mrs. Malaprop*, Mrs. Hoey as *Pauline*, and Miss Gannon as *Lydia Languish*. The unadulterated English drama here at least had found an American home, and there ensued such plays and such playing in a rapid succession of revivals, that for the present generation of then young actors was set up a school of art, the splendid results of which are seen among its graduates to-day.

How well we remember, and with what pleasant memories, the *Gertrude* of Mary Gannon, the "Little Treasure" of the New York stage twenty years ago; the *Pocahontas* of Mrs. John Wood, our "Gentle Savage;" Mrs. Vernon's *Nancy Strap* in the "Pleasant Neighbor," then a pleasant neighbor to all New York; and the *Pauline* of Mrs. Hoey, the "Lady of Lyons," and the Lion of Ladies on the metropolitan boards.

Mrs. Hoey's *Pauline* was in many respects the most satisfactory and perfect that we have ever seen, and not one of the modern *Paulines* has effaced its memory. Miss LeClerq's *Pauline* is very strong, Miss Neilson's very pretty, and Mrs. J. B. Booth's very artistic, earnest, and finished; but we always think of Mrs. Hoey as the ideal bride of Bulwer's romantic hero, and in the second act, *Claude's* poetical and supernatural birds of Como, from out their glossy bowers still in their songs syllable to us the name not so much of *Pauline* as of Mrs. Hoey. We quite approved of the taste of the gardener's son when Mrs. Hoey represented the daughter of the Deschappelles; for her sake would even have written verses, and like *Melnotte*, would have thrown down the ancestral shovel and the hoe for the sake of Mrs. *Pauline* Hoey.

No one on the stage to-day would tempt us to hang up our fiddle and our bow; but in the times of which we write, we were by no means peculiar in our devotion to the lady in question. She was considered by Young New York the very personification of all that was bright and beautiful, not only in art but in womankind; in many an air castle that was built on the Lake of Como, by the youth of her audiences, did she, no doubt, prominently figure, while many youthful dreamers will remember how poorly the eloquence of words was able in those days to translate the poetry of hearts like theirs!

The part played by Mrs. Hoey, as Miss Josephine Shaw, as Mrs. Russell and as Mrs. John Hoey, in the history of the stage in this city, has ever been a very high-principled and influential one. As artist and lady, no actress has ever been held in greater esteem, and her influence upon the "profession" and the public was always exerted for the highest good. If we have had greater actresses we certainly have had few more *generally* and more uniformly excellent than Mrs. Hoey. Everything she did was gracefully done; she was elegant, intellectual, and refined, and her like we have not looked upon since she left the stage.

Mrs. Hoey, we believe, was born in England. She came to this country when quite a young girl, and made her first appearance on the New York stage, in 1841, as *Fluvia* in "The Naiad Queen," at the National Theatre, under the management of Mr. Burton. In 1849 she joined Mr. Burton's Chambers Street Company, as Mrs. Russell, remaining until her marriage to Mr. John Hoey in 1851, when she took a farewell benefit (June 13) and retired from the stage. She was induced by Mr. Wallack upon the secession of Miss Keene to return to professional life, and made her first appearance as Mrs. John Hoey, January 30, 1854, as *Constance* in "The Love Chase." She was leading lady at Wallack's, and unquestionably the most popular leading lady in New York until 1863, when she retired abruptly and finally from the stage.

We remember particularly, besides her *Pauline* in the "Lady of Lyons," her *Pauline* in a drama of that name, her *Edith* in "Dombey and Son," her *Amy Campbell* in "Jessie Brown," *Miss Hardcastle*, *Mrs. Torrens*, *Mrs. Sternhold*, *Mrs. Lorimer*, *Henriette*, *Lady Gay Spanker*, and her *Beatrice* to the *Benedick* of the elder Wallack, the last a bit of Shakespearean comedy acting on the part of both artists that we have never seen excelled.

The elder Wallack himself we recall with the profoundest respect, for it is to him that we are indebted for a perfect realization of many of our high-art dreams. We will not speak of the past, of which we know so little except by tradition; but, has the stage since his time known a *Don Cæsar* like his? Where can we turn to match his faultless *Benedick?* Has *Shylock* lived since Wallack died? His son in these parts — *Benedick* and *Don Cæsar* — is very fine; but is the father's shadow, clearly imitating his sire in many respects, as the sire is said to have succeeded in copying much of the "dignity of movement and majesty of action" of Mr. Kemble. That Mr. Kemble's daughter was impressed greatly by Mr. Wallack's acting, her own words testify. Of his *Martin Heywood*, — a part in which many of our younger readers will remember his nephew, and a part which was not considered one of Mr. Wallack's greatest, — Miss Fanny Kemble wrote many years ago: "Wallack was to act in the 'Rent Day.' . . . . I cried most bitterly during the whole piece; for, as in the very first scene Wallack asks his wife if she will go with him to America, and she replies, 'What! leave the farm!' I set off thence and ceased no more! Wallack played admirably. I had never seen him before, and was greatly delighted with his acting. I thought him handsome, of a rustic kind — the very thing for the part he played, an English yeoman." Praise from such a source is praise indeed!

Mr. Wallack re-created, as it were, the characters of the past: in his acting, parts, obscured by the lapse of time, breathed again living, real men. His was the master hand that could retouch the lily and restore the rose. His *Shylock* we will never forget, and of

Shylock can we never think but as Wallack showed him to us. His was the Jew that Shakespeare drew; and, from the discovery of *Shylock* and *Bassanio*, in the third scene, from *Shylock's* "Three thousand ducats — well," to his final exit, his "I pray you give me leave to go from hence: I am not well. Send the deed after me and I will sign it," the rendering was immense! It is fifteen years since we saw it. "The Merchant of Venice" had an unprecedentedly long run at Wallack's Old Theatre in the winter of 1859 or 1860; but every line of it, every expression of the usurer's face, every tone of his voice, is as fresh in our memory as if we had heard it but yesterday. We had our own idea of what *Shylock* should be, and were disposed to view Mr. Wallack's rendering of it with a critic's eye; but we left the house satisfied that never before had we known *Shylock*. Every sentence he uttered had for us a new interpretation, a deeper meaning than we had ever conceived, and if Mr. Wallack had never played another part, for his *Shylock's* sake ever would we keep his memory green!

CHAPTER XIII.

THE OLD BROADWAY THEATRE. — ITS FIRST SEASON. — GEORGE BARRETT. — ROSE TELBIN. — SAMUEL LOVER.

> " Then give it your hobby-horse."
> *Othello*, Act IV. Sc. 1.

WE are all of us more or less creatures with a hobby, and no ordinary amount of obstruction can prevent our riding that hobby as long as there is anything of that hobby left us to ride. Our own hobby has been the stage, and nothing was so fascinating to us in our juvenile days as plays and players. The stage was almost all the world to us, and all the players were hardly men and women of the ordinary mould. To follow old Burton down Hudson Street as he went to his theatre in the twilight of a summer evening, and to hear the Ravels chatter in their French tongue, of which we understood not a word, while they cut their capers in the swimming baths at the Battery, was to us, in " the long ago," a delight that no sensation of the present can equal.

The leaning of the sapling towards the drama has inclined the tree in the same direction, and still the stage is our hobby, and the enjoyment of it to-day, and the lament over its days that were palmy, are among our " pet peculiarities." While actors and actresses, as we find in our association with them, are generally good fellows and estimable ladies, still they are only human; and, while virtue is not rewarded nor vice exposed in real life, as our contemplation of life on the stage led us to expect would be the case, still, for all that, there clings to us yet our belief in the drama and its representatives, whom we desire to see well used, for they are the abstracts and brief chronicles of the time.

If we do not see things dramatic, or things real, as we saw them with our youthful eyes, our juvenile vision still influences to a certain extent our maturer sight, and we cannot help comparing the present with what we saw, or thought we saw, in the past. On these past impressions we are now drawing, and if we are at fault in our reminiscences, or misjudge any of the plays and players of which and of whom we write, our readers, we trust, will not view us with a critic's eye, but, making all allowance for the riding of our hobby, and for our reverence of other days, will pass by our imperfections.

Our well-kept play-bills are to us an album of photographs; and, as we turn them over, their black letters reveal plainly to us the scenes and incidents we try to reproduce in these pages. Each name of prominence, although not always the name in the largest type, has clinging to it so many memories that we have to draw but very faintly upon our imagination for the stories we tell, and, as Mace Sloper says, "What things we keep recollecting, and recollecting, and using, as fast as we catch them, to draw in still more out of the great, deep, dark river of Old Times."

During the summer of 1847 was completed what we now remember as the Old Broadway Theatre. Located between Pearl and Worth Streets, — in those days Anthony Street, — its main entrance on Broadway, and its stage communicating with both of the side streets, it had every advantage of situation and of space, and when opened to the public on the evening of the 27th of September, its bright, cheerful, fresh appearance, its white and gold decorations, its maroon plush sofas, and its balcony circle and parquet connecting, as do those at Niblo's now, were so charmingly suggestive of comfort, that the crowded audience on its first night pronounced the house a success — a verdict against which there was never an exception taken during the long career of the "Old Broadway."

Alvah Mann, who had moved circus after circus through country town and hamlet, was the financial man of the concern. Trimble, the builder of the Olympic, was the architect, and the house was a credit to the city and to them. Bristow was the leader of the orchestra, and George Barrett was acting manager. Prices were — balcony and parquet, $1; family circle, 50 cents, and gallery, 25 cents. The great bill of the opening night is worth preserving. The "School for Scandal" was produced with the following artists cast for leading parts: —

Sir Peter Teazle	Mr. Henry Wallack.
Joseph Surface	Mr. Harry Lynne.
Charles Surface	Mr. George Barrett.
Sir Benjamin Backbite	Mr. J. M. Dawson.
Lady Teazle	Miss Rose Telbin.

After which "USED UP."

Sir Charles Coldstream	Mr. Lester.
	(His first appearance in America.)
Sir Adonis Leech	Mr. Henry Hunt.
Tom Saville	Mr. E. Shaw.
John Ironbrace	Mr. Vache.
Wurzell	Mr. Everard.
Mary Wurzell	Mrs. Watts.
Lady Clutterbuck	Miss Gordon.

We do not propose to analyze this bill, or to speak particularly of this performance; but as the management of the Broadway introduced some new faces to the American stage that have since become so prominently connected with it, and as we notice some other well-known names, though at that time better known than at the present, we feel that a slight mention of some of them may not come amiss. The most important announcement, perhaps, was the first appearance in America of Mr. Lester, the J. Lester Wallack of to-day, a name that is almost a household word in this city. As *Sir Charles Coldstream*, he achieved at once a dramatic success that he has steadily maintained during the twenty-five years of his connection with the New York stage as actor, manager, and proprietor. Probably the best actor in his line in this country, he is certainly the best known man in this metropolis, and no man now living, except, perhaps, John Brougham, has played so prominent a part in our dramatic history, or is so fully identified with the dramatic prosperity of New York. Was this opening night at the Old Broadway, of which we write, in no other way worthy of particular note, it would still be a memorable evening in the annals of the stage for having witnessed the *début* of Lester Wallack.

On this occasion Harry Lynne and J. M. Dawson, both of English extraction, made their first bow to an Amerian public as *Joseph* and *Sir Benjamin* in "School for Scandal;" and afterwards in this country, both in New York and in the Provinces, became established favorites. Mr. Henry Wallack, an old Park Theatre favorite, re-appeared as *Sir Peter*, after an absence of several years from this city, and played leading "old man" at the Broadway during its first season. Mrs. Watts is the present Mrs. John Sefton, of Wallack's Theatre, so cordially esteemed and liked in New York to-day, and one of the connecting links between these and other times. She is one of the very few ladies of the old school now left us, and our only objection to the management of Wallack's late regular seasons is, that we have not seen more of Mrs. Sefton. Her *Araminta Brown* in "David Garrick," almost the only part of any length or importance that she has played in some years, was one of the most refreshing bits of comic business in that particular line within our recollection, and would have established her reputation as a more than commonly clever artist, if she had never played anything else, or had not established for herself such a reputation twenty-five or thirty years ago.

Miss Rose Telbin, "charming Rose Telbin," is still remembered by the old "boys," sadly but pleasantly; they considered her as sweet a *Lady Teazle* as their young eyes had ever looked upon, and sincerely mourned her untimely death. Her private life was pure and without reproach, and her professional career full of promise. She was engaged to be married to Mr. Dawson of this company, whose power to win the love of such a woman was deemed by the "boys" proof of merit on his part if he had shown no other; their wedding was to have taken place at the end of the first Broadway season, but she died from the effects of a bad cold contracted in her profession, early in the spring of the same year.

George Barrett, the acting manager of the Old Broadway, during its first and many subsequent seasons, was a very old favorite in New York, his connection with our local stage dating back to the last century; it having been said that he appeared as one of the children in the "Stranger" in 1798. At all events there is in existence a bill of the Park Theatre, dated 1806, on which is seen the name of "Master George Barrett" cast as *Young Norval* in the play of "Douglas." He was at different periods manager of the Broadway, the Bowery, and of provincial theatres, always an excellent manager, but better as an actor; excelling in the "genteel comedy" parts, and winning for himself a reputation as the best light comedian of his day. He was particularly good in such characters as *Charles Surface*, which he played on this opening night, as *Beverly* in the "Gamester," *Young Rapid* and *Rover*; and in later years he was excellent as *Col. Damas*, *Sir Harcourt Courtley*, *Sir Peter Teazle*, and as *Old Dombey*, which was one of the last and most successful parts he assumed at Burton's Theatre. His manners both on and off the stage were elegant; he had a courtly old-fashioned style about him that was inimitable, and he certainly deserved the appellation of which he was so proud, that of "Gentleman George." He was also a good low comedian, and made some decided hits in low comedy parts, but this was a line of business which he rarely consented to touch, considering it beneath the dignity of so refined and intellectual an artist. Mr. Barrett retired in 1855, receiving on the 20th of November, in that year, a grand complimentary and remunerative benefit at the Academy of Music. He became subsequently a teacher of elocution, and prepared not a few pupils for the stage, but died in comparative poverty and almost forgotten on the 5th of September, 1860.

On the bills of the old Broadway during this first season we notice many prominent names other than those we have mentioned above, and its company was certainly a very brilliant one. Miss Fanny Wallack, beautiful and popular, made her first appearance here in some years in "Love's Sacrifice," playing *Margaret Elmore* to the *Matthew* of George Vandenhoff. The Monplaisir Ballet Troupe made their first bow to an American audience at this house. Mr. Murdoch, Mr. Hadaway, Madame Anna Bishop, Julia Barton, Mr. George Farren, Mr. Wm. B. Chapman, James W. Wallack, Jr., and Mr. Sam Lover, the Irish comedian and author, the last in his own and then new play, "The Emigrant's Dream," were among the strong attractions of the first fall and winter.

While Mr. Lover is better remembered and known now by his written works, his songs, novels, and dramas, his histrionic ability was considerable, and in his case, as in Mr. Dickens's, the excellent actor was lost in the successful author. As far as our recollections serve us he made but few appearances on the regular boards as his own *Phil Purcell.* His success was decided as well in the legitimate line as in his inimitable entertainments called "Irish Evenings," in which, unassisted, he gave his own songs, told his own stories, and represented the well-known characters of his own creation in a delightful manner and to delighted audiences throughout the States, from Boston to New Orleans. He was a rare humorist, had a bright Hibernian rollicking manner, a happy smile, and a rich brogue. He led the van of that noble army of British authors who have come here to show us their own heroes and heroines as they see them themselves, — to be the interpreters of their own works. His visit in every way was successful; he made hosts of friends in this country, and went back to his own with many of our dollars in his pocket, our good wishes and farewells ringing in his ears, and, as he always said, the happiest recollections of America and greatest affection for the Americans, in his heart. His entertainments were quite as popular in Great Britain as here. He never returned to the United States.

CHAPTER XIV.

THE OLD BROADWAY. — WM. RUFUS BLAKE. — SKETCH OF HIS CAREER. — HIS STRONG PARTS. — HIS JESSE RURAL.

"Here *is* a RURAL."
Antony and Cleopatra, Act V. Sc. 2.

CHARLES BURKE — poor Charley Burke — was, if we remember correctly, one of the members of the original Broadway Company in 1847, although his connection with it was short. Charley was a decided favorite with the gallery and pit; his brief career on the stage was brilliant, but he died of consumption at an early age, shortly after his first success had established his popularity. He was very funny, the drollery of his face and figure was irresistible; he was currently believed by the boys of the Bowery pit to be the great original of the familiar long-legged character on the comic almanacs: and such was his reputation for comic business that he provoked a smile from his audiences, even in his serious parts. He seemed to be made on purpose to be funny, and was naturally so funny that he could never be anything else; funny in despite of himself, even when his hacking cough and lingering slow disease saddened his many friends while they could not but laugh at and with him. He had wonderfully mobile features, and a grotesque expression that is not equalled by any comic actor of the present. In figure he was not unlike the late Nelse Seymour, or the elder of the Majiltons, long and thin, given to contortionate attitudes and to whimsicalities of gait and action, although his line, of course, was entirely different from that of the negro minstrel or the high stepping variety star.

It was said that Mr. Burton, jealous of Burke, and of his successes in some of the parts which Burton had made his own, and in which he could not endure the idea of a rival, was the cause of Burke's banishment from Broadway to the east side of the town. He was believed to be financially interested in 1849 with Mr. Marshall in the Broadway Theatre, although his name does not appear in the bills of that date, and it was said to be a part of his contract with Marshall that Burke should have no engagement at the house during Marshall's management. How true this story is we do not know; it is only remembered now as a bit of the theatrical gossip of the day. At all events, Mr. Burke never succeeded after that date in getting a position in a west side theatre, but played his unhappily too few engagements in New York to the audiences of the Bowery, where he was immensely popular, and is said to have outdone even Burton himself in *Toodles*, "cork-screwing" his legs in the drunken scenes after a fashion never accomplished before or since by any actor. He has been dead eighteen or twenty years, and is, perhaps, quite forgotten, except by his own friends and the few old play-goers who cling to the memories of the palmy days of the last generation. But by these "Poor Charley Burke" is still affectionately and kindly remembered for his many good qualities as actor and man.

William Rufus Blake, one of the finest actors who ever walked the stage of the Old Broadway, joined its company in 1847 or 1848. We find upon our old bills of that season his name as stage manager, and the announcement of his return to the New York stage, after an absence of several years. He made his first appearance at this house in the drama of "Old Heads and Young Hearts," with Lester Wallack, Hadaway, Anderson, and Miss Fanny Wallack; Mr. Blake, of course, playing *Jesse Rural*. We cannot speak too highly of his personation of the simple-hearted, ridiculed, but honest old clergyman; it was as widely known and as justly admired as is Mr. Jefferson's *Rip Van Winkle* to-day, and will be remembered as one of the most, if not *the* most, truthful pieces of acting, the most careful studies, ever seen upon the American stage, except, perhaps, Mr. Blake's own *Geoffrey Dale* in the "Last Man."

The play-going public have never witnessed anything so intense, so absolutely perfect as *Jesse Rural* in Mr. Blake's hands. He became so identified with the character, both in action and appearance, and, we believe, in feeling, that he was no longer William Blake but *Jesse Rural*, and we loved the good old man from the moment of his stepping into *Littleton's* rooms with *Tom*, in the first act, until the last act, when he blesses everybody, heads and hearts upon the stage and off it, and with tremulous voice gives the last loving advice of an old head to young hearts the world over, — love one another.

We always remember Mr. Blake as we last saw him at Laura Keene's Theatre in 1863, a few weeks before his death, when the curtain fell for the last time on *Jesse Rural*, and when Mr. Blake and *Jesse Rural* together — for we can never think of any one else in the part — passed from our sight forever.

The leading parts of the cast of this final performance of the comedy we give, having before mentioned the artists who took part in its first representation, fifteen years before.

Jesse Rural	Mr. Blake.
Tom Coke	Charles Wheatleigh.
Littleton Coke	Charles Walcott, Jr.
Lord Roebuck	Mr. Levick.
Lady Alice	Laura Keene.
Kate Rockett	Ione Burke.

During this closing engagement of Mr. Blake's professional career in New York he played *Mons. Genet* in "No Rest for the Wicked," and *Billy Bluff* in "Bantry Bay," an Irish drama. At his last appearance on the New York stage, and for his benefit, April 16, 1863, he played *Sir Anthony Absolute* and *Geoffrey Dale.* On the 21st of the same month, after playing *Sir Peter* to the *Lady Teazle* of Laura Keene in Boston, he was taken suddenly ill and died the next evening at the Parker House; his part, that of *Stout* in "Money," being played by a member of the stock company of the theatre, while he breathed his last.

The intelligence of the death of Mr. Blake, so entirely unexpected in New York, caused a profound sensation among the play-going public and among his personal friends, who had seen him on our boards so lately in the best of spirits, and apparently in the best of health. He was buried in Greenwood on the 26th of April, and his funeral, at the Wainwright Memorial Church in Hammond Street, was very largely attended, a large concourse of people being unable to enter the church at all. The theatrical profession was represented by the leading talent of the city, and no man in his public position in New York probably has been so sincerely lamented by all classes and conditions of men. He had been so long associated with the pleasant and bright memories of the town; he had in so marked a degree the faculty of drawing to himself the sympathies of his audiences, he had contributed to so much harmless pleasure and enjoyment in his profession, and his character as a man was so high, that his death was felt to be a personal bereavement not less by those who had only known him as an actor than by his nearer and more intimate friends. He is still kindly remembered by a very large class of the community, and no actor on the stage has yet been recognized as his successor in the parts he made his own.

The "Last Man," so far as we can remember, has not been put upon the stage since Mr. Blake played it, and "Old Heads and Young Hearts" is very seldom represented since his death. It was last produced in this city in December, 1873, at Daly's Fifth Avenue Theatre for one or two nights, Mr. Davidge essaying the part of *Jesse Rural*, but not even on Mr. Davidge's shoulders, nor on the shoulders of any actor of the present, has the mantle of Mr. Blake fallen.

Mr. Blake was born in Halifax, Nova Scotia, in 1805. His parentage was Irish. He made his first bow to an American audience when quite a young man, at the Old Chatham Garden Theatre, on Chatham Street, between Duane and Pearl Streets, on the 12th of July, 1824, playing *Frederick* in Coleman's "Poor Gentleman," and the three-part character of *Percival, Pertinax*, and *Peregrine Single* in an old farce, entitled "The Three Singles." He was slim of figure, graceful in carriage, and at once achieved a decided success in New York. He has been a prominent figure in the history of the American stage as actor and manager, not only in New York but in other cities. He was a man of extensive culture and of many accomplishments; his powers of conversation are said by those who had the pleasure of his acquaintance to have been of a high order; he was eloquent and fluent as a talker, bright and witty as a *raconteur*, and cordial and sympathetic in his social relations.

While Mr. Blake frequently and successfully played eccentric comedy and cockney parts, his greatest characters were his "old men." While his humor was subtle and delicate, it was often broad and hearty, and although he could move his audiences to laughter, he could also move them to shed many and real tears. Tears are not unfrequent in plays of the sensational school of the present, but we have never witnessed any mimic performance that so excited the sympathy of the public as his *Jesse Rural;* have never seen so many genuine tears shed in a theatre as have been shed over the touching actions and expressions of the poor old clergyman. Mr. Blake is said to have been the first actor who received in this country the compliment of a call before the curtain. Such compliments are common enough in this country now, but we know of no actor who has more richly merited them than he.

Mr. Blake's finest and most memorable parts, in addition to his *Jesse Rural* and his *Geoffrey Dale*, were his *Sir Anthony Absolute*, *Old Hardcastle*, *Grandfather Whitehead*, *Robert Bramble*, in the "Poor Gentleman," and his *Bullfrog*, in the "Rent Day." By his *Jesse Rural*, however, is he best remembered. The Autocrat, in one of his charming breakfast-table talks, speaking of the kindred nature of tears and laughter, says: "If you want to choke with stifled tears at the sight of this transition" — from laughter to weeping, — "as it shows itself in older years, go and see Mr. Blake play *Jesse Rural.*"

Mr. Blake's *Jesse Rural* was an art study, and as such it stands beyond the pale of criticism; over our recollections of it we linger lovingly, almost reverently, and strive here to pay to it and to him, this affectionate tribute of a young heart to an old head.

CHAPTER XV.

THE OLD BROADWAY. — MR. DAVIDGE. — MR. FORREST. — MRS. FORREST'S *DÉBUT*.

"Even those you were wont to take such delight in, — the tragedians of the City." — *Hamlet*, Act III. Sc. 2.

THE first season of the "Old Broadway" Theatre, — 1847 and 1848, — of which we have spoken in previous chapters, seems to have brought before the public almost every actor of any prominence at that time upon the New York stage, for our old bills contain the names of James Anderson, tragedian; John Collins, comedian, playing Irish parts; and John Brougham, playing *Jack Swift* in his then new five-act comedy of "Romance and Reality," in addition to the many gentlemen and ladies whom we have mentioned, or have more fully noticed.

While we have thus sketched with more regularity than we had at first intended, a regular season's business at this house, we have spared our readers more than a passing glance at the plays, new and old, good and bad, now well known or long since forgotten, which were produced during that season.

In the future, in speaking of the "Old Broadway," we shall recall plays and players as they occur to us, without regard to season or sequence; and we will in a rambling, desultory way, strive to work this mine, rich in reminiscences, in a manner that will perhaps interest the new generation of play-goers, who know only by hearsay and tradition the people and times of whom and of which we write, as well as the veterans young and old, who, before and behind the curtain, were part and parcel of those "palmy days."

We take up the following bill of an evening's entertainment, which deserves more than the passing word we give it, as introducing for the first time to an American audience, William Davidge, the ever since popular comedian; Mr. Fred. B. Conway, so well known and universally liked in his day in Brooklyn; and the sisters Gougenheim, who for several seasons were very popular.

August 19, 1850, first night of the season, and of

"THE SCHOOL FOR SCANDAL."

Sir Peter Teazle	Mr. William Davidge.
Sir Oliver Surface	Mr. George Barrett.
Charles Surface	Mr. F. B. Conway.
Joseph Surface	Mr. W. S. Fredericks.
Lady Teazle	Miss Anderton.
Maria	Miss Ada Gougenheim.

Mr. George Barrett and Mr. Fredericks were the only familiar names at the Old Broadway and in New York, the others making their first bows to an American public that August night. Of these artists, all in their way good and commendable, we will again have occasion to speak. Mr. Davidge is still with us, but Mr. Barrett and Mr. Conway are dead, and the others have not been known to our stage for some years.

During this summer of 1850 it was, we think, that the auditorium of the Old Broadway underwent a decided change; the exact date of the change we do not remember, nor is mention made of such alteration in the old note-book at our command, — the manuscript records of an old veteran's idea of matters and things theatrical in general, from which occasionally we draw our facts and fancies. But this we do remember, that a few seasons after its opening, during a summer's vacation, it was cut down, to increase the parquet's holding capacity, and the house was opened with facilities for seating a hundred or more additional people, but not at all to the satisfaction or edification of the people who were to be seated. The floor was lowered until back seats, to the juvenile portion of the audience, of which we were frequently one, were as acceptable for seeing purposes as the outside of a circus tent; and hearing, even to adults, who *could* see more than the "hoofs of the horses," was a matter of the utmost difficulty. Stage whispers and *piano* movements were lost entirely, and plots were subjects of mere speculation.

We know of one small boy who was jammed against the wall of this house one long evening, while Mr. Forrest, for whom he had an unbounded admiration, was playing *Jack Cade*, and did not get a single glimpse of the stage during all the five acts of the tragedy; only hearing distinctly one sentence of the tragedian, Mr. Forrest's passionate burst, "Aylmere, no more after this happy hour, but *CADE*, *Cade*, the bondsman!" This was hardly a fair requital for the discomfort, for the outlay of juvenile finance, and the risk of parental displeasure if the juvenile attendance at such places should be discovered. The small boy in question, "no more after that happy hour," went to the parquet of the Old Broadway, but joined the celestial band in the gallery, where he saw and heard, and drew inspiration for future recollections.

This leads us to speak of Mr. Forrest's several engagements at this house. His first, we think, was played during its second fall and winter season of 1848 and 1849, when, in the characters of *Virginius*, *Othello*, *Damon*, and *Richelieu*, and supported by such actors as John Dyott, Lester Wallack, Miss Fanny Wallack, and the strength of the Broadway company, Mr. Forrest, lately returned from Europe, played to houses crowded night after night, for a month or more, one of the most successful engagements ever remembered on the New York stage. He was then at the height of his popularity, and in his very prime as an actor; it was before the Macready riots, or the Forrest divorce suit had brought his name so unpleasantly and so unhappily before the public; and such of our readers as recall this particular series of his personations will recall Mr. Forrest at the period of his greatest histrionic ability. He was at that time in the full possession of all those wonderful physical qualifications that gave him such decided natural advantages in certain of his particular parts, and which made him almost perfect in those characters requiring the adjuncts of powerful voice and muscle. The study of foreign artists in his European tour had been decidedly to his advantage in toning down his style, and only in such parts as permitted the expression of the deepest feelings did he indulge in that rant and rampage, which before had marred many of the performances of the greatest of American actors.

He played at this house other engagements, but none so memorable or so successful as this, although, in 1852, just after the termination of the famous Forrest divorce suit, his friends and the town, anxious to see the man who was the town talk, crowded to the Broadway during the course of a prolonged engagement.

Among our old bills of Brougham's Lyceum, of about the same date, we find Mrs. Forrest under her maiden name, Catherine Sinclair, playing *Pauline* and *Lady Teazle;* in the latter character making her theatrical *début* on the 2d of February, 1852. She also drew good houses, but the Forrest divorce suit at that time was the all-pervading topic of discussion and interest; public feeling ran strongly for or against the contending parties; each had his or her sympathizers and admirers; and to this fact, did the managers of both these houses owe in a great degree the successes and profits of their rival engagements.

So strong was the public feeling that an actual "Row at the Lyceum" was greatly feared on the night of Mrs. Forrest's *début*, and hardly, except in the case of the Astor Place riots, has any event in the history of the New York stage created so much excitement in the city. The crowds were enormous. Tickets were disposed of in advance; prices were raised from fifty cents to one dollar in the lower part of the house, and from twenty-five cents to fifty in the gallery. The streets were completely blocked by the crowd long before the opening of the doors; five dollars was offered for single tickets and refused; few ladies had courage to fight their way into the building; and the scramble for places — there were no reserved seats in those days — was absolutely frightful. Out of doors order was preserved by the militia, — the 7th and 12th regiments being posted on Broome Street, by order of the Mayor, in event of their services being required. In-doors a large body of police endeavored, and for a long time in vain, to secure something like peace and quietness for the performers. The curtain did not rise for some time after the hour advertised.

Mrs. Forrest, on her entrance as *Lady Teazle*, was greeted by a perfect storm of applause, lasting many moments. She was very richly dressed, and her coolness and ease upon the stage under such trying circumstances were remarkable. The play was probably selected because of its bearing so peculiarly upon some of the incidents of the Forrest divorce suit. At all events its success and Mrs. Forrest's was great. Messrs. Brougham, Charles Walcot, Chippendale, Charles Kemble Mason, Lynne, and Mrs. Maeder, were in the cast. The *débutante* was called out at the end of the play, was cheered and applauded tumultuously, and groans were given heartily in the gallery for Mr. Forrest. Mr. Brougham, who attempted to respond for Mrs. Forrest in answer to the repeated calls for "a speech," was almost inaudible on account of the uproar, but was heard to say that this was the most brilliant triumph he had ever witnessed in New York, and that he considered Mrs. Forrest's *Lady Teazle* one of the very best he had ever seen in the world. There was no disturbance. The friends of the husband were not disposed, or did not deem it safe or expedient, to interfere with the playing of the wife.

But to return to Mr. Forrest and to the Old Broadway. Whether he ever appeared again at this house we cannot say; we do not find his name again on any of our Old Broadway bills later than this season. He has, however, repeatedly played in New York, at Niblo's and elsewhere, since that time. He last appeared before a New York audience in November, 1872, when he read "Othello" and "Hamlet" at Steinway Hall, only a few weeks before his death. His last appearance upon the New York stage in a regular dramatic performance, was at the Fourteenth Street Theatre, in February, 1871, when we saw him in "Lear," supported by Mr. Barton Hill, Mr. Tom Morris, Mr. John Matthews, Miss Lillie, and Miss Alice Placide. He played to empty benches and to cold houses, owing in part, perhaps, to the unpopularity of the Fourteenth Street house, partly to the incapacity of its management, — for he was poorly advertised, — and also to the fact that the town had forgotten Forrest, had gone after other and younger favorites, and looked upon him as the poor, infirm, and weak old man, — which personally he was, — whose day was past, whose occupation was gone. Never did he play *Lear* so well as in that last neglected, poor engagement; it was always to us the grandest of his efforts, and this, we believe, was also his own opinion; the most sublime conception of a Shakespearean character that it has been our good fortune to witness. He had lost much of his old force and fire, but nothing of his old feeling and intensity, "the trick of his voice," so well remembered, was still there, — his "every inch a king," so terribly exhaustive on the physical abilities of an actor, was magnificently rendered. He was, as he played, no longer "the ruined piece of nature," as *Lear* and as Forrest, that the *Glosters* of the tragedy and of the Press had called him, but the king, "Aye, every inch the king," he used to be.

It was the fashion in the later years of Mr. Forrest's professional life — and nearly all his life was professional — to abuse his old school of acting, to laugh at his peculiarities, to affect to pity his weaknesses, to rail on him in good set terms. He was of the old school; he had his peculiarities and his weaknesses; but where in these our younger times are we to find his like again?

> "Vex not his ghost, and let him pass; he hates him
> That would upon the rack of this tough world
> Stretch him out longer."

CHAPTER XVI.

THE OLD BROADWAY. — "ALL THAT GLITTERS." — "INGOMAR." — MR. F. B. CONWAY.

"All that glistens is not gold."
Merchant of Venice, Act II. Sc. 7.

MISS JULIA BENNETT (Mrs. Barrow) made her first appearance in New York at the Old Broadway, as *Lady Teazle*, on the evening of the 24th of February, 1851. Coming directly from the London Haymarket, she brought to this country a very favorable reputation as an artist and leading *comedienne*, and at once became a favorite with the theatre-going public of the "States." During the second week of her engagement, on the evening of March 7, she introduced for the first time in New York, and for her benefit, Morton's clever drama of "All that Glitters is not Gold," a play which from the outset took its place among the really successful productions of that season, and for some years was justly popular, and often repeated on the American stage. We reproduce this its first great cast: —

"ALL THAT GLITTERS IS NOT GOLD."

Sir Arthur Lassel	Mr. Reynolds.
Jasper Plum	Mr. Whiting.
Stephen Plum	Mr. Conway.
Frederick Plum	Mr. B. Hill.
Toby Twinkle	Mr. Davidge.
Martha Gibbs	Miss Julia Bennett.
Lady Leatherbridge	Mrs. A. Knight.
Lady Valeria	Miss A. Gougenheim.

We have a second object in the reference to this pleasant little play beyond the mere giving of its original cast as an historical record, that object being to comment briefly upon the acting of those engaged in its earliest representations, and to contrast the effect of its *morale* and tone with the unhealthful tendencies of many of the "society," "upholstery," "emotional," and "Traviata" plays of the present. We have seen this drama as played by nearly all of the dramatic combinations — star and stock — in the Northern States. We have seen amateurs and professionals wrestle with it, and win their more or less of applause, according to the merits or demerits of the performance, but by old play-goers most cheerfully is it remembered now as presented by the many good artists of this initial cast. We have seen, perhaps, better *Marthas* and better *Lady Leatherbridges* than those in the bill given above, but we do not think that the leading male parts were ever better filled than by the gentlemen who played them on this occasion.

Mr. Conway — the announcement of whose death, received last autumn while we were writing these very lines, recalls such a flood of recollections of the stage — won for himself many fresh laurels by his masterly enacting of the part of *Stephen Plum.* Both Mr. Conway and *Stephen Plum* are now, alas! men of the past; both belong to that class so sadly out of fashion now, so much derided, so utterly ignored, whose virtues in these pages we are striving to write in something more stable than water; that body of men at whom the young laugh, for whom the old sigh; that body of men, and women too, known carelessly by the many, remembered fondly by the few, and called by both "The Old

School!" *Stephen Plum* we may see again, but Mr. Conway has gone forever!

Mr. Conway belonged to a theatrical family. Tradition says he was intended for the Church; fascinated, however, by the profession of his father, a tragedian of some considerable note in England, and not unknown to our own stage, he became an actor at an early age, worked hard, and, before he came to this country in 1850, had won for himself a very fair reputation in London and the provinces. He played such parts as *Macbeth*, *Captain Absolute*, *Othello*, *Iago*, *Ingomar*, *Hamlet*, *Claude Melnotte*, and the *Stranger*, supporting Forrest, Miss Cushman, Lola Montez, Julia Dean, and other "stars" for many seasons at the Old Broadway. He was a great favorite with Mr. Forrest and with the public in the pieces in which they jointly appeared, playing second parts, and often alternating first parts, with the "old man," not only in New York, Philadelphia, and Boston, but in other cities. It is recorded that the great tragedian declared that he had found no stock actor in America to equal Conway; and, on the occasion of Mr. Forrest's farewell benefit here at the Old Broadway, in 1852, he paid Mr. Conway the handsome compliment of pronouncing him, before the curtain, in his farewell speech, "the best support he ever had!"

Mr. Conway married the present Mrs. Conway,— his second wife,— *née* Miss Sarah Crocker, in May, 1852. This was the most important and most fortunate event of his life. We have no better general actress in America to-day than Mrs. Conway. How successful she has been as a manageress and proprietress, the position of her Brooklyn Theatre to-day will testify;

while her own worth as a wife, a mother, and a lady, is universally recognized wherever she is personally known.

They made their first appearance together as Mr. and Mrs. Conway at the Metropolitan Theatre on Broadway, as *Alfred Evelyn* and *Clara Douglas*, in "Money," for the benefit of Mr. T. B. Johnstone. They "starred" about the country for some years, played an engagement in London in 1861, where they were well received; and, on the 2d of April, 1864, opened the Park Theatre in Brooklyn, with the play of "Ingomar."

Mr. Conway had been in failing health for a year or two; he relinquished active professional duties, and retired to a small country seat, where he spent the last months of his life. He was born at Clifton, England, February 10, 1819, and died near Manchester, Mass., September 7, 1874.

But to return to "All that Glitters" and the Old Broadway. Mr. Whiting — the present Mr. Whiting of the Fifth Avenue company — as *Jasper*, satisfied us so completely with his perfect rendition of the part, that we have looked in vain for an artist to succeed him in it; while Davidge as *Toby Twinkle* was irresistible. His points in the piece seemed to affect his audience with the same contagion of laughter night after night. His first pugnacious entrance in defence of *Martha*, and *Stephen's* "Why, *Martha*, what is the meaning of this?" *Martha's* agitated "I cannot speak: I refer you to *Mr. Twinkle*, sir;" and Davidge's "And *Mr. Twinkle* refers you to his nose, sir," turning and showing a naturally well developed organ, most artistically covered with painted gore, never failed to bring down, speaking figuratively, the Old Broadway. His *malap-*

ropos interference with every private conversation in his efforts to impress upon everybody his superiority to the great wizard Jacobs, his "take a card," and his shuffle of the pack, were very funny, and long to be remembered.

It is difficult for us to resist the temptation of introducing other telling quotations from the drama, in order further to illustrate the manner of the players and the style of the play; but we feel that too much have we spoken of plays that still remain on the stage, and too little of the players of whom we set out to speak, who have gone forever from our stage, or have been effectually shelved. A word or two here in regard to this really commendable drama of "All that Glitters." Plays and novels are very like men and dogs, "they have their day;" while fresh to the public, and in the first blaze of their fame, no one is apt to question the justness of their popularity. It is the fashion to see and applaud them; to read and commend them is the natural business of the hour; but sober judgment and collected second thought settle the final status of the production, and the great mellower of art — Time — can only prove how the imaginative public of a previous generation have been pleased with a rattle, or tickled with a straw.

As a work of art, "All that Glitters," tried in the crucible here set up, is a failure; for it has ceased to have any charm for the theatre-going public of the present, at least so think the managers, who never revive it on their boards; and it has not been produced here in many seasons, although in its youth it was widely and justly popular, and among our old play-bills we find it repeatedly figuring at many houses, and always with success. What has this comedy done, which in our youth amused us so, that we should neglect it now? Its pretty, *healthy*, moral little plot is still there: the lesson it teaches is as valuable and as touching now as twenty years ago. *Martha* is just as lovable, *Toby* just as funny, *Stephen* just as true; but, alas! we seem to have outgrown them and their kind; the fashions of the times are changed; we are tired of "true hearts" and "simple faith." It is only noble now not to be good, but to be emotional; to wear gorgeous toilets, and to laugh at virtue. We are running after strange comedies and dramas; we are building French idols, in which all is Glitter and not much is Gold.

The season following this of which we write opened with the same drama at the Broadway, with Conway as *Stephen Plum*, Miss Crocker (now Mrs. Conway), as *Lady Valeria*, Davidge as *Toby*, and Mrs. Vernon (her first appearance at this theatre) as *Lady Leatherbridge*, or, as *Toby* would insist upon calling her, "Old Lady Leatherbreeches." This cast was unquestionably the strongest the piece has ever known, with no dross in it, no sparkle that would not stand the assay of criticism about it, every artist having the true ring.

Another of the old plays popular in those days, and sadly out of fashion now, although very different in its style from this of which we have been writing, was "Ingomar, the Barbarian," a play for which we must confess a lingering affection, first produced in New York at the Old Broadway, on the 1st of December in this same year, 1851. Signor Salvini has lately drawn the popular attention to this drama, but does not seem to have revived the popular affection for it. He thinks the titular part, however, one worthy of his closest study, and compares it in "intensity" with the part of *Othello*. We copy from the bill the original cast, —

Will be performed for the first time, a new play in five acts, translated from the German, and altered and adapted to the English stage, by Mrs. Lovell, entitled,

"INGOMAR, THE BARBARIAN."

The new scenery by Mr. Heister. Costumes by Miss Wallis.

Greeks.

The Timarch of Massilia	Mr. Hind.
Polydor, a merchant	Mr. Thomas Barry.
Myron, an armorer	A. W. Fenno.
Lykon, a fisherman	Mr. Reynolds.
Neocles	Mr. Burgess.
Actea, Myron's wife	Mrs. Abbott.
Parthenia, her daughter	Mme. Ponisi.

Alemanni.

Ingomar, the Barbarian, leader of Alemanni	F. B. Conway.
Ambivar	Mr. Matthews.
Novio	Mr. Lyster.
Alaster	Charles Pope.
Samo	Mr. Barrett.

Barbarians, Citizens, Guards, Fishermen, etc.

It was claimed for "Ingomar," at the time of its first publication, that Mrs. Lovell had completed her task so well that to her exertions in the cause of dramatic literature, the stage was indebted for a play which, like the "School for Scandal," or "She Stoops to Conquer," would become a stock favorite, the oftener seen the better liked! How much of a "stock favorite" "Ingomar" is at present, how often repeated, and how well liked, all habitual theatre-goers know. "The language, poetry, and dramatic action have not been excelled, if equalled, in the history of the modern drama," said its original publisher. How much of its "beauty of language, poetry, and dramatic action" are remembered now? asks its present historian. Let Hercules himself do what he may, the cat has mewed, the play has had its day.

On the 1st of November, 1852, Miss Julia Dean, then in the very height of her popularity, played *Parthenia* to the *Ingomar* of Mr. F. B. Conway; and on the 29th of the same month, Mrs. Anna Cora Mowatt played the same part to the same *Ingomar* at the Old Broadway. Only once in many years has "Ingomar" been revived on our stage until Salvini's impersonation, and then but one act of it was presented, — Mr. and Mrs. Conway, at the famous Holland Testimonial Benefit at the Academy of Music, in 1871, representing the Barbarian and his faithful Grecian slave. How excellently well it was played, and how coldly it was received, many of that enormously large audience will no doubt well remember. Mr. Conway has always been the acknowledged and accepted *Ingomar* of the American stage; and as we remember him when he and *Ingomar* were better known to us, his rendering of the part suffers nothing in its comparison with that of his Italian and more pretentious rival. To his worthiness as an actor and a man we are glad to bear our testimony. May he rest in peace.

"Ingomar" is of the ultra-romantic school, with poetry and sentiment in every line; of the "two-souls-with-but-a-single-thought, two-hearts-that-beat-as-one" kind; as gushing as the "Lady of Lyons," no friends in it who are not lovers, no books that are not tales of love. It really does contain some beautiful passages, and, as a "poem," it will well repay perusal. Why should these old-fashioned plays meet with so little popular favor now? It cannot be on account of the demand for novelty on the part of the public in these days of three years of "Black Crook," and thousands of nights of "Humpty Dumpty." It must be that we are "educated up" to the modern drama and beyond the simple plays that pleased us twenty years ago.

Are we personally so very far behind the age in our affection for "Love's Sacrifice," and "Leap Year," and "All that Glitters," and "Ingomar," and were we so very much mistaken in the days of our youth when we looked upon *Matthew Elmore*, and *John Mildmay*, and *Martha Gibbs*, and *Parthenia* as the perfection of stage heroes and heroines? Are we wiser and better now than we used to be? or is our civilization a failure, and is the Caucasian played out?

CHAPTER XVII.

THE OLD BROADWAY. — "THE HUNCHBACK." — MISS JULIA DEAN. — MRS. J. M. FIELD. — OTHER JULIAS.

"O heavenly Julia."
Two Gentlemen of Verona, Act I. Sc. 3.

PERHAPS no bill in the history of the New York stage — certainly no other of the bills of the Old Broadway — is so remarkable in its chronicle of "first appearances" as this, which we copy here *verbatim*: —

On Monday Evening, August 30, 1852.
Will be performed the play, in five acts, by James Sheridan Knowles, entitled,

"THE HUNCHBACK."

Master Walter	Mr. Conway.
Sir Thomas Clifford (his first appearance) . . .	Mr. Bland.
Modus (his first appearance)	Mr. Grosvenor.
Lord Tinsel (his first appearance)	Mr. Florence.
Master Wilford (his first appearance) . . .	Mr. Sandford.
Thomas (his first appearance)	Mr. Day.
Julia (her first appearance at this theatre)	Miss Julia Dean.
Helen (first night of her engagement) .	Miss Annie Lonsdale.
Fathom	Mr. Davidge.

This was the first night of the regular fall and winter season of 1852 and 1853 at the Old Broadway, and truly if the bill is reliable, a night of *débuts*. Between "our old and faithful friends," Mr. Conway and Mr. Davidge, we find no less than seven new names and new faces — new to the boards of this house, although some of them were already well known to New York audiences, and had already established well-deserved reputations at other theatres. Mr. Humphrey Bland, the *Sir Thomas* of this night, had before appeared at the Park Theatre. He was considered the best *Jaques* on the American stage, and who that has seen him in "As You like It" will ever forget his rendition of the "Seven Ages of Man," or of kindred soliloquies. He died in 1869. In the *Modus* we recall "Joe" Grosvenor, also dead, we believe, — a quiet, conscientious actor, popular in his day. The *Tinsel* was Mr. W. J. Florence, who is above that kind of tinsel now. Mr. Sandford will be kindly remembered by the audiences of the Old Broadway; but it is to the *Julia* of the evening that we will particularly refer.

Miss Julia Dean, who figures so pleasantly in our recollections of the stage, was at this time the very ideal of *Julia* — the Julia that Knowles drew; so fitted for the part that it might have been made for her, although as the part was made before her day, she must have gone upon the stage with the special mission, and must have been created specially to play that part. As *Julia* we have never seen her equal. Her light, graceful figure, and beautiful face, won for her all the sympathy and interest in the first act that her genius and fire enabled her to maintain until the fall of the curtain. In this representation the support was in every way worthy of her. With Mr. Conway as *Master Walter*, Mr. Bland as *Sir Thomas*, and Mr. Davidge as *Fathom* — and a better *Fathom*, *Sir Thomas*, and *Master Walter* never stepped upon the stage — to encourage and sustain her, she could not but draw additional inspiration, could not but surpass herself, and delight her audience.

Those who can go back in remembrance to the *Julia*

of Miss Fanny Kemble, the original *Julia*, who played the part in London in 1832, on its first representation, to the *Master Walter* of Mr. Knowles himself, and played it subsequently in New York at the Park Theatre, supported by her father as *Sir Thomas* and with Barry, Richings, Placide, and others in the cast, still speak of it as a magnificent conception. This rendering has been the study and pattern of the score of *Julias*, good, bad, and indifferent that have come after it. But to us of a later day than Fanny Kemble's, to us to whom Fanny Kemble's *Julia* is only a tradition, Miss Julia Dean's *Julia* is the *Julia* of *Julias;* for quiet effect and subdued intensity we have seen no other to compare with it, although many other excellent actresses have played it, we know, to the equal satisfaction of many critics, who will take perhaps serious exception to our private opinion here publicly expressed. Those of our readers who remember it as it was played during this engagement, — not as she played it when Mrs. Julia Dean Hayne, after her California experiences a few years later, — will, we think, give us their endorsement of what we have here said, and sympathize with us in our perhaps too enthusiastic recollections of what we believe to have been one of the finest performances of its kind in our experience of the stage.

During this and other immediately following engagements in New York, Miss Julia Dean was decidedly and justly popular. She was so fully in sympathy with her audiences that no lady who was her contemporary on the stage could rival her in public interest. She bore herself beyond the promise of her age, and departed on her California tour, followed by the best of good wishes, and believed by her friends to be the brightest promise of the American stage.

We wish we could leave this subject here and remember this *Julia* only as we knew it first; it is not pleasant to have one's idol shattered; it is particularly unpleasant to have one's idol play the part of its own iconoclast, as did Miss Dean on her return from her trip to the Pacific.

She was very successful in San Francisco, winning applause, dollars, and a husband, but when we saw her in "The Hunchback" at Niblo's seven years later — this second bill before us is dated April 21, 1859 — she was no longer our *Julia*, Knowles' *Julia*, the *Julia* who had realized the author's ideal, the *Julia* of the past, but a *Julia* of the present, whose business seemed to be to hold up to her audiences the picture of everything that Knowles intended his *Julia* should *not* be; a picture so different from the *Julia* of Julia Dean that we could not but think she had changed her nature with her name, and had left her genius with her spinsterhood on the Pacific. What we had most to remember and admire in Miss Dean's *Julia* was the exquisite reading of the lines, and the simple, girlish grace of the actress. In Mrs. Haynes's *Julia* the contrast was great: there was hardly a sentence of pure English in the text; or a scene that was not marred by mannerisms or affectations. She mouthed and strutted, sawed the air with her hands, tore her passions to tatters, and imitated humanity as abominably as Julia Dean Hayne, as she had "o'erstepped not the modesty of Nature" as Julia Dean.

Perhaps we are at fault here in our judgment, and have done an injustice to the memory of a worthy artist. We may have rated too highly her earlier performances, as we have perhaps underestimated her later efforts, but our admiration of the one, seen perhaps through the bright spectacles of extreme youth, was so great, that our disappointment in the other, looked at perhaps with the hypercritical eyes of adolescence, was very bitter, and is still remembered.

We give here the cast of the principal parts of the "Hunchback," the last time we saw Mrs. Hayne as *Julia*, although not the last time she played the part in New York: —

NIBLO'S GARDEN. MANAGER, MR. E. EDDY.
Fourth night of the celebrated American Actress, Mrs. Julia Dean Hayne,
Who will appear, by express desire, in her great character of Julia, in the "Hunchback."
Thursday Evening, April 21, 1859.

Julia	Mrs. Julia Dean Hayne.
Master Walter	Mr. E. Eddy.
Lord Tinsel	Mr. Grosvenor.
Sir Thomas	Mr. J. B. Horne.
Fathom	Mr. Davidge.
Modus	Mr. H. Bland.

She played her farewell engagement in this city in the fall of 1867, at the Broadway Theatre (Wallack's old theatre), corner of Broadway and Broome Street, under the management of Mr. Barney Williams, when she performed such parts as *Deborah*, *Constance*, in the "Love Chase," and *Juliana* in the "Honeymoon." Her support was indifferent, and her success not great. She occasionally delighted her audiences with bursts of her old force; but the performances as a rule still continued to offer sad contrasts to her early and perfect representations.

We call this her "farewell engagement" simply because it happened to be her last. She had no idea, as far as we can remember, of bidding adieu to the stage, but died suddenly early in the next year, to the deep regret of hosts of personal and professional friends. The large crowd of citizens who attended her funeral from Christ Church, on Fifth Avenue, Sunday, October 8, 1868, attested to the regard in which she had always been held as a woman, and the admiration with which her early efforts as an actress were still remembered.

"The Hunchback" is the most original and the most successful of all of the productions of Knowles. It was first played at the Covent Garden Theatre, London, April 5, 1832, and at the Park Theatre here on the 18th June of the same year. The original casts at both houses we give below.

	Covent Garden.	Park.
Master Walter . .	J. S. Knowles . .	Mr. Barry.
Sir Thomas Clifford	C. Kemble . . .	Mr. Simpson.
Lord Tinsel . . .	Mr. Wrench . . .	Mr. Richings.
Modus	Mr. Abbott . . .	Mr. C. R. Thorne.
Fathom	Mr. Meadows . .	Mr. Henry Plaçide.
Master Wilford . .	J. Mason	Mr. Jacob Woodhull.
Gaylove	Mr. Henry . . .	Mr. Tom Placide.
Julia	Miss Fanny Kemble	Mrs. Sharpe.
Helen	Miss Taylor . . .	Mrs. Henry Wallack.

The success of the play in this country and in England was instant and decided. It enjoyed a run of many weeks in London during its first season, and is often repeated. In New York its popularity was great. It seemed to take the town by very storm, and was much the fashion for many years. Its plot and its passion appeared to tickle the popular fancy, and its language in many mouths became as familiar as household words. It was quoted in pulpits, on the platform, and in leading articles of leading journals; while its tender passages may be found yet in the albums of the young ladies of that early period, mothers and grandmothers now, with *Julias* and *Walters* of their own. "The Hunchback," thirty-five years ago, was as much a matter of common quotation as is the "other life one longs to meet, without which life one's life is incomplete," of "Led Astray," or as is *Colonel Sellers'* famous boast, "There 's millions in it," of "The Gilded Age."

Of John Keese, a well-known auctioneer in New York during the past generation, the following auction-room story is still told: At a book sale here during the first great "Hunchback" excitement, while the Kembles were nightly appearing in the play, Mr. Keese knocked down two volumes to the bid of a mild little gentleman, who, upon being asked his name, replied faintly and frightenedly, "Clifford!" Immediately striking the familiar attitude, Mr. Keese exclaimed, "'Tis Clifford's voice, if ever Clifford spoke!" and, after the storm of laughter which followed had subsided, and as the quiet gentleman, very much disconcerted, was hurrying from the room, he added, with all the pathetic intensity of Miss Kemble herself, "Clifford, why *don't* you speak to me?"

The sale was interrupted for many minutes. There was perhaps hardly a man in the room who was not as familiar with the tone and the style of Miss Kemble, and with that particular scene in the play, as was Mr. Keese; and the applause he received was as hearty as ever encouraged the best *Julia* on the professional stage. Clifford never called to claim his books.

The part of *Julia* in "The Hunchback" has always been a favorite part with our actresses, and we have had as many *Julias* on our stage as we have had leading ladies, or ladies who so considered themselves, to play it. In no other part, perhaps, have so many aspirants for dramatic fame tried their 'prentice hand as in *Julia*, and to no other do they seem to return so fondly. It is regarded as a sort of test part, and the rising star thinks if she can shine as *Julia* that she need fear no further eclipse.

The original *Julia* in America, we believe, was Miss Eliza Riddle, subsequently Mrs. J. M. Field, mother of Miss Kate Field. Miss Riddle made her theatrical *début* as *Julia* in Philadelphia, and later at the Walnut Street Theatre in that city, supported Mr. Knowles himself as *the Hunchback*, winning great praise for her careful and artistic rendering of the part. The play was presented by the Kembles at the Chestnut Street Theatre at the same time; it ran for some weeks at both houses, and the town was divided in its devotion to the rival *Julias*, Miss Riddle, as belonging to Philadelphia, — she was native there, — and as being younger in the profession, receiving, perhaps, the greater share of praise. No local reputation, however, could for a moment have rivalled successfully the popularity of Miss Frances Anne Kemble, had there been no talent behind it; and Miss Riddle, in so sharing the honors with the great artist, clearly proved herself an actress of no little promise and power. She played leading parts for many seasons, chiefly in Western and in Southern cities; she supported the elder Booth, Charles Kean, Macready, and Forrest, in frequent engagements, and made her last appearance, in Boston in 1855, as *Mrs. Mildmay*, in "Still Waters," being the original of that part, as of *Julia*, in this country. She died during a voyage to Europe in 1871.

But to return to *Julia* and "The Hunchback." New

York has seen some charming *Julias*, and many quite the reverse, from Miss Kemble, among the first, and said to have been the best, to Miss Morris, the last, and by no means the worst. Within the few years past, we have seen on our boards here and in Brooklyn, Mrs. Conway, Mrs. Bowers, Mrs. Gladstane, Mrs. Barrow, Miss Jane Coombs, Miss Cecil Rush, Miss Kate Bateman, Miss Agnes Ethel, Miss Charlotte Thompson, and others in "The Hunchback." Since 1870 the play has seen several important revivals, Miss Ethel representing *Julia* at Daly's Fifth Avenue Theatre in the month of November, 1870; Miss Leclerq appearing in the part, and very successfully, on Booth's stage, in April, 1872; Miss Neilson playing *Julia* for the first time in America at Booth's, in April, 1874; and Miss Clara Morris, for the first time on any stage, at the Union Square Theatre in October of the same year. Of the *Julia* of Mrs. Sheridan Shook, than which on the professional stage we have seen many worse, we do not, of course, as an amateur performance, speak here.

"The Hunchback" has not been so powerfully cast in many years as by the company of Miss Kate Bateman in 1862, the leading parts being filled as follows: —

Julia	Miss Kate Bateman.
Helen	Mrs. Marlowe.
Master Walter	James W. Wallack, Jr.
Sir Thomas Clifford	Edwin Adams.
Modus	A. H. Davenport.
Lord Tinsel	Owen Marlowe.
Fathom	J. E. Owens.
Thomas	Mr. Pope.

This performance we saw at the Brooklyn Academy of Music, but the company, though largely composed of "stars," was, we believe, the regular travelling company of Miss Bateman that season. The representation was in every respect admirable, and, as a whole, almost unequalled in the history of "The Hunchback" in this country. Mr. Wallack never appeared to better advantage than as *Master Walter,* nor "Dolly" Davenport than as *Modus.* It is an evening long to be remembered for the pleasure it afforded, and sadly to be remembered as the last time we saw Mr. Wallack and Mr. Davenport together on the stage.

CHAPTER XVIII.

THE OLD BROADWAY. — "BLACK-EYED SUSAN." — MR. DAVENPORT'S *WILLIAM*.

"Would cry to a sailor, Go hang."

Tempest, Act II. Sc. 2.

AMONG the many names which we recall pleasantly and fondly in our reminiscences of the Old Broadway, that of Mr. E. L. Davenport is prominent.

Before us is spread a bill of that house, dated Saturday, September 16, 1854, recording the "sixth appearance of Mr. E. L. Davenport, the eminent tragedian, returned from Europe after an absence of six years, who will present the great play, in five acts, as produced by him at the Theatre Royal, Drury Lane, with immense success, called

"ST. MARC; OR, A HUSBAND'S SACRIFICE."

By the Late John H. Wilkins, Esq.

St. Marc, a Soldier of Fortune, his original character . . . . E. L. Davenport.
Gismando, his friend, Captain of a disbanded Regiment of Fanatics . . . . F. B. Conway.
Lorenzo, Prince of Modeno . . . . Mr. Gallagher.
Rosario, his friend . . . . Mr. J. Grosvenor.
Balcastro, Minister of Finance . . . Mr. M. W. Leffingwell.
Dianora . . . . Mme. Ponisi.
Theresa, her friend . . . . Mrs. Abbott.
Carolea, a page . . . . Miss Wallis.

The whole to conclude with the Nautical Drama of

"BLACK-EYED SUSAN; OR, ALL IN THE DOWNS."

William, a sailor . . . . Mr. E. L. Davenport,

with Leffingwell as the *Admiral*, Davidge as *Gnatbrain*. Seymour as *Jacob Twigg*, Mme. Ponisi as *Susan*, and Josie Gougenheim as *Dolly Mayflower*.

The Old Broadway and its surroundings are among the things that are past and gone; but the memory of this evening is "as green as Christmas garlands," — for it was the first evening, to us personally, of E. L. Davenport, and the first time we had ever seen Jerrold's now so familiar tale of the sea. We do not know which impressed us more, the *William* of Davenport, or the "Black-Eyed Susan," not of Mme. Ponisi, though she was very good, but of Jerrold himself; whether it was the play or the player that moved us, — but moved we were, and the night we have never forgotten. Mr. Davenport had come back to his home and his American friends covered with dramatic laurels, cordially bestowed by the critics and theatre-going population of England, where he had been pronounced "an artist equalled by few, and surpassed by none, in his profession," and his reception here had been very kind and hearty. We do not propose now to comment upon *St. Marc*. Mr. Davenport has often played the part in New York, and only a few seasons ago at Wood's Museum on Broadway. Our business in this present chapter is with the after-piece of "Black-Eyed Susan."

Mr. Davenport's reputation as *William* had been established over the water, and had preceded him here; it was much discussed before it was produced; anticipation among the *habitués* of the Broadway was great; reports as to how strong a character *William*, in the hands of a true artist, could be made, were rife, and it was even currently rumored that George Frederick Cooke himself, the great nautical actor of the past, was only an ordinary seaman as compared with Davenport. His namesake, Mr. T. P. Cooke, the original *William*, — William the First of the London stage, — had rested a very successful dramatic reputation upon the part; but it was confidently stated, in advance of its presentation here, that this exponent of the character was the superior of all his predecessors. On the Saturday evening in question, the sixth night of his engagement, but the first, we believe, of "Black-Eyed Susan," the critics (there were not many of them professional critics in those days, for dramatic editors were not so common then as now) were present in full force; and the denizens of the old right-hand corner of the pit still speak enthusiastically of the occasion.

The five acts of "St. Marc" were duly listened to and enjoyed, and the event of the evening was "rung up" on a house well filled and kindly disposed. The opening scenes were not of thrilling interest; *Susan* was duly admired, and the usual sympathy felt for her and for "the pangs, the dreadful pangs, that tear the sailor's wife, as, wakeful on her tear-wet pillow, she lists and trembles at the roaring sea." *Doggrass* made himself odious in the eyes of the gallery; *Gnatbrain* threw the rolling-pin at him, and won a round of gallery applause; *Hatchet* paid the rent; *Susan* retired to her tear-wet pillow to list again, and so forth, when scene fourth is on, "All in the Downs," and enter Davenport as *William;* and oh, how briny a *William* in every look, and action, and accent, and hitch of trowsers, of the salt sea salty was *William.*

What a shivering of timbers was there, and what splicings of the main brace, what belayings and what running over at the scuppers, ye lubbers! were there when he embraced his *Susan!* The first three scenes were but the prologue, and the play itself did not begin until *William* appeared, or the interest ripen, until actual trouble came to *Susan's* natural protector, when the *Captain* was upset, and the audience discovered who the victim of the protector's just indignation was, and the result to *William* of such a blow to his superior officer.

Davenport's acting in the final scene of the first act, when it was divested of the "clapping-on-of-the-main-top-bowline," and all of that ordinary nautical-drama business, was very powerful, and marked with an earnestness and artistic effect that the part of *William*, or its kindred parts, rarely receives; and it became apparent to the audience that rumor for the once had been correct, and that there was something very much out of the common in the representation. What has been poetically called "the sugar of the performance" seemed, as it were, to have been salted to the listeners; the curtain went down on the first grand tableau to slow music, and on an audience whose subdued silence attested the strong effect produced, — the whole house seeming to have entered into the nautical spirit of the play, and to have tapped its briny!

With Act II., "The Court Martial," we were particularly impressed. Hardly, we think, in the range of drama, can the proverb of the short step from the sublime to the ridiculous find so apt an illustration as in an indifferent, and, if indifferent, necessarily ridiculous, performance of this court-martial scene. In an artist's hands, and with artistic support, it is as sublime, *almost*, as *Portia's* famous scene with the Jew before the Duke and the Magnificoes of Venice; but, when badly played, how flat, stale, and unprofitable it becomes. We remember, not many years ago, how the miseries of a very creditable *William* were entirely forgotten by a Brooklyn audience one evening, on account of the ridiculous bearing of the supers who played the twelve post-captains of the fleet, and by the mirth-provoking delivery of "Witnesses for the Prisoner," "The Prisoner," "*The Prisoner*," as passed on by the prompter.

But to return to Mr. Davenport and this performance in question. There are occasions when the almost magnetic influence of a thoroughly appreciative audience can so stimulate and exalt an actor, that the character he enacts becomes an inspiration in his hands, and for this *William* and its impersonator, this first time we saw Mr. Davenport in the part, we claim this inspiration; he carried the house with him; and this fact, and the fact that he felt it, added "fresh fuel to the fire of his genius." One of the standard jokes of the play, the only "funny business" in the trial scene, the reply of the boatswain, *Mr. Quid*, to the Admiral's inquiry as to *William's* moral character: "His moral character, your honor? Why, he plays on the fiddle like an angel!" provoked not a smile; it seemed irreverent to laugh, the audience grasping at any straw in *William's* favor. The decision of the Court, "Guilty," and the reading of the sentence, "Death," were terrible blows to *William's* scores of friends before the footlights; and *William's* subdued "Poor *Susan*," found echo in every sympathizing heart in the audience.

The interest in the drama, however, did not reach its intensest point until the last scene of all — the execution. The farewells with his shipmates and friends, the last dying gifts and bequests, and his parting from

Susan, were all very harrowing, and very real, and very choking; but the culmination was *William's* standing under the yard-arm, his bare neck ready for the rope that was "to launch" him, the parson on the black platform, the twelve melancholy-looking captains, the grief-stricken *Admiral* Leffingwell, and the entrance of *Captain Crosstree* with his pardon, and his honorable and explanatory speech. Never was a *Captain Crosstree* so well received!

We do not recall many evenings where a single great actor has so controlled and moved his audience as did Mr. Davenport on that occasion; and, as we look back upon it, and compare it with the playing of other actors, we can only account for it as being a true artist's handling of an impressive part. When *William* was finally released and congratulated, and when he took his *Black-eyed Susan* in his arms, the audience made a personal matter of it, and cried over it as if it were their own personal and particular joy, and the Young Veteran, and all the rest of the boys in the pit, went home to their little beds, resolved, with the young Columbus, "to go and be sailor boys, by jingo, or die."

CHAPTER XIX.

THE OLD BROADWAY. — THE ORIGINAL "CAMILLE." — MISS J. M. DAVENPORT. — MISS HERON.

"The acting of a dreadful thing."
Julius Cæsar, Act II. Sc. 1.

AMONG our bills of the later seasons of the Old Broadway we find the following, so interesting in itself, and so valuable as giving an idea of the strength of the Broadway company at that time, that we reproduce it in full: —

This evening, Thursday, November 30, 1854, will be performed a new play in five acts, adapted from the French for Miss Davenport, by J. Wilkins, Esq., author of "Civilization," etc., and entitled

"CAMILLE; OR, THE FATE OF A COQUETTE."

Camille Gautier . . . by . . .	Miss Davenport.
Helene	Miss J. Gougenheim.
Mme. Babillard	Miss France.
Michette	Mrs. Nagle.
Nanette	Miss Seymour.
Anabelle	Miss Barnard.
Armand Duval	Mr. F. B. Conway.
Mons. Duval	Mr. Leffingwell.
St. Frivole	Mr. W. Davidge.
Gustave	Mr. Sandford.
De Varville	Mr. Lanergan.
Albert (a peasant)	Mr. Cutter.
Louis (a servant)	Mr. Wright.
Gregoire	Mr. Jones.
Gaston	Mr. McDowell.
Arthur	Mr. Vincent.

Act I. March — Supper Scene.
Act II. April — Spring.
Act III. August — Summer.
Act IV. October — Autumn.
Act V. New Years Day — Winter.

"All nature hopes for Spring, and why not I?"

Old play-goers will remember this performance pleasantly, if not enthusiastically. There was nothing particularly remarkable or brilliant in the play itself, and nothing decidedly superlative in the rendering of it; but it was in every part well played, and it was itself the original "Camille," the grand prototype of the whole sensational school of drama and of acting; the father, or mother, of all the "Formosas" and "Frou-Frous," and "Jezebels" and "Women Without Hearts," that have followed it *ad nauseam*.

This was not the first season of the production of "Camille," — Miss Davenport brought it out at the Broadway on the 9th of December, 1853, — although it was the first season of its success. The year before it had failed to attract; the public, in all of the bliss of ignorance, had not yet been educated up to that style of dramatic entertainment; the curtain went down to unsympathetic, and, happily, unappreciative audiences, and "Camille" was shelved, to make way for other and better-drawing novelties. On the night of its revival, with a cast in very slight degree differing from the first cast, excepting that Mrs. Vernon was the original *Mme. Babillard*, the result was different; the house was crowded, and the audience, becoming familiar with the face, first endured, then pitied, and finally embraced "Camille."

Miss Davenport's picture of the *traviata* was in its

way certainly exquisitely drawn; it was painfully realistic and harrowingly true to the life she portrayed. She was, as we remember her in the part, *the Camille* of all the *Camilles* who have come after her. The play was successful from the outset of its second production, and Miss Jean Margaret Davenport, always popular, became at once the great dramatic sensation of the day. Pope's well-known lines admirably describe the career of this drama "of so frightful mien." Acts I. and II., "March" and "April," were listened to indifferently — were patiently "endured;" Act III., "Summer," to some extent thawed the ice of critical reserve; in Act IV., "Autumn," interest and sympathy for *Camille* began to ripen; she was "pitied;" and in Act V., "Winter" — "a sad tale 's best for winter" — [*Shakespeare*] — the house, weeping over the misery of *Camille*, established her as a success, — "embraced" her.

Miss Davenport was happy in her support. In no other part has Mr. Conway appeared to better advantage than as *Armand Duval*, and no *Armand Duval* have we since seen on the stage better than his. On this very account, because of his so clever personation of the lover, should he be held with Miss Davenport as jointly responsible for "Camille," and for the subsequent deluge of its kindred plays that have flooded the stage for twenty years, and have to such a degree reduced the standard of the drama.

The original *Armand* fairly divided the honors with the original *Camille*. Mr. Conway seemed to be made for the part, as the part, if not made, was probably "adapted" for him. When in the fourth act, he scattered the bank notes and shower of gold on *Camille's* head as she lay exhausted on the sofa of the *salon*, and in reply to *Gustave's* "Unlucky in the game of love, lucky in the game of hearts," uttered his famous line, "Hearts! Diamonds! Play diamonds if you would win woman," he towered away above himself and was almost grand, if an actor in such a part can be grand; he absolutely "enthused" his audience, until that time not disposed to be enthusiastic over the play, or anything in it, and made "Camille;" "Camille" at the same time, perhaps, doing a great deal towards the making of Conway.

We find among our old bills records of these artists playing *Armand* and *Camille*, and find other *Camilles* and other *Armands* elsewhere in New York, but no traces of "Camille" again on the Broadway boards. Miss Davenport, a few years later, we discover at the "Metropolitan Theatre, late Burton's," under the management of Mr. F. B. Conway, playing, so says the bill, "'Camille' to overflowing houses nightly assembled to greet the great and eminent artist, who will this evening and every evening, in compliance with universal request, resume her great impersonation of the part in the drama of the same name, as played originally by her to crowded and enthusiastic houses," etc., etc., and so on. This bill is dated April 9, 1859, and in the cast were Mrs. F. B. Conway as *Helene*, Mrs. W. H. Smith as *Madame Babillard*, F. B. Conway as *Armand*, W. Reynolds as *De Varville*, Charles Fisher as *M. Duval*, Mr. Dawson as *St. Frivole*, and T. Baker as *Gustave*.

Miss Davenport's great rival in this part in the meantime had come upon the boards, Miss Matilda Heron making a great success as *Camille* two or three years before, at Wallack's Theatre, and playing during the next season at Niblo's Garden a long and profitable engagement, Mr. Eddy as manager, on his play-bills soaring quite as high in his descriptive adjectives as did Mr. Conway in his "establishment over the way." In presenting this play for the 526th time, and for the first time in New York for three years, Mr. Eddy felt that he was meeting with the general wish of his patrons, etc., in large type, to considerable extent. Miss Heron, during this engagement at Niblo's in November, 1859, was supported by Charles Fisher as *Armand*, George Farren as the *Elder Duval*, Aiken as *Gaston*, Mrs. Eddy as *Prudence*, and Ida Vernon as *Minchette*. In her original cast at Wallack's Old Theatre in January, 1857, Mr. Sothern played *Armand*, Mrs. Vernon *Prudence*, and the support included such artists as Mrs. J. H. Allen, Miss Charlotte Thompson, C. Stuart, G. T. Lee, and Mr. Reynolds. The drama ran for some two months, not a common dramatic success twelve or fifteen years ago.

Miss Heron was at this time at the zenith of her fame as an actress, looked upon by her admirers, who were many, as one of the most fascinating and brilliant ladies on the stage. She and "Camille" were the rage; her picture was to be seen in the illustrated journals of the day; she was the object of masculine devotion and the recipient of serenades. On this bill before us is the announcement, that between the third and fourth acts will be performed by the orchestra, under the direction of R. Stoepel, the "Matilda Heron March," dedicated to Miss Heron by R. Stoepel himself. She became Mrs. Stoepel within a few months. The unhappy termination to their married life is well known.

Miss Heron's last important engagement in New

York, as far as we remember, was at Niblo's, in 1864. We must crave the indulgence of our readers in presenting its cast, promising in future not to devote so much space to hard dramatic facts, or to uninteresting dramatic statistics. This was in many respects so strong a cast, and contained so many well-known and favorite names, that we cannot resist giving its main parts: —

Camille	Matilda Heron.
Mons. Duval	J. G. Burnett.
Gaston	B. T. Ringgold.
Minchette	Mrs. Skerrett.
Armand	B. Macaulay.
De Varville	J. W. Collier.
Prudence	Miss Mary Wells.
Nannie	Miss Fisher.
Olympe	Miss Ione Burke.

This version of the play was "adapted for the American stage by Miss Heron." It differed materially from Miss Davenport's version, and from still another, presented in the form of a dream, by Miss Laura Keene. The names of many of the characters, it will be seen, were unlike those in the elder translation, as was also her division of the acts. As "Act II. — April, the Pledge of Love;" "Act III. — August, the Sacrifice;" "Act IV. — October, the *Fête;*" "Act V. — Winter, the Eleventh Hour," etc. As we remember them now, and as they were compared at the time of their original production, of the three versions, that of Miss Davenport, the earliest, was the best. Most artistic in a literary point of view, and least objectionable in point of morals.

In an old dramatic scrap-book we find a "Card" of Miss Heron's, cut from the *New York Herald*, bearing no date, and signed Matilda Heron Stoepel, in which she defends her rights to "Camille," particularly against Miss Charlotte Thompson, who seems to have been playing the drama without her authority in Philadelphia, and generally against the whole profession, who do not seem disposed to give Miss Heron credit for her own version of the play. In this card she claims that Miss Davenport's version is entirely different from her own, and from Dumas, the leading incident being left out, and a new scene in the last act introduced. Miss Heron further states that "Camille" — her own version — has been played in every leading city of the Union, and by almost every lady in the profession who could recite the words; that in her own case she had at that time given over seven hundred representations of the part during the five years she had been playing it; she had, "out of pure devotion to her art, given to every detail of it the utmost of her power of body, heart, and mind, to perfect each element of it, to prune its blemishes, erase its defects, harmonize its beauties, elevate its tone" — (elevate its tone!) — "sublimate its passion, to celebrate its love; in a word, to bring it to that state of powerful fascination, poetic interest, and immortal life which, on its first representation, the warmest hearts and best pens of the country predicted it was capable of, and which to-day the entire press of New York pronounces accomplished."

The success of Miss Heron in the part was wonderful; she did win from the press of the country the highest praise; she did certainly deserve very much of the praise and success she received; she was devoted to her art, and gave to the elaboration of the part her utmost power of body, heart, and mind; and she certainly was entitled to the copyright of the particular version of the play she produced; but her version was not the first nor do we think it was the best; she was not the original *Camille* in America, nor do we think she was the best; and we cannot agree with her that "Camille" possesses powerful fascination, poetic interest, or immortal life.

It is said that Miss Heron made her first appearance on the New York stage on the 23d of August, 1852, at the Bowery, playing *Lady Macbeth* to the *Macbeth* of Hamblin. She made her last appearance in the same part at Booth's on Christmas Day last (1874), supported by Mr. Vandenhoff as *Macbeth*, and by Mr. Fred B. Warde as *Macduff*. She has not been often seen before the public in late years, but she has taken no public farewell of the stage, and is not likely to retire absolutely into private life. When she does take such a step, she leaves behind her a worthy successor in her little daughter, Bijou Heron, the brightest, most highly gifted, most wonderfully precocious child our stage has had upon it for many years, — already a brilliant actress, for whom, if she lives and remains in the profession, we venture to prophesy the most decided success.

To return to "Camille." Long is the list of leading ladies, as Miss Heron has said, who have played the part; the last and by no means the least of these being Miss Clara Morris, who, on the 26th of March, 1874, at the Lyceum Theatre, Fourteenth Street, for the benefit of the poor of the city, first assumed the character. She played it subsequently for four weeks in the months of May and June of the same year, at the Union Square Theatre, when she drew full houses and had many admirers. Her *Camille* is of the school of Miss Heron, of whom in the part she often reminded us.

As Miss Heron believes of Miss Morris that she (Miss Morris) is her only worthy successor as *Camille*, we give here the cast of " Camille " on the occasion of Miss Morris's *début* in the *rôle*.

Camille Gauthier (La Dame aux Camelias)	Miss Clara Morris.
Prudence	Miss Marie Wilkins.
Nichette	Miss Kate Claxton.
Olympe	Miss Louise Henderson.
Nannie	Miss Kate Holland.
Armand Duval	Mr. Frank Mayo.
Gaston Rieux	Mr. George Fawcett Rowe.
Monsieur Duval	Mr. F. F. Mackaye.
Gustave	Mr. Joseph B. Polk.
Monsieur de Varville	Mr. W. B. Laurens.

Miss Agnes Ethel, Miss Charlotte Thompson, Miss Morris, and the other later *Camilles*, have not one of them achieved anything approaching the success of Miss Davenport and of Miss Heron in the part on its first production here, and in the first flush of its youth and novelty ; and the success achieved by these ladies was very different.

To contrast the acting of Miss Heron and of Miss Davenport would be unfair to both ; as actresses there was little in common between them. Miss Jean Davenport, the present Mrs. Lander, so well and so favorably known to-day by the name she now so honorably bears, was and is an artist ! Dogberry says that " comparisons are oderous," and indeed they are. It is not our purpose here to champion one of these ladies at the expense of the other. Miss Heron at once won a success in the part that Miss Davenport had required slow and laborious study to attain. The pictures of *Camille*, both in their way almost perfect, were in every way dissimilar. They were entire and distinct

Camilles. In Miss Davenport's impersonation *Camille* was French; slowly and by degrees we were led to realize that the relations that existed in the play were French, and because French not so odious, less objectionable, — French pitch being considered as not quite so defiling. While, on the other hand, no one could for a moment doubt the status and nationality of the rival *Camille.* And it is just here that Dogberry may be congratulated upon the strength of his adjective, and the force of his English.

CHAPTER XX.

THE OLD BROADWAY. — MISS LOUISA PYNE. — "THE SKYLARK."

"Doth sing as sweetly as the lark."
Merchant of Venice, Act V. Sc. 1.

Of what benefit to us have been our early lessons in the lore and literature of fairyland, unless it be to set us dreaming now, and of what benefit is our dreaming, or what pleasure in the dreaming have we, if there is no probability of a realization of our dreams? The present is too positive, the future too unsubstantial, and to the past, therefore, — that past with which in these pages we have tried to deal, — must we go, abjuring both present and future in dreamland, building no new castles, but wandering about the ruins of the castles of other days in search of our idols, seeing visions that are not all visions, and dreaming dreams that were very real to us once.

Of all the fairy tales that were ever written, "Cinderella" was to us the loveliest and truest and best, and of all the Cinderellas we have ever dreamed there has been no Cinderella like the *Cinderella* of Louisa Pyne. We have found her name on the play-bills of the Old Broadway; and who can say there is no poetry in old play-bills which have set us dreaming thus?

The arrival of the Pyne-Harrison Opera Troupe in America was an era in our dramatic, or rather, perhaps, operatic history, although at that time it was not so regarded. On the 9th of October, 1854, we had reached what may be called "a period."

Our bill of that day says: —

"La Sonnambula."

First appearance in America of the Pyne and Harrison Troupe.

Count	Mr. Borrani.
Elvino	Mr. W. Harrison.
Amina	Miss Louisa Pyne.
Liza	Miss Susan Pyne.

Modest, very modest this; and nowhere in our records are we apprised of the result of this initial performance. No sensation was created; we give it only for its simplicity, its historical value, and pass it without comment other than this:—

The several versions of the different operas had been sung in English here, with not a great deal of popular favor, and with very little financial success. Miss Louisa Pyne, an English lady, arrived in this country at a period when an English reputation was everything to a *débutante* here, before we had established sufficient faith in our own opinion of art and artists to accept as very fine anything or anybody who brought not the indorsement of our cousins over the water. The lady in question came to us quite unheralded, and none of the gentlemen or ladies who were to be her support, as far as they were known, promised to be more than ordinarily clever in their performances, or to add any great charm to her proposed entertainments. Miss Louisa Pyne, as we remember her then, was a modest, retiring young woman, still in her teens, not handsome, barely pretty; not very tall nor very short, nor very plump nor very thin, with nothing at all in her personal appearance that was remarkable, or promising of decided success in a profession where so much depends upon physical beauty; "a gentle body," a fair, fresh, Saxon-faced girl — nothing more; a face that suggested a good, lovable, sisterly friend, and one that moved the observer, while watching it in repose, to wonder why Miss Pyne had ever become an artist, or wherein lay her powers. Her mild blue eye we have seen so quiet and subdued, that it seemed as if no "ripple in the tide of song" could ever disturb its calmness; but, again, how changed when her art inspired her. Her almost homely face became radiant with the brightest beauty, and the transformation was complete; everything was forgotten; she forgot herself, and stood before us the Queen of Song, the like of whom we had scarcely heard till then.

The particular play-bill over which we are dreaming bears date Saturday evening, January 20, 1855, and thus it reads: —

To-night will be performed the Grand Opera and Fairy Spectacle of

"CINDERELLA; OR, THE LITTLE GLASS SLIPPER."

With the following unequalled cast of Characters: —

Prince Felix	Mr. W. Harrison.
Alidoro, his tutor	Mr. S. Rea.
Dandini, the Prince's valet	Mr. Borrani.
Baron Pompolini	Mr. Horncastle.
Pedro, the Baron's servant	Mr. Davidge.
Clorinda	Miss Susan Pyne.
Thisbe	Miss Carlotta Pozzoni.
Fairy Queen	Mrs. Reeves.
Cinderella	Miss Louisa Pyne.

In Act III. Miss Louisa Pyne will introduce a new aria, composed by Jules Benedict, Esq., called "The Skylark."

Here follows almost a yard more of play-bill, a description of the good things in prospective for this night, and for other nights of the engagement.

The story of Cinderella and the Glass Slipper was by no means new. We had often heard it in opera and in burlesque; still it was ever fresh to us, — and when will it not be? People, young and old, always did go to see it, and always will go as long as it is played and sung; for what will so thoroughly entertain old and young as "Cinderella" and its kindred stories on the stage? — the young for its freshness and realness, and the maturer in years for the sake of the days when it was real and fresh to them. Who of us, male or female, has not at some time played in our dreams *Prince* or *Cinder* to the *Cinder* or *Prince* of some little sweetheart to whom we have long, long ago sung "Good-by, Sweetheart, good-by!" Those rats and mice, that golden pumpkin, that Fairy Godmother, that Grand Duke's ball, have been at certain periods of our life absolute reality to most of us, and it will not be until young men have passed away, and until old men have ceased to dream, that "Cinderella" and the Glass Slipper will be "shelved" forever.

On this night of "Cinderella" the house was comfortably full. The performance had been up to the usual standard, all good, nothing great. There had been no enthusiasm. The third act was "on," but the audience was evidently so taken up with the usual business of the piece, that it had lost sight of, or had attached no particular importance to the promised aria of Jules Benedict, Esq., when Miss *Cinderella* Pyne walked down to the foot-lights, took her position in the "special song" style, and "sang such notes as, warbled to the string of Orpheus, drew iron tears down Pluto's cheek." (Milton.) Many of our readers will remember the surprising effect of this song of the skylark upon the audience, the entranced silence during the rendering of it, and the spontaneous burst of applause that followed the last sweet notes, as *encores*, *bravas*, and every demonstration of delight were expressed by the astonished house. Not one, nor two, nor three repetitions were enough, nor cheers, nor ladies rising in their seats, nor hats nor handkerchiefs thrown in the air. The house seemed to be in a frenzy of admiration, such as is rarely witnessed in this undemonstrative metropolis of ours, and the people realized that they had found at last that they had a song-bird among them, too long neglected because her feathers were russet.

This *diva* never had cause to complain of neglect again. No nightingale in gilded cage was half so petted, no skylark free was half so loved, as Louisa Pyne in America after that evening. We had discovered an artist that English audiences had failed to appreciate: she seemed to belong to us by right of this discovery, and we were as proud and as fond of her as if she had belonged to the family of our own National Bird. It is difficult now to determine whose astonishment was greatest at this skylark's sudden and overwhelming success, — that of stage or house, or of the singer herself; she did not seem to understand what it all meant, or what she had done to deserve it, and blushed and faltered and looked as if she would have run away had she dared, when the house rose to do her honor. Her pleasure and excitement were pretty to look upon, but the lark sang none the less charmingly for the fluttering of its wings.

From this time forward there were no more grumblings of manager or treasurer, both strong box and auditorium were filled to everybody's satisfaction; and from this Saturday evening's "Cinderella," and from the first notes of this skylark of which we write, date the extraordinary successes, financial and artistic, of Miss Louisa Pyne, not only in America, but subsequently in Europe.

As *Arline*, in the "Bohemian Girl," *Zerlina*, in "Fra Diavolo," *La Catarina*, in "Crown Diamonds," *Amina*, in "Sonnambula," and *Stella*, in the "Enchantress," she has probably never been surpassed either on the English or Italian stage. Her English and Scotch ballads were particularly charming, and she sang "Waes me for Prince Charlie" as sweetly as if she had been born upon the heather, and after a fashion that moved to rank Jacobinism every Scotchman who ever heard her.

Her return to England was followed by a repetition of her successes here, and she became at once the recognized leader of the English operatic stage. Whether she is still before the public we cannot say. We heard of her marriage a few years ago. She never returned to this country.

NOTE. — It may not be amiss here, in these times of high prices and of four dollars for seats to hear Nillson or Lucca, to mention the scale of prices at the Old Broadway during the engagement of the Pyne and Harrison Troupe: —

"Dress Circle and Parquette, fifty cents; Family and Third Circles, twenty-five cents; Gallery, twelve and a-half cents; Private Boxes, five and six dollars."

These are the days we dream of now.

CHAPTER XXI.

THE FASHION OF PLAY-BILLS. — A PRODIGAL PROGRAMME. — THE RIVAL "MIDSUMMER NIGHT'S DREAMS."

Grumio. — "Error i' the bill, sir ; Error i' the bill."
Petruchio. — "Aye, there 's the villainy."
The Taming of the Shrew, Act IV. Sc. 3.

THERE is as much fashion in play-bills as there is in the cut of a coat or the shape of a bonnet. Fashion as to their length, their breadth, their size, their color; different styles predominating at different periods and in different parts of the town — the very name itself, play-bill, being out of fashion now. Locality has something to do with this; the Bowery bill is long and broad, hearty in look, perhaps a little coarse in texture, with plenty of big lettering and a certain Bowery air about it that is unmistakable — the old-fashioned bill we used to know; while the bill of the Broadway to-day is dainty and perfumed, contains society gossip, elegant *bon mots*, sometimes the portrait of a leading-lady or of a masculine star; never condescends to the clap-trap of large print, which is vulgar; calls itself the *Programme*, and is the index of fashion, the vane of the *beau monde*.

The success of a season has also something to do with the fashion of the bill of the present. It had a great deal to do with the fashion of the bills of the past. Many are the fashions and styles of the collections of play-bills before us which date back so many years, and aid so materially our recollections of the stage.

Here are the bills of the Park, the original Park, long, narrow, compact specimens of bills, showing the gentility of a close corporation, while the bills of the old Bowery, twenty years old, are flaming spread-eagle bills, often illustrated with graphic wood-cuts of the entertainments they chronicle ; studied by the boys of the pit before the play, as perfect pictures of the glories to come, preserved after the play as delightful souvenirs of the glories that were. The bills of the Old Broadway are, in themselves, apart from their associations, curiosities to-day. The printed matter in single columns is eight to ten inches wide, not unfrequently with double sheets, long in proportion and containing sometimes as much matter as the play itself.

We have fallen upon a certain bill of a certain play, dated June 2, 1851, which, even in its old age, startles us by its proportions and adornments, and, recalling other bills of its kind, leads us thus to moralize on bills. The play is forgotten, no doubt is out of print, but the bill remains. It announces itself as the herald of "The Romantic and Operatic Spectacle of Azael, the Prodigal, now performing in Paris and London to crowded houses." We quote no more. Our readers have done us no harm ; our publisher has borne patiently with us, and has printed for us without protest, casts of plays innumerable, and we will not presume upon your good-nature or his by the infliction of this. In order to give some idea of the immensity of the document and the ponderosity of its contents, the amount of hard reading the audiences were forced to do in order to arrive at what the bill set forth, we will give simple dimensions of its proportions. It is twenty-four inches long by eighteen inches wide, and in double columns at that. It is filled with startling announcements, quotations from the poets, and heart-thrilling situations. Compare this with a programme of the present, which by chance lies near it, the bill of the opening night of Mr. Daly's new theatre, a dainty blue satin bill, not much larger than the one-dollar bill that paid for our standing room only, and led us on to "Fortune."

In the length of our bills, both as to size and contents we are degenerating; there is a falling off also in the quantity of our theatrical representations every evening, my countrymen. We do not get half so much as of old for our twice as much money, and has the quality improved?

But to return to our bills of the last decade, this of "Azael the Prodigal" and its kindred. They were prodigal of promises, and were too apt to promise more than was fulfilled. They were rather an advertisement of the house than a chronicle of the play; they were found in the hotels and in the ferries, in Clarke & Brown's chop-house, and in Kipp & Brown's stages. They took the place of posters, and were almost as large, and like some of the posters of the present, they were little to be relied upon.

To how many plays in the palmy days of twenty years ago have we gone, drawn out only by the attractions offered in the bills. How many curtains have we seen go up on first acts that found us full of blissful expectations, which went down on last acts leaving us full of disappointment and disgust at the result; and how often, mentally contrasting the size of the bill with the size of the house, the nature of the promise with the manner of the performance, realizing that the bill and not the play had drawn, have we been tempted to cry, with the amiable and exemplary *Mr. Fagin*, in "Oliver Twist," that "BILL did it! BILL did it!"

Of this play, "Azael," we may mention, that we saw a representation on the stage of one of the leading theatres of the South a few years later, in 1858 or 1859. We remember it only as a spectacular, and it is remembered by us particularly as introducing the Keller Troupe, with their mysterious announcement of "Mythological Reproductions;" a series of classical groupings that in their own way have never been excelled in the whole range of art. Mr. Keller had not been successful in New York; the Press and the public, while they praised the beauty and faithfulness of his pictures, with one voice condemned, and justly perhaps, the impropriety of putting upon the dramatic stage the subjects of his representations. They were living tableaux, reproductions in flesh and blood of certain of the famous Scriptural paintings of the old masters, such as Rubens' "Descent from the Cross," and other equally well-known works of art. They were, some of them, marvellous copies of the originals, and with all of the stage accessories of lights and hangings, were absolutely startling in their effect. Mr. Keller was at Niblo's in the summer of 1859, under the management of Mr. Eddy, who had brought his Broadway Company to that house on the final closing of the Old Broadway in April of the same year. In his historical tableaux and military pictures, Mr. Keller was more successful; his ideas were good and his ideals high, but New York did not appreciate his entertainment, and we do not remember his being on our boards since that time.

But to turn to pleasanter and more legitimate stage pictures, rival pictures of the poet's fancy, more cheerful and enjoyable in every respect. Pictures of a dramatic contest memorable in its way, particularly remarkable for the fact that high art, not low art was the bone of contention, and the bone no less a bone than the "Midsummer Night's Dream" of the immortal William himself.

Under date of February 11, 1854, we find at the Broadway the announcement as follows: —

Will be performed for the first time at this theatre, Shakespeare's famed comedy and great fairy spectacle, —

"A MIDSUMMER NIGHT'S DREAM."

Should we reproduce the bill *verbatim* we would more than fill our limited space, and o'erstep the bounds of that brevity which we know to be the soul of wit. We will strive to condense, and content ourself with the mention of leading parts and comments thereon. *Theseus* was played by Conway, *Lysander* and *Demetrius* by James Lanergan and Joseph Grosvenor. Little Viola Crocker, as pretty as a pictured fairy, was the *Puck;* Mrs. Nagle, a beautiful woman, played *Hermia;* Ada Gougenheim, *Helena;* Madame Ponisi and Mrs. Abbott, *Oberon* and *Titania;* Moses Fiske doing *Snug, the Joiner;* and William Davidge, *Sweet Billy Bottom.*

At Burton's Chambers Street Theatre, at the same time, the piece was produced with a cast of unexceptionable strength in male parts, one of the weak features in the performance at this latter house being the lack of beauty in the ladies of the company, always an important item of dramatic success, particularly in fairy or spectacular plays.

The principal parts as filled at Burton's Theatre we give here: —

Theseus, Duke of Athens	Mr. Charles Fisher.
Lysander } in love with Hermia	Mr. George Jordan.
Demetrius } in love with Hermia	Mr. W. H. Norton.
Quince, the carpenter	Mr. Tom Johnstone.
Snug, the joiner	Mr. Henry Russell.
Bottom, the weaver	Mr. Burton.
Flute, the bellows-mender	Mr. G. Barrett.
Snout, the tinker	Mr. George H. Andrews.
Starveling, the tailor	Mr. Paul.
Puck	Master Charles Parsloe.
Oberon	Miss Emeline Raymond.
Titania	Mrs. Burton.
Hermia	Mrs. Lotty Hough.

Mr. Burton was anxious to match his reputation with that of Mr. Davidge as *Bottom*, and the rivalry was prolonged throughout the season, both houses and both representations having their own partisans and strong admirers. In our own humble estimation, however, the presentation of the part of *Bottom* by Mr. Davidge has had no equal before or since. The play and the characters in it were at this time almost entirely new to the theatre-going public, as it had not been produced in over fifteen years in New York, — even then had but a short run at the Park, — and public interest was now excited and full houses the result. At the Broadway the entertainment was well worthy its popularity and success. The play was beautifully mounted, and the parts admirably played.

We have seen latterly in print, articles on the splendor of theatrical representations of the present, that ignore the magnificence of the scenic effects of other days, but we have had on our stage nothing more gorgeous in late years than the settings of the "Midsummer Night's Dream" at the Broadway in the season of which we write. Particularly fine, as we remember it, was the panorama of fairy land, done by the "compounding of flats," and the artistic adjustment of lights. George Heister, the scenic artist of the Broadway, may have been wanting in some of the improvements and inventions of modern stage craft, but his taste was then as artistic and correct in its judgment of effects, as is seen displayed in anything of the "Black Crook" transformation school of the present; and the piece as a whole is recalled by old theatre-goers as one of those bright particular productions, when master, art, artist, and public were in perfect accord.

Of the controversy that then arose over the respective merits of the rival personations of the part of *Bottom* we will not now speak, only remarking that every true Shakespearean comedian considers it within his range of parts, although very few actors have influence enough with managements to induce a revival of the comedy on their account.

"The Midsummer Night's Dream," it is recorded in the history of the old Park Theatre, was at that house on the 9th of November 1826, for the first time played in America. Mr. and Mrs. Thomas Hilson were the *Bottom* and the *Puck*, Peter Richings played *Oberon*, and Mr. Henry Placide *Snout*. It was last produced at the Grand Opera House on the 18th October, 1873, with George L. Fox as *Bottom*. Miss Laura Keene brought it out at the present "Olympic," then "Laura Keene's Theatre," in the spring of 1859. Miss Keene herself playing *Puck*, and no less an artist doing the *Bottom* than Wm. Rufus Blake.

Mr. Fox in the part displays decided talents as a comedian, which those who have seen nothing but his

"Humpty Dumpty" business would never credit him with possessing; but William Davidge, we think, and he alone of the present school, has fully comprehended the part, and has the artistic ability to portray it as the text demands.

CHAPTER XXII.

J. B. BUCKSTONE'S "LEAP YEAR." — MRS. HOEY AND MR. BROUGHAM.

——— "And wished myself a man,
Or that we women had men's privilege
Of speaking first."

Troilus and Cressida, Act III. Sc. 2.

MR. J. B. BUCKSTONE has in his time written many pleasant comedies, and has played many parts. It is not generally remembered that in 1840 he played a successful engagement in this country, making his *début* in America at the old Park Theatre, New York, in August of that year. The theatre-goers of five and thirty years ago are not many of them habitual theatre-goers to-day, and by this present generation Mr. Buckstone is much better known on this side of the water as a writer of plays than as a player in them. His "Married Life," and "Single Life," and "Green Bushes," and "Breach of Promise," and "Rural Felicity," are occasionally produced here; but "Leap Year," one of the brightest and most sparkling of his comedies, has not been seen upon our stage in some years. It was first presented in this country at Burton's Theatre on Friday evening, March 1st, 1850, so says the bill, the cast of which we copy *verbatim*:

A New Three Act Comedy called
"LEAP YEAR, OR THE LADIES' PRIVILEGE."
By J. B. Buckstone, Esq., with the following cast: —

Bachelors:

Mr. Charles Dimple . . . . Mr. Burton.
Sir Solomon Solus . . . . Mr. T. B. Johnstone.

Captain Mouser, a fortune hunter	Mr. Holman.
Walker, Mrs. Flowerdew's footman . . .	Mr. John Brougham.
John Thong, Mr. Solomon's coachman	Mr. Rea.
Joseph, a page	Mr. Levere.
Diggs, a gardener	Mr. Hurley.
Widows:	
Mrs. Flora Flowerdew	Mrs. Russell.
Mrs. Crisp, a lady's-maid	Mrs. Holman.
Spinsters:	
Miss O'Leary	Mrs. Brougham.
Miss Desperate	Mrs. Hughes.
Susan, a housemaid	Miss Barber.
Betty, a chambermaid	Mrs. Rea.

The comedy was hardly original with Mr. Buckstone, although he claimed it as such and said in the preface to the printed book of the play, that he drew his inspiration from no novel or French play, but that an old English statute law, entitled "An Act to Amend the Laws of Courtship and Matrimony," said to be found in certain old volumes, suggested the idea and plot of the story.

As a bit of curious and obsolete legal literature, and as a matter of slight interest to the "Bachelors," and "Widows" and "Spinsters" of to-day, we give the act in full, somewhat modernizing the spelling, and not at all vouching for its value or authenticity: "Albeit it is now become part of the common law in regard to the social relations of life, that as often as every bissextile year doth return the ladyes have the sole privilege of making love unto the men, which they doe either by wordes or lookes as unto them seemeth proper; and no man will be entitled to the benefit of clergy who doth refuse to accept the offer of a ladye, or who doth in any-wise treat her proposal with neglect or contumely."

This is the keynote of Mr. Buckstone's "Leap Year;" on this hint hath he spoken, and out of these scant materials he has woven one of those amusing sketches for which he has become so famous, and which the several artists enumerated in the above cast knew so well how to enact. There is much pleasure to us in the retrospection, as we contemplate this bill of the Chambers Street house, a bill that has so little of the twinkle, twinkle of the star about it, and so much of the steady light of "our rare old stock" in its unpretending small capitals and modest announcements throughout. What names there were among the "Widows," and "Spinsters," and "Bachelors," not one of them in larger type than the rest, and all of them great in mouths of wisest censure. What would we of the present think of Wm. E. Burton, John Brougham, Tom Johnstone, Holman, Mrs. Russell (now Mrs. Hoey), Mrs. Brougham, and Mrs. Hughes in the cast of an unpretending comedy, and a "first night" at that! There were giants in those days!

In order that we may fully understand the entertainment in question, and appreciate the good things of which it consisted, we will take a brief glance at the plot of the play, not so familiar as it should be to the audiences of to-day. *Mrs. Flowerdew* Russell (widow), must, so says her husband's will, marry within two years of her husband's death — the late *Mr. Flowerdew* could not have been an ordinary man — or forfeit her inheritance of her husband's estate. *Miss O'Leary* Brougham (spinster), an old schoolmate, comes to the rescue as the prescribed time of widowhood draws to its close, and by her advice, and with her assistance, certain of the male friends and relatives of *Mrs. Flowerdew* Russell are introduced into the house, with the idea of some day becoming permanently established as its head and master. Prominent among these are *Mr. Dimple* Burton; *Captain Mouser* Holman, and *Sir Solomon* Johnstone (bachelors), whose efforts and plots to circumvent each other, and secure their own election by the widow, their combined efforts to circumvent the heir-at-law — now distant in spirit but present in flesh — and this heir-at-law's strategetic schemes to circumvent everybody else, made up a comedy which "I must confess made mine eyes water, but more merry tears the passion of loud laughter never shed."

That our readers may more fully comprehend the subject and period of which we write, it will be well to remind them, perhaps, that the art of acting had arrived at such a point in Burton's Theatre that to play a comedy well was not enough. Everything was so well done, so perfect in every respect, mere excellence was so much a matter of course, was so positive, on the Chambers Street boards, that there was but little room for the comparative, and the superlative itself was necessary to create a sensation. This evening the sensation was created!

Who that has ever seen it will forget Mr. Burton in the part, — his easy, self-satisfied air, as his friend *Miss O'Leary* assures him of the prosperity of his suit, and that he has only to exercise his boasted qualifications: "fortitude, forbearance, and a sweet temper," in order to carry everything before him? Who will ever forget, too, the assurance of *Captain Mouser* Holman, who, when all his protestations of love and constancy had failed to win the widow, presented his little bill of £700 for attendance upon the lady, with his explanations thereof? The proverbial trait, "stage impudence," was never carried further or more unblushingly than this. The *Sir Solomon* of this cast, Tom Johnstone ("the Old Dutch Governor"), was particularly happy and amusing. A nervous, haunted, and hunted man he was, the victim of an astrology-mad old maid, *Miss Desperate* Hughes (spinster), who was bound to marry him, whom she considered her destiny, ere her star of hope had waned, or the sun had set on her forty-ninth summer. This was a part into which he seemed determined to concentrate all of his powers of eccentric comedy, and all that was great in his early successes; and his *Toots*, and *Quilp*, and *Uriah Heep*, each in its way a perfect picture, the brightest of "star performances," paled for a time in the lustre of his *Sir Solomon Solus*.

Our next act shifts, and the distant relative, the heir-at-law, the disguised *Walker*, *Mrs. Flowerdew's* poetical footman, the inimitable John Brougham (to whom his mistress, to get rid of everybody else, exercises "man's privilege, and speaks first"), wins the widow, declares himself to be the rightful heir, blesses everybody, while everybody blesses him, embraces *Flora*, while everybody is embracing everybody else; and, when *Flora* asks for a couplet or verse adapted to this occasion, quotes his farewell lines: —

I calmed her fears, and she was calm,
  And told her love with gentle pride;
And so I won my *Flowerdew*,
  My bright, my beauteous bride.

(Curtain.)

That was Leap Year in 1850!

Mr. Buckstone, as a writer, is essentially a *farceur*: he is given to extravagances of plot and of dialogue even in what he calls his comedies; many of these, as "Married Life," being nothing better than farces in three acts. He is certainly clever as an actor and as an author; he is very funny, and is very popular in London; but his popularity is among the frequenters of the pit rather than among the loungers of the boxes. Those who remember him during his engagement here, or in later years have seen him on his own London stage, have noticed, no doubt, about his acting, something that is almost a lack of refinement, a something which, as it approached the broad joke, or the *double entendre*, reminds us of our own Burton. As a comedian, Mr. Buckstone is truly a low comedian; as an author, although he is hardly low, still he is scarcely high: he is farcical, fond of absurd surprises, abounding in ludicrous situations; still he is fresh, often original, and always amusing. His "Leap Year" is as happy as anything he has written; it is bright in its language, and it is not absolutely unnatural. *Mrs. Flowerdew* unconsciously is attracted by the good looks and by the elegant style of *Walker*, — he is something more than a footman to her; he is a confidant, almost a friend; and, before she fully realizes her own position, or understands her own feelings, she becomes desperately in love with him. Such things have happened even in real life. His attentions are so delicately shown, — by such a *Walker* as Brougham, — he anticipates her every want so intelligently, makes himself so indispensable, is so full of tact in his speeches, and so apt in his quotations, that the widow, in spite of herself, is won.

The main idea of the plot of "Leap Year," the falling in love of the lady with the page, is taken from an almost forgotten play of Sheridan Knowles's, called "Love; or, the Countess and the Serf," first produced at the Bowery Theatre in 1839 by Hamblin and Mrs.

Shaw. In Knowles's play, however, the servant *is* a servant, who, by his own efforts, makes for himself a name and a fortune; while in "Leap Year" the footman is simply a footman in disguise, and never a very probable footman at that.

The part of *Mrs. Flowerdew* was not one of Mrs. Hoey's greatest parts; it gave her no chance for the display of magnificent histrionic talent; but, to be at all an acceptable part, it demanded grace, delicacy, and sparkle, — all of these it found as Mrs. Hoey represented it; and *Mrs. Flowerdew's* conflict between her love and her pride, as Mrs. Hoey showed it to us, was artistically and charmingly rendered.

We have seen Mr. Brougham in many parts; we have seen him in strange company, and in many companies, — how many and how strange we have related before, — but his *Walker*, as we remember it on this occasion, and on other evenings later, is one of the brightest and most artistic of all his conceptions. It was with him purely an original part, — Charles Kean playing it originally at the Haymarket, in London, to the *Mrs. Flowerdew* of Mrs. Kean, in the same year, — a new *rôle*, a mine of richness in its droll situations and innumerable quotations from the poets, which the "silver-tongued" John worked with a master hand. This was at a period in the history of the stage in New York, as we have said above, when the acting of the regular companies, particularly of Burton's, was, probably, as perfect in all respects as was ever seen, or will be ever seen again. Burton, Johnstone, Holman, Mrs. Brougham, Mrs. Hughes, and Mrs. Russell, were in their prime. In "Leap Year," as in all other comedies, every part was so perfectly filled that nothing more in the way of excellence could be looked or wished for; and *Walker*, by Brougham, stood prominent above all the others, and remains in our memory the pleasantest picture in a pleasant comedy.

To the manager and proprietor of our oldest comedy theatre we are indebted for many revivals of old comedies, that have shown us many of our friends of the olden time in their olden parts; we owe to him in late seasons the picture of Mr. Gilbert's perfect *Lord Ogleby*, *Sir Peter*, *Lord Duberly*, and *Old Dornton*. We owe to Mr. Wallack the picture of Mr. Floyd's inimitable *Sir Frederic Blount*, than which there can be no better; the picture of Mr. Polk's *Dolly Spanker*, the best our stage has seen since the days of Dolly Davenport; of Mme. Ponisi's *Mrs. Malaprop*, almost perfection in its way; of Mr. Beckett's *Bob Acres*, as good to-day as our stage can show; the picture of his own *Alfred Evelyn*, *Young Marlow*, *Charles Courtley*, which no actor on the stage, in our day or in his, has rivalled; he has shown us Brougham as *Sir Lucius O'Callaghan*, *Dazzle*, and *Stout*. Are we ever again to see "Leap Year," with the great and only *Walker*, Brougham?

CHAPTER XXIII.

HOLIDAY BILLS. — "DOT" AND "SMIKE."

"For now I am in a holiday humor."
As You Like It, Act IV. Sc. 1.

THERE is a flavor of holiday seasons lingering about the play-bill we are ruminating over to-night; a flavor of past holidays, it is true, but so fresh and so green in our recollection that they seem but cheerful yesterdays to us now; and a thousand fantasies begin to throng into our memory, of calling shapes, and beckoning shadows dire, and airy tongues, that syllable men's names and women's names on sands and shores and musty, faded play-bills! What peaceful hours we once enjoyed, how sweet their memory still, though they have left an aching void which the stage of to-day seems not quite able to fill!

Saturday and Wednesday matinees are of weekly and common occurrence to-day, but a few years ago they were almost unknown. Only on great or holiday occasions were the public treated to afternoon performances, and even then, by the vast majority of the play-going population, was the evening preferred as the legitimate time for dramatic entertainment. Our Christmas and Thanksgiving Days were devoted to the historical turkey and the traditional pumpkin pie, but when these — the business of the time — were disposed of, how naturally followed the pleasure; after the wine and the walnuts, what more fitting termination to the day than the drama? The Christmas pantomime we did not inherit from our progenitors over the water, and "Boxing Night" has not come down to us as a particular institution of Christmas week, but to the theatre on holiday nights, in our younger days, we did like to go; and a little beyond the ordinary were the inducements our managers held out to us; the houses were crowded with happy, good-natured, and not altogether habitual crowds, and long remembered were the entertainments by the smaller fry of the audiences.

It was not by any means the least important part of the celebration of Thanksgiving or Christmas Day, this going to the theatre; and grave thought and deliberation were given to the subject; much delightful anticipation was indulged in for days, and many family discussions were often held before the momentous question, which should it be, was finally settled. Between so many attractive sweetmeats, difficult was the choice of one that should properly close our holiday feast, and leave in our mouths that proper "taste of sweetness" which was to be desired; not "that little more than a little thereof, which was so apt to be by much too much!"

We have before us holiday bills going back to the days of the Park, before our own days, but remembered well and fondly by our sires; bills showing that the Seguin Troupe were singing the "Bohemian Girl" there in 1846, on Christmas Day, and singing it as well, so think our sires, as it has ever since been sung. We find a Thanksgiving bill of the next year, and of the same house, with Shakespeare's "King John" as the play; produced at "unheard-of cost" and with "undreamed-of magnificence;" Charles Kean playing *King*

John and Mrs. Kean *Lady Constance*, "superbly supported," but losing all the money they had invested, in their attempt to gratify New York audiences with what is still remembered as one of the most correct, meritorious, and expensive productions of a Shakespearean play that this country has ever known.

We have 4th of July bills at Burton's of "Toodles" and the "Serious Family;" Christmas bills of the Ravels, with yards of attractions; the bill of "Our American Cousin," in all its original strength and with all its original glory, dated December 25, 1858; the bill of Christmas Eve, 1855, at Wallack's, announcing the first night's performance of "Pocahontas, or the Gentle Savage," by John Brougham, with Walcot as *John Smith*, Peters as *Rolff*, Miss Hodson as *Pocahontas*, and Brougham himself as the smoking, joking *Powhatan*, the King of the Tuscaroras. We have Christmas bills of Bryant's Minstrels in Mechanic's Hall and of Italian opera at the Academy of Music, of Nixon's Circus at Niblo's and of Dickens's Readings at Steinway Hall, December 26, 1869. Very many and very varied are these Christmas bills, and they come down to Christmas 1873, with "Gabriel Grub" at the Olympic, and to Christmas, 1874, when Miss Heron at Booth's played *Lady Macbeth.*

It is, however, upon one particular and well remembered holiday bill that we would dwell in this chapter, and to which all of this talk of holiday memories is but the prologue.

Winter Garden, a Conservatory of the Arts, Dedicated to the Culture of Comedy, Music, Ballet, by Miss Agnes Robertson. This establishment has been newly constructed and decorated from plans furnished by Mr. Dion Boucicault.

THANKSGIVING NIGHT, NOV. 1859.

In consequence of the great entertainment to-night, and to enable families and children to reach their homes in early season, the curtain will rise at 7 o'clock. The new Domestic Drama in a Fairy Frame called

"Dot,"

Representing Charles Dickens's beautiful story, "The Cricket on the Hearth." The characters will be sustained by the following artists: —

John Perrybingle . . . . Mr. Harry Pearson.
Dot, his wife . . . . Miss Agnes Robertson.
(In which character she will sing "Auld Robin Gray.")
Tilly Slowboy, a charity girl who takes care of the baby . . . . Miss Morton.
Caleb Plummer, a toy maker . . . . Joseph Jefferson.
Bertha, his blind daughter . . . . Sara Stevens.
Edward Plummer, his son . . . . . . A. H. (Dolly) Davenport.
Mrs. Fielding, reduced in circumstances in consequence of a crisis in the indigo trade . Mrs. W. R. Blake.
May Fielding, Edward's sweetheart . . . . Mrs. J. H. Allen.
Tackleton, a toy merchant, Master to Caleb . . T. B. Johnstone.

CHARACTERS IN THE FAIRY PROLOGUE.

Oberon . . . . Miss Secor.
Titania . . . . Miss Fielding.
Puck . . . . Miss Gimber.
Ariel . . . . Miss Clinton.

Latter Day Fairies, strong, hard-working, useful little things, not at all proud.

Home . . . . Miss Barnett.
Kettle . . . . Miss Denham.
Cradle . . . . Miss Clinton.
The Cricket . . . . Miss Burke.

To conclude with

"Smike."

Act 1. — Ralph Nickleby's Office in Golden Square.
Act 2. — A Room at Madame Mantilini's.
Act 3. — The School-room at Dotheboy's Hall.

Ralph Nickleby, a lawyer and money lender . . Mr. Stoddart.
Newman Noggs, his clerk . . . . Joseph Jefferson.

Scaly, a Sheriff's officer / Tompkins, specimen boy	George Holland.
Nicholas Nickleby	Mr. Harrison.
Mantilini	"Dolly" Davenport.
Mrs. Squeers	Mrs. Blake.
Mme. Mantilini	Mrs. J. H. Allen.
Kate Nickleby	Miss Secor.
John Brodie	Harry Pearson.
John	Mr. Ponisi.
Fanny Squeers	Miss Burke.
Miss Price	Miss Gimber.
Miss Jones	Miss Clinton.
Squeers, a Yorkshire schoolmaster	T. B. Johnstone.
Smike, an orphan	Miss Agnes Robertson.

This was the first season of Winter Garden *as* Winter Garden; the lessees were William Stuart and Boucicault, and the house had been previously known as the Metropolitan Theatre.

These adaptations of Dickens's "Smike" and "Dot," both by Boucicault, were, as plays and in a mere literary point of view, as clever and successful as any version of a novelist's work that we have ever seen on our stage; and never — and we make *no* exception — were dramatized novels so thoroughly satisfactory, and so charmingly played from first to last, as were these on this particular night and during this particular season.

This Thanksgiving Night was not the first night of either of these plays singly, for "Dot" was first produced on the 14th of September, the opening night of the house under its new name and under the Boucicault management, when Mrs. John Wood was the *Tilly Slowboy;* and "Smike" was produced a few months later, but this was the first occasion, so far as we can now remember, when both were given on the same evening. The same artists, it will be seen, were in the cast of both, and in characters as widely different in many cases as the whole range of the drama contains. Where can be found a greater contrast than between *Dot* and *Smike; Newman Noggs* and *Caleb Plummer; Mme. Mantilini* and *May Fielding; Fanny Squeers* and a "Latter Day Fairy?" Although the contrast between *Tackleton* and *Squeers*, and between *John Brodie* and *John Perrybingle* was not so decided, the very fact of there being a similarity, and the fact of the one part following so closely upon the other in one night, made them very difficult and trying parts for their representatives.

The desire to see and to compare them was great, and crowded was the house this holiday evening; not so much with the regulation and ordinary holiday crowds, as with *habitués* of the house who had frequently seen and enjoyed each play separately before.

We have sometimes feared that in these reminiscences we have shown too much enthusiasm, and have been too wholesale in our commendation and admiration of each particular occasion or artist, of which or of whom we may have happened to write; have claimed so much superlative excellence for so many performances and for so many companies; have employed so many adjectives in praise of so many actors, that we have earned in the minds of such of our readers as have had patience to follow us so far, a reputation of unreliability and of "gush."

We have chronicled other evening's performances that have been on many accounts very enjoyable, and long to be remembered; but we can think of no evening's entertainment so perfectly admirable and memorable in every respect as this, the close of a Thanksgiving Day for which to give thanks, a feast of reason by the side of which all others of our dramatic holiday banquets have been as ordinary restaurant regimen.

We have always noticed at holiday plays an easy disposition on the part of audiences to enjoy the dishes set before them, even though they are barely palatable and fall far short of the promises contained in the bill of fare. Good nature, however, was not imposed upon, nor critical taste shocked on this occasion by such shortcomings — the feast was a feast, almost a surfeiture of good things, and no Oliver could reasonably cry for more.

CHAPTER XXIV.

"DOT" AND "SMIKE." — JOSEPH JEFFERSON AND AGNES ROBERTSON.

"And crickets sing at the oven's mouth."
Pericles, Act III. Gower.

A PRESENTATION copy of Dickens's "Cricket on the Hearth" is said to be in existence in England with this inscription in Mr. Dickens's own hand-writing: "To Wm. M. Thackeray, from Charles Dickens, whom he made very happy once when a long way from home."

How very happy and how much better we have all been made by Charles Dickens himself, and by his Christmas stories, at home and a long way from it, who can say? The "Carol" and the "Chimes" would have stamped him the "master" if he had written nothing more, but the purest, simplest, sweetest story in the whole range of English literature we claim to be this story of "Dot," and Agnes Robertson was the very *Dot* that Dickens drew. We can only describe her acting of the part as the master described the little woman herself in the tale — "fair she was and young, though something of the dumpling shape, but I don't object to that." Who could object to that? When during "Chirp the First" she looked out of the window for *John's* return and saw nothing, owing to the darkness, but her own face mirrored in the glass, we quite agree with the "Master" that "she might have looked a long way, and have seen nothing half so agreeable."

A coy Dot was she, a motherly little Dot, a matronly little Dot, watching her Dot of a daughter; the very Dot the fairy and the cricket showed John in his dreams; the Dot who was John's darling and the "Master's" best creation, never to be seen again so well and so perfectly represented on any stage. Miss Robertson was, in her way, and still is, in her womanly, natural, gentle way, the most charming and perfect actress we have ever known; her *Jessie Brown* was simply inimitable, but her *Dot* in its homely home-like setting, more delicious even than her lowly romantic Scottish heroine of Lucknow!

Mr. Dickens might have gone very far before he could have found his ideals so absolutely realized as in almost every case they were by the Winter Garden Company in the plays of which we write; for Harry Pearson's *John Perrybingle* and Jefferson's *Caleb Plummer* were in every way fit to be companion pictures to Miss Robertson's *Dot.* Mr. Pearson's Lancashire or Yorkshire origin had endowed him with a dialect, and nature herself had given him a face and a figure, that fitted him admirably to play the part of *John, the Carter*, and to look it too. "This lumbering, slow, honest John; this John so heavy, but so light of spirit; so rough upon surface, but so gentle at the core; so dull without, so quick within; so stolid, but so good!" We can find no better words to tell of *John* as Pearson played him, than Dickens's own; and of Pearson we always think when we think of John.

Jefferson's *Caleb Plummer*, with all respect for his *Rip Van Winkle*, and in all affection for his *Asa Trenchard*, is the best thing that he ever played! Why will he not gratify the many who knew and loved him as *Caleb* years ago, by giving them an opportunity to know and love him as *Caleb* again? Why is he content to spend his glorious prime in his unceasing Rippings about the country? Can the voice of no familiar Cricket wake him from the twenty years' sleep into which he has fallen, and in which he seems disposed to dream forever?

Over his *Caleb* in our reminiscences we like to linger. We saw it often, never wearied of it, and were willing to go to Winter Garden at least once a week to sympathize with *Caleb*, to laugh at and rejoice with him, and to shed over him tears which we could not restrain, and of which we had no reason to be ashamed. There were not many dry eyes in the house those nights when the old man in "Chirp the Last" began to realize that his dear boy from the golden South Americas was alive again and before him; and when he tried to tell his blind girl how for love of her he had deceived her, how the eyes in which she had put her trust had been false to her during all those years, we have known eyes to fill and to run over, even on the stage itself.

How plainly we can recall that scene in the toymaker's cottage; the dolls, and Noah's arks, and small fiddles, and barking dogs; *Bertha* making the dolls' dresses; and *Caleb* in his sackcloth coat, which she, in her blindness and her fondness, believed to be a garment that the Lord Mayor might have been proud of, finishing up a great toy horse. How plainly we can see the thorough *goodness* of the old man, as he described to *Bertha* the beautiful things by which they were surrounded, and which existed only in his loving, doting old heart; that quaint, humorous look on *Caleb's* face as he painted the numerous circles, and dots, and stripes, which gave to his preposterous horse a likeness to nothing known in natural history, and held it up with the satisfied, contented remark that he did not see how he could outlay any more talent on the animal, at the price. He was not Joseph Jefferson, but *Caleb Plummer* himself; this was not a play, but the story realized; and yet the man who can accomplish so much of this has played but one star part, and that *not* his best, in New York for many years.

But to return to the cast of "Dot." *Bertha* was simply charmingly played by Sara Stevens, who, the year before, had made so many friends as the original *Mary Meredith* of "Our American Cousin," — both of them the innocent, lovable sort of characters which she was so fitted in manner and appearance to represent. Mrs. J. H. Allen, beautiful and talented (the Mrs. Louise Allen, to-day, of Daly's company), was irresistible as *May*; and Mrs. Blake, as *Edward's* mother-in-law, under the blight of the indigo trade, was everything that could be expected of a mother-in-law on the stage and in books. Tom Johnstone, as *Tackleton*, was perfect, as he was in every part he undertook, ugly enough in looks to have made a wooden nut-cracker, and to have been sold among his own toys, crushing the imaginary crickets with his heel, and with the most scr-r-r-aunching of sounds. Of Miss Morton, the *Tilly Slowboy* this evening, we can, alas! remember nothing; she has completely paled in the brilliant light cast by the original *Tilly*, Mrs. John Wood, who, when the play was first produced, was the wildest, roughest, most heathenish, most impossible of nursemaids, treating the baby as no real baby could have been treated, and lived, and conducting herself in a way that would have insured her discharge in five minutes from the worst regulated household in England. *Tilly Slowboy* and the baby — the latter furnished by the property man — were the only overdrawn and unnatural part in the play.

We have before remarked that the representation on the stage of well-known characters of romance is the most difficult and thankless task the actor has to perform, as the dramatization of a popular novel is the most unsatisfactory work of the playwright. Except in such rare cases as "Masks and Faces," and in the later dramatization of the "New Magdalen," where the work is done by the author of the book, a play which is an adaptation is rarely a success. It invites comparisons, and the comparisons are invariably odious to the play. Excellent actors, male and female, who have created scores of characters, and have won fame and profit out of them, have failed entirely in the rendering of a character which, in the pages of fiction or history, has made itself familiar to all readers. Every reader is apt insensibly to form his own opinion of the men and women who figure in the books he reads, each opinion of each reader being entirely different from every other opinion, and being regarded by that reader as the only one worth having. More particularly is this true of Dickens's characters; and we claim that Miss Robertson and Mr. Jefferson, in impressing audiences of thousands of people who had *Dots* and *Caleb Plummers* of their own, that her *Dot* and his *Caleb* were the only true and acceptable *Dot* and *Caleb*, have won the highest triumph of dramatic art. Other artists, however, have accomplished almost as much. Wallack as *Fagin*, Davenport as *William Sikes*, Burton as *Micawber* and *Cap-*

tain Cuttle, Brougham as *Bunsby*, Johnstone and Raymond as *Toots*, and Mrs. Vernon and Mrs. Hughes as *Mrs. Skewton*, have played their parts so well and so positively "to the life," that if they have not actually realized our ideals, they have created for us new conceptions, which we have accepted as the only true ones, and which Mr. Dickens himself, in his readings, in many cases failed entirely to reach.

We have read and studied Dickens's books, we cannot say how often, and have seen every dramatization of them, good, bad, and indifferent, that has been put upon our stage during the last twenty years. When he came here to show his creations as he saw them himself, many of our idols were shattered by the hands of the man who made them. *Lady Creamly*, in the "Serious Family," observes that "the truth when it is useful, ought to be told!" It is a sad but useful truth, to prove the strength of the argument, that we were far from being satisfied, in Dickens's interpretations of his own creations, and by these interpretations, lost many an old friend forever,— *Toots* and *Winkle*, and *Buzfuz* and the *Wellers*, and many more of them, as we had known them all our lives, faded into thin air, in the light that Dickens cast upon them at Steinway Hall.

We have had but one *Smike*, and he was Agnes Robertson's; but one *Newman Noggs*, and he was Joseph Jefferson's. She was the miserable, friendless, orphan boy from the pages of the book itself; he, the rusty, goggle-eyed, cadaverous clerk, whose whole existence might have been spent in that rusty office in Golden Square, and the incessant cracking of whose knuckles was heard distinctly in every part of the house!

We have said little here of the play of "Smike." As

an adaptation it was quite as good as that of "Dot," and was by all the actors in the cast quite as well played. It had, however, this disadvantage, that it followed too immediately after the masterwork of its author, and as a story was less hearty in tone, and infinitely more sad; the brighter portions of "Nicholas Nickleby," the Cheeryble brothers, Miss La Creevy, and Manager Crummles finding no place in the play. We had only to abominate the *Squeers*, to sympathize with *Kate*, to love poor *Newman* while we pitied him, and to weep for *Smike*. All this we did and heartily; and "Smike" and "Dot" are still remembered as among the saddest and the brightest, the purest and the whitest of all our holiday bills.

CHAPTER XXV.

AGNES ROBERTSON AND *JESSIE BROWN.* — MRS. BOUCICAULT'S PLAYING. — MR. BOUCICAULT'S PLAYS.

"In mine eyes she is the sweetest lady I ever looked on."
"*Much Ado,*" Act I. Sc. 1.

"For look you, how he writes."
Second Part "*Henry IV.*," Act. II. Sc. 2.

It seems no longer than yesterday that we shed our first tear over the miseries of the siege of Lucknow, as presented on the stage of Wallack's old theatre, and fell first in love with *Jessie Brown.* It was about our first stage love, and we confess to a little of it lingering yet. We were only a school-boy in those days, semi-Scotch at that, and the effect was tremendous. Up to that period of our existence the height of our ambition was to be one of Marryat's midshipmen, wear a dirk, cut out pirate cutters, and play tricks on the purser. But now we aspired higher, we 'd be a *Geordie McGreggor* at least; we did once aim even as high as *Randal,* but we had no noticeable moustache, and no confidence in the size and shape of our own legs for kilts, and then, too, *Geordie* was nearer our own age. We sympathized with his "flenching," his "business" we thought would suit us better, and, moreover, as *Sweenie* was to marry *Jessie,* we preferred next to her *Alice,* played in those days by Mrs. J. H. Allen. Those were indeed palmy days of the drama at Wallack's. Boucicault played his own *Nana Sahib* and of course played it well. Lester

Wallack was *Randal McGreggor*, very dashing, very heroic, and very handsome in his highland costume. He was then known as Mr. Lester on the bills, although we find him cast as J. Lester Wallack, in his own play of the *Veteran* the next year, 1859. "Dolly" Davenport was *Geordie* and a good one; his drunk in the first act, was particularly good. T. B. Johnstone played *Sweenie* —poor Tom Johnstone, a general favorite in his time, and now so long dead that he is almost forgotton. Blake was the *Chaplain*. Mr. Sloan played *Cassidy*, and *Amy Campbell* was played by Mrs Hoey.

This was sixteen or seventeen years ago. Blake, Johnstone, Davenport, Sloan, are dead. Mrs. Hoey is in honorable retirement. Wallack's Theatre has been moved to its present position; the old corner of Broadway and Broome street is now covered with marble stores; another generation of play-goers is among us; times and men and things are changed; but Agnes Robertson, when we saw her last at Booth's as *Jessie Brown* in the fall of 1872, fourteen years after her first appearance in the part, came trippingly on the stage in her Scotch plaid, and her blue stockings, driving her lovers and her *bairns* before her, as bright, and fresh, and pretty, and young as ever; the same "sprig of heather from the Highland moors," singing the same old Scottish ballads in that same sweet voice that "Nature has put into the prettiest throat that ever had arm around it." She was a little stouter but in no other respect altered, and was as worthy of the devotion of *Sweenie* and *Cassidy*, and of the eight hundred men of the seventy-eighth regiment in the play, and of the ever so many hundreds of men in her audiences, when we saw her last as when we saw her first. We thought with 'Zekle in 1858 that—

"'Twas kin' o' kingdom-come to look
On sech a blessed cretur,"

and even now we must confess that —

"A dog-rose blushin' to a brook
Ain't modester nor sweeter."

She has still the prettiest Scottish accent we ever heard on or off the stage; the first word she uttered at Booth's in 1872, as *Jessie Brown*, brought back to us a flood of recollections; and although we are a regular play-goer, and are not given to much emotion at plays, we found our vision dimmed as we watched her through our opera glass; we half cried, half laughed as we thought of the days and the scenes her presence recalled. We became —

"All kin' o' smily roun' the lips,
An' teary roun' the lashes —"

not so much on account of the play or the player, as on account of "the days of auld lang syne" of which she sang so sweetly.

The chief attraction of Agnes Robertson's acting is the modest refinement of her manner. Her chief personal attraction, we are inclined to think, is the simple way in which she wears her hair — the same simple, pretty way of fifteen years ago, when fashions were sensible and *chignons* unknown. We will venture to assert that there is hardly a male play-goer in New York who, remembering her as she was and is, does not long for the *coiffure* of other days.

She belongs to a school of actresses now, alas, almost extinct, of which she and Mrs. Frank Chanfrau and one or two *womanly* women, are the only representatives; actresses who depend more upon their own gentle manners and winning ways, than upon all the accessories of paint, powder, blond hair, long trains, and magnificent toilettes of the period, actresses of whom we think and say, "How prettily she looked," "How charmingly she acted," not "How elegantly she was gotten up."

Miss Robertson was born in Edinborough on the 25th of December, 1833, so said a usually truthful historian on her first coming to this country many years ago. She is said also to have been descended from the great Scottish ducal house of Buccleuch, which may perhaps account for the purity and refinement of her Scottish accent. A pretty little story of her early career we remember to have heard, which, without vouching for its truth or entering into its details, we venture to repeat here.

Her first public appearance was made in her native city as a singer, as early as 1844. At thirteen years of age she began her theatrical career, appearing in the larger of the provincial cities of Great Britain, and by her own exertions supporting, until their death, her parents and her brothers. Her London *début* was made at the Princess's Theatre in 1851. She played the part of *Narcissa* in "The Merchant of Venice." The Queen, who was present, was much impressed by the young girl, and at the royal request she was taken after the performance by her manager, Mr. Charles Kean, into the royal box. She subsequently took a leading part in the private theatrical entertainments given at Windsor Castle, and on one occasion she went with the young Queen into the nursery of young royalty, and there among the youthful princes told to her majesty much of the story of her eventful life. The kindly notice of royal circles was of great advantage to the rising artist, both socially and in her profession; she received much flattering attention and made many powerful friends. No one who remembers her as she came to this country in the glorious prime of her comely womanhood, can doubt that she had many lovers. Among the most persistent and ardent of these was a young earl, then one of the wealthiest peers of Scotland; so marked was his attention that his family, dreading what they termed a misalliance, even begged the interference of the Queen, who declined to use her influence. The mother of the enamoured youth finally offered to Miss Robertson a fortune of £10,000 if she would marry at once some one in her own walk of life, and thus remove from his Earlship the possibility of his making her his wife. This, Miss Robertson indignantly refused, writing that "Lord H. had commenced his suit so offensively, and his first offer had shown so little respect for her, that she could never feel anything but aversion for a person who had not scrupled to insult her feelings. Therefore, presuming that Lady H.'s offer was intended as an inducement to discourage her son, she begged while declining it, to assure her ladyship, that neither the rank nor the fortune of the Earl could make her bestow her hand where she could not give her love or her esteem."

The young Earl, driven to desperation, publicly laid his coronet and his wealth at her feet, and all London was thunderstruck at the open rejection of one of the best matches of the season by a simple actress. She became Mrs. Boucicault in 1853.

This is the story. It is good enough to be true. That Miss Robertson did enjoy the friendship of the Queen, however, we believe there can be little doubt; a friendship that reflected credit on the heart and the head, not only of a good woman who was merely an actress, but of a good Queen who was after all only a woman!

The career of Dion Boucicault as an actor and playwright has been remarkable. He was born in Dublin of French parentage in 1822, and educated, we believe, at the University of London. His career as a dramatic author commenced with the production of "London Assurance," March 4th, 1841, at the Theatre Royal, Covent Garden, in London; and where it will end no man can say. He is said to be the author of over four hundred different theatrical pieces, all of which have been performed. The names of the most successful of these, and the number of times each is said to have been played, we noticed in a late newspaper paragraph, which seems to be given upon authority, and which as one of the curiosities of literature we transcribe here. "The Colleen Bawn" has been played 3,100 times; "Arrah-na-Pogue," 2,400 times; "London Assurance," 2,900 times; "Rip Van Winkle," 1,400 times; "Old Heads and Young Hearts," 1,250 times; "The Octoroon," 1,800 times; "Formosa," 1,100 times; "Jessie Brown," 820 times; "The Corsican Brothers," 2,200 times; "Don Cæsar de Bazan," 1,700 times; "Used up," 1,350 times; "The Willow Copse, 1,110 times; "The Streets of New York," 2,860 times; "Led Astray," 498 times. These are the leading plays; others have enjoyed runs of from 100 to 1,000 nights each. The entire number of all of these performances must have been almost 50,000. Estimating that the receipts at each performance averaged five hundred dollars, the public must have paid the enormous sum of twenty-five millions of dollars ($25,000,000) to witness the plays of this one man.

Among those productions of which we have not spoken above as "leading," may be mentioned, "Kerry," "Daddy O'Dowd," "The Irish Heiress," "Mimi," "Love and Money," "Jezebel," "Lost at Sea," "Jennie Deans," "Hunted Down," "After Dark," "Dot," "The Life of an Actress," "Smike," "Flying Scud," "Belle Lamar," "Mora," "The Long Strike," "How She Loves Him," "The Man of Honor," "The Shaughraun," and many others, more or less familiarly known to New York. Of these, however, many are adaptations, translations, and dramatizations, and are acknowledged as such, and some of them are not the only versions of the play known to our stage. For instance "Used Up," as played here by Charles Mathews, was adapted from the original French of *L'Homme Blasé*, by Mr. Mathews himself; "Jennie Deans, or the Heart of Midlothian," was known to our stage before Mr. Boucicault was born; and "Don Cæsar de Bazan," as played at Mitchell's Olympic in 1844, was translated during the same year by G. A. A' Beckett and Mark Lemon for the Princess's Theatre in London. Mr. Boucicault's version was brought out almost simultaneously at the Adelphi, and still another by Mr. Mathews at the Haymarket.

Mr. Boucicault, with his four hundred plays, may be regarded as one of the most prolific writers that the whole history of literature contains. We know of no other pen that can approach his in this respect. There are plenty of playwrights who have written plenty of plays, unaccepted, and never likely to see the light of the foot lights; but all of Mr. Boucicault's four hundred plays have been played, and abused, and derided, and played again. They have been received as "standard" and are likely to be long lived; while some of his char-

14

acters are almost destined to be immortal. *Jesse Rural*, *Dolly Spanker*, and *Lady Gay* we venture to assert will live as long as *Sir Anthony Absolute*, *Lady Teazle*, or as *Tony Lumpkin*, himself.

As a producer of plays and not as a player, will Mr. Boucicault be remembered by posterity; still Mr. Boucicault is by no means a poor player; his *Grimaldi* in his own "Life of an Actress," his *Nana Sahib* in "Jessie Brown," his *Bernard* in "Pauvrette," his *Spectre* in "The Vampire," his *Counsel for Defence* in "The Heart of Midlothian," his *Myles na Coppaleen* in "The Colleen Bawn," his *Mantalini* in "Smike," and his *Wah-no-tee* in "The Octoroon," in other days, were all strongly played; while in these days his *Daddy O'Dowd*, his *Kerry*, and his *Con the Shaughraun* are inimitable. In all of these late plays in which he has himself assumed the central and titular part, his object, he claims, has been to elevate the stage Irishman to something like nature, "to give a truthful stage portraiture of Irish life, manner, and character; and to obliterate the gross caricature the public had received from the stage — a caricature that had been mainly instrumental in forming a popular and very false impression of Irish nature." His *Daddy O'Dowd* we consider a beautiful bit of character acting, equal to his *Kerry*, which was saying very much for it, and fit to rank with Fisher's *Triplet* or Jefferson's *Rip Van Winkle*.

Mr. and Mrs. Boucicault came to this country in 1853. Miss Agnes Robertson made her first appearance in New York on Burton's stage, October 22, 1853, as *Maria* in "The Young Actress." Mr. Boucicault made his first appearance on the 10th of November in the next year at the Broadway, as *Sir Charles Coldstream*, in "Used Up," at his wife's benefit.

"Jessie Brown" was first produced at Wallack's on the 22d February, 1858, with the cast as we have given it above, and was played for some time to full houses. The Boucicaults appeared in it for two weeks of the same year, beginning September 6th at Niblo's Garden, George Jordan playing *Randal McGreggor*. And on the 2d, 3d, and 4th of July, 1860, we noticed the fact that "Miss Agnes Robertson, previous to her departure from the United States, will take her farewell benefit at Winter Garden as *Jessie Brown*," making her last appearance in America in the *Colleen Bawn*, July 5, 1860.

The Boucicaults returned to New York in the summer of 1872, and at Booth's Theatre on the 23d of September, opened in "Arrah-na-Pogue." "Jessie Brown" and "Kerry" were produced on the 26th of October. "Jessie Brown," in leading parts, cast as follows: —

Jessie Brown, a Scotch girl . .	Miss Agnes Robertson.
Amy Campbell	Miss Kate Newton.
Alice	Miss Geraldine Stuart.
Mary	Miss Livingstone.
The Nana Sahib	Mr. Joseph Wheelock.
Randal McGreggor	Mr. Geo. Becks.
Geordie McGreggor	Mr. C. Alexander.
Rev. David Blount	Mr. A. W. Fenno.
Sweenie	Mr. Neilson Decker.
Cassidy	Mr. Shiel Barry.

It ran until the 16th of November, the close of their engagement in this house, and is the last part that Mrs. Boucicault has played in New York.

Very pretty is the story of "Jessie Brown," and a pretty little play has Boucicault made of it; inventing and adding the first two acts, and working up the incidents to the climax in the last. The story originally appeared in our papers at the time of the height of public interest in the Indian mutiny of 1857, in the shape of a letter from an English lady, Boucicault's *Amy Campbell*, who had taken part in the awful scenes enacted at Lucknow, and wrote of them to her people at home. The story was very simply and pathetically told, and were it not so long and so well known, would well bear repetition here. It was universally copied throughout the country, was much commented upon, and was even read by Edward Everett in his matchless way, at one of his lectures in the Academy of Music. Dion Boucicault's quick eye for dramatic situation saw its dramatic power at once, and recognized the fitness of his own wife for such a character as *Jessie;* and Mrs. Boucicault's Scottish heart, warming to the part that her Scottish accent and homely, womanly ways enable her so fittingly to play, gave us *Jessie Brown*, one of the most agreeable remembrances of the play-goers of another decade.

"Jessie Brown" has been played at the Bowery Theatre in this city, and was produced by Mrs. Conway at the Park Theatre, Brooklyn, in March, 1868; but never until its last representation at Booth's so satisfactorily as on its first production in 1858, nobody of course ever equalling Miss Robertson in the titular part, a part with which she has so thoroughly identified herself, and made so real, that although the truth of the original story has been more than doubted, and the existence of an actual *Jessie Brown* even denied, we believe in her as thoroughly as in Grace Darling, or in Florence Nightingale.

CHAPTER XXVI.

THE MARSHALL TESTIMONIAL IN 1851.

"A merited benefit."
Measure for Measure, Act III. Sc. 1.

OPEN as day for melting charity always is the hand of the actor, ever ready is he to aid the sick and the miserable of his own profession, and never unwilling is he to come to the assistance of the needy in any other. That benevolence which he certainly exercises ought surely to cover the multitude of sins he is charged with committing. Among no class of people is so much thorough good-fellowship shown as among players, a good-fellowship that might well serve as a copy to many of the moralists of our times, who condemn the stage and everything and everybody connected with it.

The noble Charity Benefits which our theatrical managers have so generously organized in late seasons, to which our actors have so generously donated their talents and their time, and which have given to the poor of the city and to the widows and orphans of the profession, so many thousands of dollars, are only fair examples of what the stage has done, and is always doing, for the relief of the distressed.

Our recollections of complimentary and charity benefit performances are very many and varied, and the bills of these are among the most valued and interesting of our collection. One of the most remarkable of these bills, one which recalls the most remarkable entertainment probably ever given in this city, opens as follows: —

"Programme of the Performance at the Grand Dramatic Jubilee in honor of Ethelbert A. Marshall, Lessee of the Broadway Theatre, New York, and of the Walnut Street Theatre, Philadelphia, to be given by the Citizens of New York at Castle Garden, on Tuesday, August 12, 1851, through the voluntary aid of the principal artists in the United States. The performances will commence at precisely 10 o'clock, A. M., and will terminate at 11 o'clock at night. Doors open at 8 A. M. Admission tickets to the entire performance One Dollar each."

At Castle Garden! How oddly now reads the announcement, and how many pleasant associations are connected with the spot, for many years the temple of the drama, now only the scene of the Emigrant's Dream, the first American home of the Exiles of Erin.

At Castle Garden Jenny Lind made her first bow to an American audience, and John N. Genin, the Knox of other days, paid the fabulous sum of $225 for first choice of seats at her first concert, September 11th, 1850.

At Castle Garden that same summer Max Maretzek, then comparatively new to New York, had presented Italian opera with Marini, Lorini, Beneventano, Baratini, Bossio, Steffanone, and other artists whose names are now forgotten, but who were as popular then as Cary, Campanini, and Capoul to-day — and the admission was fifty cents. Those were seasons when the great public got for its money its full value in song, and seasons when the Battery was the aristocratic part of the town, before fashionable society had learned to ignore the world below Fourteenth Street.

At Castle Garden, too, were held the fairs of the American Institute, with their countless delights to the boy of that period; their models of full-rigged yachts, their wonderful glass blowers, and the marvellous machines to pare apples and to wring clothes, which were to revolutionize our entire domestic economy, and which never worked when we got them home. At one particular fair was an instrument that would have stamped the Castle Garden forever in our memory, if nothing else had done so, an instrument — a chopper of some kind, for sausages perhaps — about which we used to linger with a weird sort of fascination never to be forgotten; an instrument in which some rash youth had left four of his fingers, and which has ever since served as an awful warning to us to keep our "hands off" everything at fairs.

To Castle Garden also came the first and only Chinese Junk, and to Castle Garden, to see and wonder at it, down Broadway came all the good people of Gotham.

At Castle Garden, too, best of all, were those peep-holes in the gallery, which we can remember so long ago that we had to be lifted up by paternal arms to look into them. Cosmorama or diorama were they called? and what pictures were revealed of impossible deluges, with pre-Raphaelite waters, and a pink-colored Duke of Wellington at a very blood-red battle of Waterloo! The cyclorama of Paris by Night, or London by Day, is nothing to these battle scenes of Castle Garden, as real to us in those days as war itself. The exercise of a very little "make believe" invested in the old fort a personal interest in all of its battles, and the peep-holes became port-holes to us, through which many a time and oft, with General Taylor, we have bombarded Monterey, or have died on the Plains of Abraham with General Wolfe.

Of Castle Garden hardly can we speak without some mention of the promenade on the outer balcony, so popular on fine nights when the moon, the inconstant moon, shone on the sparkling river and the Jersey shore; and the music of the orchestra, with its voluptuous swell, mingling so harmoniously with the melodious "clink, clink" of the ice in the julep glasses, added such charms to the opera. There are old married people we wot of, whose silver wedding day is not far distant, who still contend that never sounded music so sweetly, never shone moon so brightly, as on that balcony of Castle Garden a quarter of a century ago. Of this, personally, we cannot speak; it is mere tradition, and as such is recorded here.

The coming of Jullien and his orchestra, over which New York went mad, and his first appearance in America at Castle Garden in 1853, is almost too important an event in the history of music in New York to pass with mere mention here; but it is not of Jullien, or music, or Castle Garden itself, and the scores of cheerful and pleasant recollections that are connected with its time-honored walls, that we have to do at present. Our purpose in this chapter is to place on record a benefit entertainment which is recalled, as one of the most remarkable in the recollection of play-goers, — remarkable in this, that it combined operatic, dramatic, and other "combination of talent," that could hardly have been enlisted, no matter how meritorious or important the object, at any subsequent period.

Mr. E. A. Marshall had, like many other of the managers of that day, exhausted his means in his efforts to please the public. At the Old Broadway he left no stone unturned to win popular applause, and to reap the benefits of popular appreciation; for at no period since his management have companies been stronger, stage-settings more appropriate, or scenic displays more generous. The results, however, were not happy. Disheartened, he determined to abandon the enterprise, and had so announced, when the testimonial of which we write was tendered him. We will give here merely a few "head-lines" of the bill of the entertainment, that our readers may compare this with benefits of the present, and learn how really earnest were the public and the players of a quarter of a century ago, to do a good deed when it was felt that the object was a worthy one.

In the correspondence that preceded the benefit, a letter dated July 12th, 1851, and addressed to Mr. Marshall, was signed by Henry F. Quackenboss, as secretary, and by some two hundred and fifty of the prominent citizens of New York, his Excellency Governor Washington Hunt heading the list. This letter informed Mr. Marshall that "the subscribers, his fellow-citizens, desirous of testifying their respect for his zeal and efforts in upholding the cause of the drama during his managerial career in this and other cities of the Union, more particularly for his able management of the Broadway Theatre, had determined," etc., etc. We give here as briefly as possible "the programme which the executive committee had the honor to announce," with the time at which each performance commenced: —

At ten o'clock, A. M., precisely, grand overture by the orchestra, leader, Dr. Connington; followed by the third act of "Rob Roy." Titular part by Mr. Anderson ("The Wizard of the North"); *Bailie Nicol Jarvie*, W. H. Chippendale; *Captain Thornton*, George

Jordan; *Francis*, W. H. Hamilton; *Helen McGregor*, Mme. Ponisi; *Di Vernon*, Mrs. Conway.

At twenty minutes before eleven, a Pas de Deux, by Mlle. Adeline and Signor Neri.

At eleven, A. M., "How to Pay the Rent," with Collins as *Rattler*; Whiting, *Mr. Miller;* Haines, as *Swell Billy;* Mrs. Vernon as *Mrs. Conscience;* and Josie Gougenheim as *Kitty*.

At forty-five minutes after eleven, a Pas Seul, Polka Mazourka, by Miss Julia Turnbull.

At twelve o'clock, "Un Acte de Kean par Alexandre Dumas." Principal parts by Robert Kemp and Mlle. D'Armant.

At twenty-five minutes past twelve, the Martinetti Family. Extraordinary chair feats by the Martinetti's; astonishing feats on the stilts by M. Julien ("on which he will throw a summersault, one of the greatest feats ever attempted").

At fifty minutes after twelve, the company of the German National Theatre, from the Olympic, Manager C. Burgthal, were announced to perform with their full strength "Die Weibliche Schildwache" ("The Female Sentinel").

At two o'clock precisely, the Grand Italian Opera Company, under the direction of Max Maretzek, were to present the first act of "Ernani," cast as follows: —

Elvira . . . . Signora Truffi-Beneditti.
Ernani . . . . Signor Bettini.
Carlo V. . . . . Signor Beneventano.
Sylva . . . . Signor Marini.

Followed by "LA DONNA DEL LAGO." One Act.

Recitative Cavatina . . . . Signora Caroline Vietti.
Aria . . . . Miss Virginia Whiting.

"LUCIA DI LAMMERMOOR." Second Act.

Lucia	Signora Angiolina Bossio.
Edgardo	Signor Bettini.
Karmondo	Signor Colletti.
Henri Ashton	Signor Badiali.

"LA FAVORITA." Fourth Act.

Leonora	Truffi-Beneditti.

"LUCREZIA BORGIA." Second Act.

Lucrezia	Bossio.
Gennaro	Salvi.
Alfonso	Marini.

With the Grand Chorus of the Company.

We will pause a moment here to breathe, as did the audience and performers. The operatic part of the entertainment occupied some four hours.

After the intermission, at half-past six, P. M., was presented the "School for Scandal," with Peter Richings, Couldock, Buchanan, Brougham (as *Sir Benjamin*), C. W. Clarke, Charles Pope, Whiting (as *Crabtree*), Mme. Ponisi (as *Lady Teazle*), Kate Horn, Mrs. Abbott, and Ada Gougenheim in the cast.

At the Academy of Music on the 19th March, 1874, "The School for Scandal" was presented with the last great cast it has seen in New York, only noticeable here, however, from the fact that Mr. Brougham played *Sir Oliver*, Mr. Whiting, *Rowly*, and Mme. Ponisi *Lady Sneerwell*, hardly such juvenile parts as they filled for Mr. Marshall's benefit so many years before.

At a quarter after nine o'clock Mr. Richings made an address on behalf of the beneficiary.

At half-past nine there was a "Grand Divertisement by the Roussel Family." At ten o'clock the entertainments in the Garden concluded with the "varied and extraordinary performances of the Ravel Family," "Classic Scenes," by François, Antoine, and Jerome, and surprising and wonderful feats on the tight rope by the daring Blondin. (We do not find Blondin's name among our bills before this date.) "The Grand Jubilee to conclude with magnificent displays of Fireworks on the Battery for a premium offered by the Committee." Curtain!

We must again apologize for the quantity of play-bill we quote, but we have done our utmost to be brief, and in our page or two here, have condensed the matter contained in twelve pages of printed programme.

The "Grand Jubilee" was in every way a success. There are among our oldest inhabitants men still living, participants before and behind the curtain, in the Marshall Testimonial, who gather their children and grandchildren about them, and tell great stories of the operatic, dramatic, pyrotechnic, and gymnastic doings of that long August day in 1851 at Castle Garden; how they took it all in from Dr. Connington's overture at ten, A. M. to the capers cut by Paul Brillant, of the Ravel Troupe, thirteen hours later; how good and commendable was it all; and standing up are ready to say to all the world:—"This was a benefit!"

The receipts were $10,000.

CHAPTER XXVII.

FAREWELL BENEFITS AND LAST APPEARANCES. — THE TESTIMONIAL TO MISS CUSHMAN IN 1874.

"And farewell, friends;
Thus Thisbe ends;
Adieu! adieu!! adieu!!"
Midsummer Night's Dream, Act V. Sc. 1.

Of all sad words of tongue or pen, the saddest are *not* "It might have been," but "It never can be more." There can be no sorrow over a mere contingency half so intense as the lament over an actual possession that is gone forever; no regret over a vain hope can equal the regret for vanished realizations, all the poets to the contrary notwithstanding.

The judge who rode on and left the fair haymaker in the field alone, never regretted half so sincerely his not winning that same sweet Maud Muller with the hazel eyes, as he would have regretted her won and worn, when the sad day came of their earthly parting. Alexander, who wept because there were no more worlds to conquer, would certainly have had something more serious to weep over if he had lost the world he had already won; the child who cries for the moon, certainly in mental and in corporal sufferance finds a pang fully twice as great in the loss of his dinner; the parent who buries his child, surely suffers greater sorrow than the childless man, who thinks of the children he might have had but never knew; to put it more practically, the man who sees how he could have made his fortune in the "selling short" of the proper stock at the proper time, feels not half so acutely the loss of that fortune, as the man who had a fortune, and with it undertook to "corner" hops or cheese! No! Let poets grieve over their "might have been," we who have tears to shed will reserve them for the loss of the things that were.

We cannot greatly grieve when we reflect what a perfect actor Dickens would have made had he adopted the drama as his profession; nor even can we weep when we think how glorious is the talent born to blush almost unseen and to hide its greatness on the amateur dramatic stage; but we can, and we do, look back with sincere regret upon the records of the actors whom we have known, who have delighted us in our youth and in our riper age, and whom upon the stage we feel we are to see no more; and sad as words of pen or tongue can express them are the farewells we utter to such accomplished artists as Miss Cushman and her peers!

Honorable retirement from any profession, or from any active walk in life, while it is looked for and is welcome, bears with it a sadness that is not to be shaken off; even sad to young hearts who know so little sadness, is the leaving of school; as Tom Brown of Oxford says, it is no light thing to fold up and lay by forever any portion of one's life, even when it can be laid by with honor and in thankfulness. Particularly sad, we think, to actors and to audiences are farewells to the stage; sad to the audiences when the actor who bids farewell, a long farewell to all his greatness, is really a great actor, and sad, very sad, to that *Othello* who feels his occupation gone.

This feeling of regret and home sickness is stronger

in old actors than in any other class of veteran men. Old merchants quit their markets, old preachers leave their pulpits, old soldiers hang up their swords, old sailors settle on shore, almost always with a better grace and with lighter hearts than is felt or shown by old actors in retirement; and this is proven by the desire of many of our comedians and tragedians to go back to the scenes of their labors and their successes, "their short retirement urging sweet return."

How great is the longing on the part of actors and actresses whose days are past, for the return of the happy and hard-working days of their professional life, all readers familiar with the biographies of the eminent players of past generations must well remember. Mrs. Siddons, who took her farewell of the stage as *Lady Macbeth* in 1812, and lived in honorable retirement for nearly twenty years longer, was never happy after the last performance, missing sadly the excitement and fascination of theatrical life. She was very fond, until the day of her death, of telling stories of her theatrical career, remarking as she sat in the quiet — no doubt to her monotonous quiet — of her own apartments, at the time of the rising of the curtain in the theatres of the world outside, how at that moment she would have been dressing for her part, now awaiting the signal of the call boy, now before the house, now making her best points, — and seeming to hunger and thirst for the popular applause that was never more to reach her ears! Miss Maria Tree is said to have walked across the stage upon one occasion, long after her withdrawal from it, merely for the sake of "sniffing the foot-lights," the very perfume of which was so delightful to her.

How many of the artists of our own day have retired

from the stage only to return to it? Mrs. Russell withdrew into private life in 1851, when she took an affectionate farewell of a regretful public on Burton's stage, and was presented on that occasion with a diamond ring by the manager; but she returned to it in a few years as Mrs. John Hoey, and for many seasons thereafter was the respected and admired leading lady of Wallack's Theatre. Miss Henriques quitted Mr. Wallack's company and the profession upon her marriage; she played for the last time *Peg Woffington* in "Masks and Faces," made a pretty little valedictory speech, which greatly moved the hearts of all the young men in front of the house (and the house was crowded), but stepped back again upon the same stage ere many seasons to play another successful although brief engagement.

We remember a retirement of Miss Jane Coombs some ten years since, yet we saw her play *Lady Teazle* at the Lyceum Theatre on Fourteenth street in the Spring of 1874. Miss Jean Margaret Davenport left the stage upon her marriage in 1860, but returned to it after the war, one of its very brightest ornaments, as Mrs. Lander. Mr. George Vandenhoff, whose support of Miss Cushman during her farewell engagement here was so scholarly and so effective, although he never took formal farewell of the stage, except in the pages of his pleasant "Leaves from an Actor's Note Book," adopted the legal as his profession in 1858, and since that time, with the present exception, has only been known to the public as a reader; but a reader who will be remembered in New York until Dr. Holmes's "Last Reader reads no more."

Miss Cushman herself, to whom the Arcadian Club,

the dramatic profession, the guild of literature and art in New York, and the whole city full of her friends and admirers, paid such a touching and well merited tribute at Booth's, on the occasion of her last retirement, has more than once before retired from the stage, wept, honored, and sung; only to return to it, always heartily welcomed by the most affectionate applause, and by the richest accounts of fullest boxes and benches.

In one of these farewells, at least, did Mr. Vandenhoff, as in this, participate, when he played *Benedick* to her *Beatrice* at the Old Park Theatre, October 25, 1844, on her farewell to the New York stage, previous to her first, and so decidedly successful essay in Europe.

On the 15th of May, 1852, at the Old Broadway, she made what the bill before us calls "her last appearance on the stage," as *Meg Merrilies*, with Fenno as *Colonel Mannering*, Reynolds as *Harry Bertram*, Davidge as *Dominie Sampson*, Whiting as *Dandy Dinmont*, Pope as *Dick Hatterick*, and Julia Gould as *Lucy*.

She played also a farewell engagement at Niblo's in 1858, which lasted two weeks, when she appeared as *Meg Merrilies*, *Lady Macbeth*, *Queen Katherine*, *Lady Gay Spanker*, *Romeo*, *Mrs. Haller*, and *Lady Teazle*. The cast of the leading parts of the "School for Scandal" will give some idea of her strong support this season: —

Sir Peter Teazle	Mr. Henry Placide.
Sir Oliver Surface	Mr. John Gilbert.
Charles Surface	Mr. E. L. Davenport.
Sir Benjamin	Mr. John Brougham.
Crabtree	Mr. Wm. R. Blake.
Lady Teazle	Miss Charlotte Cushman.

The *Maria* was Miss Mary Devlin, the first Mrs. Edwin Booth, whose New York *début* was made this season at that house, although not, we believe, in the same part.

Miss Cushman, on the sixth of July, 1858, the day before her sailing for Liverpool, played *Lady Macbeth* to an overflowing house. At the close of the performance she was led before the curtain by the *Macbeth* of the evening, Mr. E. L. Davenport, and made a few valedictory remarks. It was her intention, she said, to leave her country for a two years' sojourn in Europe, never to return to the stage unless fortune should prove adverse to her. She acknowledged with gratitude the kindness she had received in New York, and trusted she would never be forgotten.

While we sympathized sincerely with Miss Cushman in the reverses of fortune which subsequently brought her out of her retirement, we could not but congratulate ourselves that her ill wind had blown us so much good, had blown her back over the Atlantic, and had given us other opportunities to enjoy her matchless performances.

She appeared here in 1860, 1861, and again in 1871, at Booth's. For the "Benefit of the American Dramatic Fund," on the 21st of March, 1861, at the Academy of Music, we saw Miss Cushman as *Lady Macbeth*, in the strongest cast of the tragedy it has known, certainly in the memory of this generation; and we give its principal parts: —

Macbeth . . . . Edwin Booth.
Duncan . . . . C. Kemble Mason.
Malcolm . . . . O. B. Collins.
Banquo . . . . A. W. Fenno.

Macduff / Lenox / Rosse	Noblemen of Scotland . .	Charles Fisher. / T. Weymiss. / T. Hamblin.
Bleeding Officer	. . . .	Felix Rogers.
First Murderer	. . . .	Mr. Williamson.
Lady Macbeth	. . . .	Miss Cushman.
Principal Singing Witch	. . . .	Mme. Anna Bishop.
First Witch	. . . .	Harry Pearson.
Second Witch	. . . .	John Sefton.
Third Witch	. . . .	James Lingard.

Alas, we are to see Miss Cushman as *Lady Macbeth* no longer " on the mimic stage." No sad " might have been " is half so sad as such a thought as this! As Miss Cushman leaves the stage, *Meg Merrilies*, *Queen Katherine*, *Lady Macbeth* themselves, too soon, leave with her.

> " *Seyton.* — The *Queen*, my lord, is dead!
> *Macbeth.* — She should have died hereafter;
> There would have been time for such a word,
> To-morrow, and to-morrow, and to-morrow " ——

Miss Cushman stands at the very head of her profession. She is the greatest native American actress. A good woman too, a woman whose reputation, in her professional and in her private life, is absolutely without the shadow of reproach. We do not propose here to enter into the details of her eventful dramatic career. She was born in Boston, Massachusetts, about the year 1818. She appeared originally as a singer; her *début* before the public being made at a concert in Boston, in 1830. Her *début* upon the operatic stage was made in the same city, April 8th, 1835, at the Tremont Theatre as the *Countess of Almavia* in " The Marriage of Figaro." She made her first appearance upon the dramatic stage as *Lady Macbeth*, in New Orleans in the same year, and her first appearance upon the New York stage, September 12th, 1836, as *Lady Macbeth* at the Bowery. The bill of this performance unhappily is not preserved. Mr. Hamblin played *Macbeth* and Mr. H. B. Harrison *Macduff*. She first played *Meg Merrilies* at the National Theatre on the 8th of May, 1837. On the 7th of February, 1839, she first played *Nancy Sykes* at the Park.

Her favorite parts have been *Queen Katherine*, *Lady Macbeth*, *Nancy Sykes*, and *Meg Merrilies*. As *Nancy Sykes*, she made her first great hit; as *Meg Merrilies*, perhaps, she has appeared to greatest advantage, and in this part will she be most fondly remembered. She has played it many hundreds of times, and in many cities of the Union. Although in itself the part of *Meg Merrilies* has but little to recommend it, by the force of her genius she has made it immense. The look, the tone, the figure, the gesture, the gait by which she puts beauty into language the most indifferent, are beyond all critical praise.

She has played in New York almost all the leading parts in comedy and tragedy; not only the female parts, but in frequent instances the male characters. She has been *Lady Teazle*, *Katherine* ("Katherine and Petruchio"), *Bianca*, *Constance*, *Rosalind*, *Helen McGregor*, *Queen Gertrude*, *Lady Gay Spanker*, *Helen*, *Mrs. Haller*, *Janet Pride*, *Julia*, *Juliana*, *Beatrice*, *Hermione*, *Mrs. Simpson*, and many more.

As *Bianca*, in "Fazio," she made her London *début*, at the Princess's Theatre, in 1845, meeting in England at once with decided success. She played the part for the first time at the Old Broadway, January 5th, 1850. Her representation of the ungovernable and frenzied passion of the jealous woman, was very powerful, and she was enthusiastically called before the curtain every night of its performance. Her acting at the close of the trial scene, was certainly very beautiful in its subdued and touching portrayal of misery and self-accusation. Her *Lady Teazle* was an original and a new conception, a "creation" of Miss Cushman's. She made her *Ladyship* a thoroughly rustic beauty, fresh and hoydenish in her pouting and quarrelling with *Sir Peter*, — homely and countrified in her wheedling and her coaxing him. She was a rural belle, who only imitated the high-bred airs and graces of the fine city ladies who were professors in the School for Scandal which had just received her as an undergraduate. Her *Lady Teazle* had many admirers.

Romeo, *Claude Melnotte*, *Cardinal Wolsey*, and *Hamlet*, are among the most prominent of the male parts she has played. Her *Cardinal Wolsey* was a most remarkable performance. She is no doubt the only woman who has had the courage and the ability to undertake it. Another marvellous assumption of hers was *Romeo;* she was earnest, intense, and natural. The constitutional susceptibility of *Romeo's* character was depicted by her in its boldest relief, — a particular phase of the nature of the young *Montague*, which no male actor, unless he were a mere youth, could efficiently and satisfactorily portray.

In the "Lady of Lyons" she has played the *Widow Melnotte*, — she was the original *Widow Melnotte* in New York, — *Pauline*, and *Claude*. She acquired high repute for her *Claude* in England, and drew crowded houses at the Old Broadway, in 1850, when she first assumed it; the public seemed greatly to relish the earnest and truthful manner with which she rendered the familiar and celebrated character. It was said over twenty-five years ago, that while women ordinarily fail when they assume male parts, Miss Cushman always succeeds. She succeeded not only in the portrayal of male, but of female, characters; and on her final retirement from the New York stage, on the 7th of November, 1874, she was the recipient of one of the handsomest and most flattering testimonials from the press, the public, and the profession, that has ever been paid to any artist in any country in the whole history of the stage.

At the end of a brief engagement at Booth's Theatre, then under the management of Messrs. Jarret & Palmer, her farewell of the New York public was formally announced; the house was crowded with the finest audience it has ever seen, — the bar, the press, the pulpit, art, literature, were all magnificently represented, and the play selected was "Macbeth." We give the cast of its principal parts: —

Lady Macbeth	Miss Charlotte Cushman.
Macbeth	Mr. George Vandenhoff.
Macduff	Mr. Frederic B. Warde.
Duncan	Mr. Edwin Sheppard.
Banquo	Mr. Charles Wheatleigh.
Malcolm	Mr. Charles Rockwell.
Hecate	Miss Annie Kemp Bowler.
Gentlewoman	Miss Emma Grattan.
First Witch	Mr. Charles Le Clerq.
Second Witch	Miss Mary Wells.
Third Witch	Mr. J. W. Brutone.

After the play was finished, the curtain was raised, and on the stage, crowded with the most prominent men in every walk of life in New York, were discovered Miss Cushman, Mr. William Cullen Bryant, and the members of the dramatic company. Mr. Charles Roberts read an ode written for the occasion by Mr. Richard Henry Stoddard. Mr. Bryant, in behalf of the Arcadian Club, in a happy speech, presented to Miss Cushman a Crown of Laurel, "as a token of what is conceded to her, as a symbol of the regal state in her profession to which she had risen, and which she so illustriously holds." Miss Cushman responded in a speech equally happy, but full of deep feeling, earnest, and tender. Miss Anne Kemp Bowler sang "Auld Lang Syne," and Miss Cushman made her last bow.

Certainly we have never uttered our farewell to any artist in her profession with more sincere regret than to Miss Cushman; and no actress who has ever left our stage has been more worthy, personally and professionally, of such an honor.

The testimonial, and the manner of its presentation, was unique in dramatic history, and without precedent in the annals of our own stage. The gentlemen of the Arcadian Club who suggested it, and by whose efforts it was so ably carried out, are deserving of much praise.

It is a coincidence, and a very pleasant and remarkable one, that England's greatest tragic actress should have taken her farewell of the stage in the same great character, and under many similar circumstances.

On the 29th of June, 1812, Mrs. Siddons made her last appearance on any stage, and played *Lady Macbeth.* The crowd at the theatre, we are told, was immense. At the sleep-walking scene the excitement was so great that the audience stood on the benches and demanded that the performance should end with that scene. The curtain was then dropped for twenty minutes, and, when it rose, Mrs. Siddons was discovered at a table, dressed in white. She came forward amid a perfect thunder-storm of applause, which endured many minutes. Silence being obtained, she recited an address, toward the conclusion of which she exhibited deep emotion. The closing lines were, —

"Judges and friends, to whom the magic strain
Of nature's feelings never spoke in vain,
Perhaps your hearts when years have glided by,
And past emotions wake a fleeting sigh,
May think on her whose lips have poured so long
The charmèd sorrows of your Shakespeare's song;
On her, who parting to return no more,
Is now the mourner she but seemed before;
Herself subdued resigns the melting spell,
And breathes with swelling heart, her long, her last farewell."

The occasion of Mr. Macready's final retirement from the stage at the Haymarket in London in 1851, is still remembered. He played *Macbeth*, and those who witnessed the performance state that the tragedian could never have been greater than on this touching occasion. After the play he too came before the audience, and addressed the enormous assemblage in sad words of farewell, which we will not quote. Tennyson's well-known lines addressed to him at that time, we cannot resist paraphrasing, expressing so feelingly as we are satisfied they will, the affectionate and honorable regard still felt in New York for Miss Cushman: —

Farewell, Miss Cushman, since to-night we part:
Full-handed thunders often have confest
Thy power, well used to move the public breast.
We thank thee with one voice, and from the heart.
Farewell, Miss Cushman, since this night we part.
Go! take thine honors home, rank with the best;
Kemble, and statelier Siddons, and the rest,
Who made a nation purer through their art.
Thine is it that our drama did not die,

Nor flicker down to brainless pantomime,
And those gilt gauds men-children swarm to see.
Farewell, Miss Cushman; moral, grave, sublime,
Our Shakespeare's bland and universal eye
Dwells pleased, through twice an hundred years on thee.

CHAPTER XXVIII.

LAST APPEARANCE OF MR. BURTON AND OF MRS. HUGHES.

"The humorous man shall end his part in peace."
Hamlet, Act II. Sc. 2.

We have spoken many a time and oft in previous chapters of first nights, new plays, with new players and in new play-houses; have copied first bills and original casts, and have given our recollections of scenes, incidents, and impressions of first appearances and first successes; in a late chapter we spoke of farewell benefits, drawing a moral from the lessons they taught; perhaps a few facts and a few reminiscences of last nights and last appearances may be of interest here, and may strike a pleasant, although perhaps a melancholy chord in the play-going breast.

We will not speak of the farewells of Mrs. Hoey in 1851, nor of Miss Henriques in 1867; of the farewells of Miss Coombs, Miss J. M. Davenport, nor Mr. Vandenhoff, all of whom said *adieu* to the stage when *au revoir* would have been the more appropriate term, because on all of these we have already touched. We will not dwell upon the final and actual farewell of Miss Charlotte Cushman at Booth's Theatre, in the fall of 1874, because we have just devoted an entire chapter to that memorable occasion; nor will we dwell upon the farewell benefit of Miss Mary Taylor, who absolutely retired on her marriage to Mr. Ewen in 1852, because the story of her leave-taking we told in full, when we paid our little tribute to the good and sunny memory of "Our Mary;" nor yet here will we tell the sad story of George Holland's farewell to the public on Mr. Daly's stage in January, 1870, because there is nothing more of that story to tell than we have already told; how the good old man, more sinned against than sinning, when the curtain rose upon him for the last time showed that he felt it was the last time, and how keenly, and sitting in the midst of the younger members of Mr. Daly's Company, who stood affectionately and sadly about him, uttered his now famous farewell speech, the saddest, simplest, and most affecting perhaps that was ever spoken on the stage,—"God bless you all;" but of the last appearance upon our stage of such old and valued public favorites as Burton, Blake, Forrest, Wallack, Setchell, Mark Smith, Mrs. Hughes, Mrs. Vernon, Miss Mary Gannon, and others, who left our stage without the proper accompaniment of leave-taking, but who nevertheless have left many a trace behind, we must say something; relating facts historical which we feel assured will be of interest to the general theatre-going public, and placing upon record, for the sake of the few enthusiastic collectors of stage stories, certain bills and incidents of final appearances which we feel satisfied have never before been collectively preserved.

All mankind innately are hero worshippers; we all are born with a desire to idolize and idealize some hero, actual or fictional, and all of us who go to the theatre, and are not too familiar with theatrical people in their private lives, have worshipped at some time some stage hero; not for his personal qualifications, of which perhaps we know nothing, but for the stage heroism he has assumed for our gratification and his own benefit. Surely the end of that hero's heroics, which we now present, cannot fail to be more interesting to his worshippers than the story of any other part of his career.

We all like to know something of the last hours and death of the man or woman whose life and life's doings have interested and impressed us. The last picture of Landseer, the last novel of Thackeray, the last Mass of Mozart, the last speech of Webster, the last fight of any warrior, though he may not have died with his harness on his back, has a sad interest for us on this very account which no other painting, novel, musical composition, oration, or battle scene can excite. No bill of all the many bills of "Toodles," the very mention of which moves to laughter so many old admirers of the immortal *Timothy* and of the never-to-be-forgotten *Mrs. T.* can be half so worthy of preservation as the bill of "Toodles" at Niblo's Garden, Saturday, October 15th, 1859, with the names of Burton and Mrs. Hughes cast as *Mr.* and *Mrs. Toodles;* the last time that either Burton's or Mrs. Hughes's name was seen on any bill of the New York stage, although neither at the time had any idea of final retirement.

Burton was probably the funniest man that ever lived. Certainly there lives no man to-day who can remember seeing or hearing of a man who was funnier than Burton. Burton in his day was the best known man in New York, if not in America, while Burton's Theatre in Chambers Street was better known throughout the United States, than any other public building in the Union, not even excepting the Capitol at Washington. Never came a stranger to New York, who ever went to theatres at all, but went to Burton's, and he had in his audiences many men who never entered theatre elsewhere, before or since. The very name itself is a synonym now for everything that is pleasant, cheerful, funny in the past; and if we would call up thousands of brightest reminiscences of uproarious farces, wittiest travesties, most sparkling comedies, we have only now to mention Burton's. Perhaps no theatre in the world, in so short a time, and with so brief a career, has formed for itself so world-wide and enduring a reputation as this, and yet Burton's was only in existence for eight years, from 1848 to 1856; we refer, of course, to the Chambers Street House: the Metropolitan on Broadway, his new theatre, while it was, it is true, for some seasons under his management, and bore his name, was never "Burton's."

We do not purpose to speak of Mr. Burton's success as an actor and manager on his own boards; of the members of his company during the different seasons, of the Blakes and Broughams, Mrs. Russell (Hoey), Mrs. Vernon, Mr. Lester (Wallack), Mr. Holland, Mr. Bland; to enumerate the favorite artists whom he introduced to the New York public, "Joe" Grosvenor, J. H. Stoddart, Charles Fisher, J. K. Mortimer, O. B. Raymond, T. B. Johnstone, — or to speak even of the new plays that "drew" so enormously, and added so decidedly to his fortune and his fame; all of these being foreign to our present subject, — his last appearance on the New York stage. Nevertheless, these and many more of the familiar scenes and well-remembered faces force themselves upon our notice, and insist upon straying into our memorial like Mr. Dick's Charles the First.

Dear Mr. Dick! We missed him sadly in "David Copperfield" as dramatized for Burton's stage. Burton was *Micawber*, of course; George Jordan, *Copperfield*, Lester Wallack a very handsome *Steerforth*, Tom Johnstone a perfect *Uriah Heep*, Blake and Bland were great as *Peggotty* and *Ham*, Mrs. Hughes was *Betsy Trotwood*, Mrs. Hoey, *Rose Dartle*, with a pretty scar; but there was no Janet, no donkeys, and no Mr. Dick!

Burton's *Micawber* has never been equalled, and Mrs. Hughes's *Betsy Trotwood*, except perhaps by Mrs. Vernon's, has never been approached. Mrs. Vernon and Mrs. Hughes were contemporary "leading old ladies" for many years on the New York stage, playing the same parts and playing them so equally well, that no critical Paris of the day was able to decide to whom belonged the apple of superiority. In the case of their *Betsy Trotwood* and *Mrs. Skewton* the apple was divided, a half given to each. Mrs. Vernon, the survivor, on the retirement of Mrs. Hughes, inheriting both portions of the "Pomarian Prize," left the entire apple on her death, in 1869, to Mrs. W. H. Gilbert of Daly's present company, the only worthy representative of their particular school of "old lady" whom we have upon our stage to-day. Of Mrs. Vernon we will speak again.

Mrs. Hughes was very happy in such parts as *Lady Sowerby Creamly* in the "Serious Family," *Lucretia MacTab* in the "Poor Gentleman," *Madame Deschappelles* in the "Lady of Lyons," *Mrs. Trapper* in the "Breach of Promise," *Lady Duberly* in the "Heir at Law," *Mrs. Hector Sternhold* in "Still Waters," *Mrs. Triplet* in "Masks and Faces," *Miss Desperate* in "Leap Year," *Mrs. Hardcastle* in "She Stoops to Conquer," and as *Mrs. Toodles* of that ilk. She is remembered as a good *Lady Teazle* in her young days, but these were long before our days. We were particularly impressed by her *Mrs. Sternhold* in "Still Waters." She was, we think, the original of the part in this city, and we have never forgotten the impression she made upon us in the part at Burton's, when she turned up the gas in the first act, and discovered herself to *Hawksley* in the conservatory. It was a simple action; for a minute nothing was said; but the attitude and expression of the insulted woman, at bay and full of scorn, was magnificent. George Jordan was the *Captain Hawksley*, Mr. Burton the *John Mildmay*, but the *Mrs. Mildmay* we have quite forgotten.

Mrs. Hughes was a member of Mr. Burton's Chambers Street House for many seasons, and until he closed that establishment. She went with him to the Metropolitan, and on his final retirement from theatrical management in 1859, travelled with him as joint "star." In the summer of 1859 they played a short engagement of two or three weeks at Niblo's, under the management of Mr. Eddy, and again in October appeared on the same boards.

During this last engagement Mr. Burton appeared as *Aminadab Sleek*, *Van Dunder* in the "Old Dutch Governor," *Captain Copp* in "Charles the Second," *Paul Pry*, *Munns the Buttonmaker* in "Forty Winks," *Tobias Shortcut the Cockney* in "The Spitfire," *Samuel Coddle* in "Married Life" (the *Mrs. Coddle* was Madame Ponisi), *Mr. Sudden* in "Breach of Promise," and *Captain Cuttle* in "Dombey;" Mrs. Hughes throughout giving him excellent support. Their *Mr.* and *Mrs. Toodles* who will ever forget?

On the 15th of October, 1859, the bills contained the following announcement: —

"Benefit and Last Appearance of Mr. Burton, the Great Comedian, in which he will appear in Two Grand Performances, Afternoon and Evening. Extraordinary Attractions."

Burton . . . . as . . . . Mr. Sudden.
Burton . . . . as . . . . Mr. Micawber.
Burton . . . . as . . . . Toby Tramp.
Burton . . . . as . . . . The Mummy.
Burton . . . . as . . . The Eminent Tragedian.

Afternoon: "Toodles" and "Secrets of State."

Mr. Toodles . . . . Mr. Burton.
Mrs. Toodles . . . . Mrs. Hughes.

Evening: "Breach of Promise," "Mummy," and "David Copperfield."

"BREACH OF PROMISE."

Mr. Sudden . . . . Mr. Burton.
Mrs. Trapper . . . . Mrs. Hughes.

"DAVID COPPERFIELD."

MR. MICAWBER . . . . MR. BURTON.
Peggotty . . . . Mr. Charles Fisher.
Mrs. Micawber . . . . Mrs. Eddy.
Rose Dartle . . . . Mme. Ponisi.
MISS BETSY TROTWOOD . . . . MRS. HUGHES.

We never saw Burton or Mrs. Hughes again. Mrs. Hughes quietly retired to private life. Mr. Burton played for a few weeks in other cities, but came back to New York quite broken in health, and died at his residence in Hudson Street on the 10th of February, 1860. He was the greatest comedian of our day, and his place is not likely to be filled in our generation. No man now living will probably ever be able to affect so many people by his comic powers as could Burton. He newly-created many parts, and invested *rôles* with peculiarities and stage business of which the author never dreamed. His *Toodles* and *Sleek* were so absolutely his own, that the daring man who plays them now plays Burton's *Toodles* and Burton's *Sleek*, and not the *Sleek* of Morris Barnet's "Serious Family," or the *Mr. Tweedle* in the "Broken Heart," who was the present *Mr. Toodles* in "Toodles," as Burton found him.

Mr. Burton was a man of large culture, had collected a very extensive and valuable library; and the care and correct elaboration of many of his Shakespearean revivals will testify how great he was as a Shakespearean scholar. Although they are not now remembered as are many of his other and characteristic parts, his *Caliban*, *Dogberry*, *Autolycus*, *Nick Bottom*, *Verges*, *Touchstone*, and his *Falstaff*, are by competent and impartial judges said to have been among the most complete embodiments of the great poet's ideas, that his works have ever seen. We are all familiar with his pathos, and know that he could, if he would, move his great audiences to tears as readily as to laughter.

Mr. Burton was buried in Greenwood, and for fourteen years his grave was unmarked by any stone or emblem. Only within a few months has the shaft been raised that now stands above poor Yorick's skull, and the following is its simple inscription: —

"In Memory of
William E. Burton,
Born September 24th, 1804.
Died Feb. 10th, 1860."

CHAPTER XXIX.

LAST APPEARANCE OF MR. BLAKE, MR. WALLACK, MR. FORREST, AND MR. SETCHELL.

"A well-graced actor leaves the stage."
King Richard II., Act V. Sc. 2.

IT is a peculiarly striking fact that the last part played by Mr. Blake in New York was that of *Geoffrey Dale*, in "The Last Man," which had been his best and favorite part for so many years.

At Laura Keene's Theatre, April 16th, 1863, Mr. Blake's benefit was announced in the play of the "Rivals," cast as follows: —

Sir Anthony Absolute	Mr. Wm. R. Blake.
Captain Absolute	Mr. Charles Walcot, Jr.
Sir Lucius O'Trigger	Mr. Charles Wheatleigh.
Bob Acres	Mr. Stuart Robson.
David	Mr. Peters.
Faulkland	Mr. H. F. Daly.
Lydia Languish	Miss Laura Keene.
Julia	Miss Nickinson.
Lucy	Miss Ione Burke.

To conclude with (first time in this theatre) the thrilling drama, in two acts, entitled,

"THE LAST MAN."

Mr. Blake in his great character of Geoffrey Dale.

Strange as it may seem, the name of the lady who personated *Mrs. Malaprop*, in the "Rivals," was not mentioned in the play-bill. We do not remember who enacted the part, nor do we find it recorded.

The story of Mr. Blake's death in Boston a few days after this performance, with a short and imperfect sketch of his career, we have given in a previous chapter.

One of the daily journals here, in speaking of Mr. Blake's benefit, carelessly, as the best of journals sometimes will speak, had alluded to it as his "farewell appearance in New York," and the very day of his death had published a card from him, stating that he by no means intended to retire from the stage, but hoped to meet his friends again and often on the metropolitan boards. Very prophetic was the announcement, however, and sadly prophetic was the final scene of the "Last Man," and the last words he uttered as *Geoffrey Dale* before the public that had known him so long and had liked him so sincerely: "May we be remembered on earth when our shadows have followed the western sun, so that a shade be not left on our characters behind. Peace to all, my friends, my children; my club is broken up. Peace to all, and heaven's blessings on the last man."

Mr. Blake was the recipient of a grand complimentary benefit March 20th, 1850, on his retirement from the management of the Broadway Theatre. The bill of the evening is before us. "The Poor Gentleman" was presented, with Mr. Placide as *Dr. Ollapod*, Mr. Blake as *Sir Robert Bramble*, Mr. Lester Wallack as *Frederick*, Lynne as the *Lieutenant*, George Jordan as *Sir Charles*, and Mrs. Blake as *Lucretia MacTab*. Burton and Brougham followed as "The Siamese Twins" — imagine Burton and Brougham as *Chang* and *Eng*. Brougham was the drinking twin; Burton the twin who had to get drunk. Mr. Hamblin and Mrs. J. W.

Wallack, Jr., wound up the performance as *Katherine* and *Petruchio*. At the close of the play, in the green-room of the theatre, a richly engraven silver cup and salver were presented to Mr. Blake by Dr. James Powell, as a token of regard towards the ex-manager by the members of the company, and by a few of his professional, non-professional, and personal friends. The speeches, of course, were happy and brilliant, and the occasion was made doubly pleasant and interesting to Mr. Blake by the presence of many men distinguished in literature, the drama, and art, who crowded the green-room to witness the presentation, and to add their own expressions of esteem and good will.

History repeats itself, even dramatic history; and nothing under the sun, even on the stage, is new. Whether Dr. James Powell and Mr. Blake's many friends in New York in 1850 were familiar with the fact, we know not, but there was a precedent for their presentation of the silver cup to the retiring manager; — a similar compliment having been paid to Mr. King, the original *Sir Peter Teazle*, on his bidding farewell to the stage, in 1802, at Drury Lane. On the 24th of May, Mr. King played *Sir Peter* for the last time, just twenty-five years after the first presentation of the comedy, and after a dramatic career of fifty-four years. The old man, we read in the "Life of Sheridan," very aged and very feeble, with trembling lips and faltering voice delivered an address to the audience, written by Cumberland, of which the following lines are part: —

"Patrons, farewell!
Though you still kindly my defects may spare,
Constant indulgence who would wish to bear?
Who that retains the sense of brighter days,
Can sue for pardon, while he pants for praise?

On well-earned fame the mind with pride reflects,
And pity sinks the man whom it protects.
Your fathers had my strength, my only claim
Was zeal; their favor was my only fame."

Amidst shouts of applause the venerable actor made his bow, and retired to the green-room, where, as in the case of Mr. Blake fifty years later, a handsome compliment awaited him from his dramatic brethren, in the shape of a silver cup, with an engraved motto from "Henry V.," happily adapted for the occasion, —

"If he be not fellow with the best king,
Thou shalt find him the best king of good fellows."

From this cup his health was drunk, and he returned the compliment almost overpowered with the intensity of his feelings.

We have no little pleasure in recalling this incident, and in comparing the scenes in the two green-rooms, so far distant in space and time. The inscription on Mr. Blake's cup we do not remember, but very many of his friends will agree with us that he also was fitted to rank with "the best king of good fellows." It was affectionately said of Mr. King on his retirement that *Sir Peter Teazle* died with him. That *Jesse Rural* and *Geoffrey Dale* died with Mr. Blake, we feel satisfied is already proven.

As a coincidence it is somewhat peculiar that Mr. Blake, Mr. Burton, and Mr. Wallack the elder, three of the best known actors and managers of the last generation, each in his own line excelling every other actor, should each have made his last appearance at his own benefit, without any ceremony and without any idea of leave-taking, and in his favorite and best part; the part in which perhaps he is now best remembered and which perhaps of all others he would have wished to have made his last, — Mr. Blake as *Geoffrey Dale*, Mr. Burton as *Timothy Toodles*, and Mr. Wallack as *Benedick* in "Much Ado."

Mr. Wallack's *Benedick* was one of the best, if not the very best, the American stage has ever known. Between his *Benedick* and his *Shylock*, so totally different, but both so admirable in his hands, his critics were never able to show even "the most shallow spirit of judgment." His *Benedick* was inimitable, his *Shylock* perfection, and which was the better no doctor could decide. He played *Shylock* for the last time on the 15th of January, 1859, at the "old theatre," Broadway and Broome Street. Mrs. Hoey was the *Portia*, and his son, Mr. Lester Wallack, played *Bassanio*. On the 14th of May in the same year he played *Benedick*, and was never seen in character on the stage again.

From this last bill of Mr. Wallack's we quote: —

Benefit of Mr. Wallack, May 14, 1859, being his 135th night and positively the last night of his appearance this season. For this evening only

"MUCH ADO ABOUT NOTHING."

Benedick	Mr. Wallack.
Dogberry	Mr. Brougham.
Leonato	Mr. Dyott.
Claudio	Mr. Wheatleigh.
Don Pedro	Mr. Bangs.
Borachio	Mr. Floyd.
Verges	Mr. Sloan.
Antonio	Mr. F. Chippendale.
Beatrice	Mrs. Hoey.
Hero	Mrs. Sloan.
Ursula	Mrs. Reeves.

Mr. Wallack appeared upon the stage of the new and present Wallack's Theatre on the opening night, 21st of

September, 1861, and in evening dress made the opening speech. He appeared before the curtain on several subsequent occasions in response to cries for the "manager," but his name was never seen in any bill subsequent to this one of "Much Ado" we have given above.

Richelieu was the last part played by Mr. Forrest in New York. His greatest part was probably *Lear*. *Richelieu* was certainly not his greatest part, and we have always regretted that the abrupt termination to his final engagement here should not have come before "Richelieu" was put on. Personally, we liked his *Lear* better than anything the "old man" ever played; it was the last part in which we saw him, and we would like to think of him as making his last exit here in that character.

On the 6th of February, 1871, he commenced an engagement of three weeks at the Fourteenth Street Theatre (present Lyceum Theatre), playing five nights a week. He represented *Lear* for ten nights, and on the 19th as *Richelieu*, he promised Mr. Tom Morris a Bishopric as *Joseph*, befriended Mr. Barton Hill as *Du Mauprat*, drew the awful circle around the form of Miss Lille as *Julie*, threatened to launch the curse of Rome against Mr. Arnold as *Baradas*, and confronted a very intelligent stock company as "courtiers, pages, conspirators, soldiers," etc.

Mr. Forrest was the original *Richelieu* in this country. He played the part first at Wallack's Old National Theatre in 1841, supported by Corson W. Clarke, George Jamieson, J. W. Wallack, Jr., Mrs. W. Sefton (as *François*), and Miss Virginia Monier as *Julie*. He received the manuscript from Mr. Bulwer direct for production in America, and brought it out almost simultaneously with its original production by Macready at the Covent Garden in London. The question of Mr. Forrest's personation of the "wily Cardinal" we will not discuss; many of his friends claim that it alone was sufficient to establish his claims to a lasting histrionic reputation; in our own estimation it has been surpassed by the *Richelieu* of Booth. How well Mr. Forrest may have played the part in his youth and vigor, thirty-five years ago, of course we cannot say by personal observation; but certainly during his last engagement here, four years ago, he was too much broken in health to portray even the feeble Cardinal; he struggled through it for a night or two, broke down completely, and the house was closed.

Mr. Forrest of course was not the original *Lear* in this country, and who was the original *Lear* in England we believe is not recorded. When Mr. Forrest first played *Lear* we do not know, nor is it perhaps of much moment; but *Lear* was the last part he really played in New York, and we give its cast here for preservation, because we feel that it is as the Mad King, "the feeble, miserable, but still royal old man," that the curtain, by all the rights of Poetic Justice, should fall on Edwin Forrest: —

FOURTEENTH STREET THEATRE, FEBRUARY 16, 1871.

"KING LEAR."

KING LEAR	MR. FORREST.
Edgar	Mr. Harris.
Edmund	Mr. Allerton.
Kent	Mr. T. E. Morris.
Gloster	Mr. Arnold.
Albany	Mr. Lowry.
Cornwall	Mr. Collins.

Burgundy	Mr. Smith.
Goneril	Miss Placide.
Regan	Miss Walters.
Cordelia	Miss Lillie.

With one more farewell bill we will close this chapter of farewells. Another bill, as we are dealing in coincidences, of "Leah," but a "Leah" as widely differing from Shakespeare's "Lear" as can be imagined; a *Leah* no more like unto Forrest's *Lear* than I to Hercules, but still a great *Leah;* greater, perhaps, than even Miss Bateman's *Leah*, a burlesque of which it was. We refer to poor Dan Setchell's *Leah*, in "Leah, the Forsook."

Mr. Setchell was not so distinguished an actor as Mr. Forrest, Mr. Wallack, Mr. Blake, or Mr. Burton. He was barely more than thirty years of age when he left our stage. He had only been known to the stage for a few years, but he was much liked in New York, and had before him what promised to be a brilliant career. He added greatly to the amusement of the town in a pleasant, hearty way, and the bill of his last performance in New York — even if it did not contain an unusually strong list of names, and was not something of a curiosity now in itself — would be well worthy a place in the histrionic archives of the metropolis, on Mr. Setchell's own account. We condense it here: —

Winter Garden, under the management of Mr. Mark Smith and Miss Emily Thorne. To-night, Saturday, August 8, 1863, last night of the season, and benefit of Mr. Mark Smith. Twenty-fourth and positively last night of Mr. Frank Wood's successful burlesqué "Leah, the Forsook," preceded by

"California Diamonds."

Mr. Kerr Mudgeon	Mr. Setchell.

Mr. Danby Symes	Mr. Mark Smith.
Mr. Rigsby	Mr. Sol. Smith, Jr.
Mrs. Kerr Mudgeon	Miss Emily Thorne.
Mrs. Danby Symes	Mrs. H. F. Grattan.
Betsey	Mrs. Flynn.

"LEAH, THE FORSOOK."

Leah, a Shewish Maiden	Mr. Setchell.
Rudolph, who loves her and then don't	Miss Emily Thorne.
Madeline, Leah's rival	Mr. Mark Smith.
Nathan, the Apostate	Mr. Harry Pearson.
The Doctor, with his Stock remark	Mr. A. H. Davenport.
Father Abraham, familiarly known as Old Abe	Mr. Sol. Smith, Jr.
Father Lorrenz, Rudolph's pa	Mr. Tom Morris.
The infant Child, a pretty prattler	Mr. C. T. Parsloe, Jr.

Villagers, Lager, Retainers, Sweetzer-Kaisers, etc., etc., etc.

The synopsis of scenery and incidents we spare our readers. Suffice it to say it begins "Act 1st, Scene 1st. The Happy Village Green, Conventional gathering of the Happy Village Greenies," and ends "Act 2d, Scene 3d. Grand Finale, Happiness Lying Around Loose."

How much fun and absurdity was lying around loose, during the whole two hours or so of the performance, nobody who ever saw it is likely to forget. The burlesque was one of the brightest and cleverest of Mr. Frank Wood's clever productions, and the cast was very strong for such an entertainment. Mr. Setchell and Mr. Mark Smith as the "Maidens" were very funny, and notwithstanding the heat of the July and August weather, the hardness of the war times, and the excitement of the draft riots, the houses were good. During the engagement, which lasted three weeks, Mr. Setchell played *Hugh de Brass* in a "Regular Fix," and appeared in the "Serious Family," "Poor Pillicoddy," "Loan of a Lover," "Nine Points of the Law," and in other pieces of that stamp. He never played again in New York.

His first appearance here was at Barnum's Museum in 1853. He was a member of Burton's Company in 1856–7 and '57–8, and played other engagements at other houses at different periods. About the first of January, 1866, he sailed from San Francisco for New Zealand in a small vessel, of which nothing has since been heard; she is supposed to have foundered at sea and all on board to have perished, —

"Soft sigh the winds of heaven o'er his grave."

CHAPTER XXX.

THE LAST APPEARANCE OF MISS MARY GANNON AND MRS. VERNON.

"Good-night, ladies ; good-night, sweet ladies ; good-night, good-night."
Hamlet, Act IV. Sc. 5.

NEVER does the King of Terrors bring so many terrors in his train, as when he strikes the actor on the stage, in the midst of his professional duties and with his harness on his back. Coming to the bridal chamber; coming in consumption's ghastly form; coming to the mother when she feels for the first time her first-born's breath, death is terrible enough; but coming to the mimic king upon his mimic throne; to the professional jester in the midst of his jests; to the player who counterfeits death before the hundreds of spectators who have come to laugh and to be amused, death is horrible.

Happily, in the history of our own stage, cases of death to the actor while before the curtain, or even the stroke that precedes death, are rare; and never, so far as we can remember, during the twenty years of which we write, has any actor in presence of the audience, finished indeed his mortal act. In other lands, however, such ghastly events as these have been not infrequent. Palmer, the original *Joseph Surface*, who died in Liverpool in 1798, is said to have fallen lifeless upon the stage while performing the character of the *Stranger*, and just as he had pronounced the words "There is another and a better world." Edmund Kean, it will be remembered, made his last appearance upon the stage at Covent Garden, in London, in 1833, when he played *Othello* at the benefit of his son Charles Kean, who enacted *Iago*. Although not an old man, the elder Kean, wasted by disease and by a misspent life, was so feeble when he stepped upon the stage that the mere dressing for his part had almost exhausted him, and so shattered were his nerves that he was almost overpowered by the dread of the disaster he felt was to follow. It was touchingly said of him that "he went through his part dying as he went," until he came to the farewell, ending "Othello's occupation gone," when his head fell upon his son's shoulder, and the curtain fell upon him forever.

More awful even than these was the stroke of paralysis that horrified the large audience in this same Covent Garden in May, 1757, and drove forever from the stage what a few moments before had been the saucy, bewitching Peg Woffington. She was playing *Rosalind* in "As You Like It," this Peg Woffington — not the *Peg Woffington* of Charles Reade's and Tom Taylor's "Masks and Faces," but the Peg Woffington of history, the independent, wayward, and not too-good Peg Woffington, who never visited *Triplet's* garret, and who had never come under the refining influence of a virtuous *Mabel Vane*. She had not been very well in health that miserable night, but, like Kean on the same stage many years later, fought against the coming blow; throughout all of the five acts of the comedy she played with almost her wonted force, and had nearly reached the end of the epilogue when the blow was struck. She is said to have uttered with frightful gayety the words: "If I were among you, I'd kiss as many of you as had beards that pleased me," when her tongue became powerless, and her face horribly distorted ; she tried in vain to proceed, realized the fearful sense of her position, and was carried shrieking from the stage, nevermore to be seen upon it. She survived a few years in privacy and in penitence, but died before she had reached the age of forty.

Two of the favorite actresses of our own day, not so great, perhaps, in the profession as the Woffington, but purer in their lives, narrowly escaped meeting the Woffington's unhappy fate. Emma Taylor, it will be remembered, while running off the stage at the close of the performance at Hartford, struck the projecting scenery in such a way as produced convulsions and subsequently her death. Mary Gannon, who made her last appearance upon the stage at Wallack's as *Mary Nettley* in Robertson's "Ours," on the night of January 27th, 1868, was so feeble in health that she finished the part with difficulty and was taken home to die. Mrs. Clara Jennings the next evening assumed the character, and Miss Gannon lived only until the 22d of February. She was buried on the 27th from her residence by the good Dr. Houghton, who even then had proven himself the actor's friend, although his church had not yet been called that "Little one round the corner."

The last bill that contained Mary Gannon's name, for her memory's sake, is well worth preserving : —

Monday, January 27, 1868. Grand revival of Mr. Robertson's Comedy of

"OURS,"

With the following cast : —

Hugh Chalcote . . . . Mr. Lester Wallack.
Colonel Shendyn . . . . Mr. John Gilbert.
Sergeant Jones . . . . A. W. Young.
Angus McAllister . . . . B. T. Ringgold.

Prince Perovsky . . . . J. B. Polk.
Major Samprey . . . . J. W. Leonard.
Mary Nettley . . . . Miss Mary Gannon.
Lady Shendyn . . . . Miss Fanny Morant.
Blanche Haye . . . . Miss Kate Ranoe.

A little more than a year later, we find another bill of Wallack's that contained for the last time the name of an estimable lady, who had been known well and fondly to the New York stage for many years, and who had been seen in many pleasant comedies with Mary Gannon on Wallack's boards. We refer to Mrs. Vernon. She made her last appearance as *Mrs. Sutcliffe*, in Robertson's "School," on the 3d of April, 1869. This is the date of our bill, and if this was not Mrs. Vernon's very last night, she played but a few nights later, and the bill remained unchanged as long as she was in the cast: —

Every evening until further notice, and Saturday matinee, Mr. T. W. Robertson's last new and successful comedy, entitled, —

"SCHOOL."

Jack Poyntz . . . . Mr. Lester Wallack.
Dr. Sutcliffe, Principal of Cedar Grove House Mr. John Gilbert.
Beau Farintosh . . . . Mr. Charles Fisher.
Mr. Kruz, Assistant at Cedar Grove House Mr. J. H. Stoddard.
Lord Beaufoy . . . . Mr. Owen Marlowe.
Vaughan . . . . Mr. T. Ward.
James, a Tiger . . . . Mr. E. Cashin.
Gamekeepers . . . . Messrs. Arnold and Clarke.
Naomi Tighe, an East Indian Heiress . . . Miss Effie Germon.
Bella, a Dependent Pupil . . . . Mrs. Clara Jennings.
Mrs. Sutcliffe, Governess of Cedar Grove House . Mrs. Vernon.

And so in the last act, blessing *Bella*, who in a bridal wreath had just become *Lady Beaufoy;* and blessing *Naomi*, who with the stick of candy in one hand and

Jack Poyntz in the other, was about to become *Mrs. Poyntz*, good Mrs. Vernon passed out of our sight and into our memory, one of the very best of "old ladies," not only in her professional, but in her private life. Mrs. Vernon survived her retirement for two months, dying on the 4th of June, 1869, in the seventy-seventh year of her age, and in the forty-second year of her connection with the New York stage.

During the ten or more years that are among the pleasantest of our theatre-going experiences, when Wallack's Theatre, New and Old, was the pleasantest theatrical spot in New York, Mrs. Vernon and Miss Gannon were the brightest objects on Wallack's boards. We never went to Wallack's without finding the name of one or both on the bills; we never knew either of them to assume any part that was not played almost to perfection; and we never saw Wallack's stage when it was not the better for their being on it.

With Mrs. Vernon or with Miss Gannon we had no personal acquaintance. We have no recollection of ever having seen either of them, except across that fiery chasm which the foot-lights mark, but we felt in the death of each an individual loss, and personally mourned sincerely for them both; grieving particularly at the death of Mrs. Vernon, whom knowing in a professional way from our infancy, we had learned to regard, professionally, in a truly filial light.

How often have we seen these ladies together in old comedy parts, which no other two ladies on any stage have been able so satisfactorily to fill. How often have we found them creating new comedy parts, in which they have scarcely found worthy successors. When have we ever had a better *Sophia* or a better *Widow*

Crabtree in the "Road to Ruin" than Miss Gannon's and Mrs. Vernon's? Where a better *Blanche d'Ivry* and *Mrs. McShake* than theirs in the "Veteran?" Miss Gannon's *Lydia Languish*, in the "Rivals," was the best this stage has seen in many a year; and Mrs. Vernon's *Mrs. Malaprop* was immense. Her "choice of epitaphs" was almost sublime; she was a "perfect mistress of orthodoxy in her mis-pronunciations;" and her *Malaprop-isms* fell as trippingly from her tongue as if she herself had been a "progeny of learning." In "Rosedale," her discovery of the rats in the jam-closet was ridiculously natural; while Miss Gannon's "Good-night, *Elliot*," from the top of that long flight of steps that led out of *Elliot's* gothic room in the Manor House, was as refreshing a bit of artistic *naïveté* as we have ever met out of real life. How many of us have known in our lives just such old housekeepers, just such old maiden aunts — if not our own, somebody else's — as Mrs. Vernon's *Tabitha Stork;* or have met at some time just such a bewitching maiden, ingenuous, but coquettish, as Miss Gannon's *Rosa Leigh*, — one who would most artlessly call us by our Christian name, and most insidiously at the same time peck away at the heart we carry inside of our waistcoat.

The great charm in the acting of both these ladies was their perfect ease and naturalness, and the spirit with which they entered into all their parts. When Miss Gannon made the pie in *Matthew Leigh's* cottage in "Rosedale," she went about it, or seemed to go about it, as if her whole heart were set on pie-making. Everybody in the audience felt satisfied that the pie would be a good pie, and wanted to try it when finished; and nobody in the audience enjoyed the discomfiture of poor *Banberry Kobb* when caught in the act of helping himself to *Miss Tabitha Stork's* pickles and jam, or seemed to enjoy it, more than did Mrs. Vernon herself. "Rosedale" was very melancholy to us when we saw it last, simply because we missed so sadly the original *Rosa* and *Tabitha*, and because George Holland, the original *Banberry Kobb*, in his "beautiful pumps," was never more to dance at the Rifle Ball.

We can remember Miss Gannon and Mrs. Vernon as *Mrs. Delmain* and *Lady Creamly* in the "Serious Family;" *Betty* and *Mrs. Heidelberg* in the "Clandestine Marriage;" *Mme. Aubrey* and *Mme. Laroque* in the "Romance of a Poor Young Man;" *Mrs. Dr. Savage* and the *Widow Crabstick* in Brougham's "Playing with Fire;" *Mrs. Cox* and *Mrs. Box* in "Box and Cox;" *Miss Hardcastle* and *Mrs. Hardcastle* in "She Stoops to Conquer," with Holland as *Tony Lumpkin*, and Lester Wallack as *Young Marlow;* and we remember them as *Gertrude* and *Mrs. Meddleton* in "The Little Treasure." *Gertrude* was a favorite part of Miss Gannon's; she selected it often on her benefit nights, and certainly she was the very best we have ever known. In her white dimity dress, and with her innocent, girlish ways, she was perfectly irresistible as *Gertrude*, even in her middle age; and the play without her — we have never seen it without her, and do not want to — would be as hollow and as lifeless as the "Last Man" without Blake, "Toodles" without Burton, or "The Gilded Age" without Raymond himself.

CHAPTER XXXI.

MARK SMITH.

" Thou art a goodly Mark."
Troilus and Cressida, Act V. Sc. 6.

MARK SMITH is the last prominent and popular actor for whom the profession has been called upon to mourn. The last part he played upon the New York stage, or upon any stage, was that of *Jacques Fauvel* in Hart Jackson's adaptation of "Le Centenaire." Those who knew him best could have hoped he would have lived long enough to have played the part without "making up" for it, might himself have been "An Hundred Years Old."

Mr. Smith had many friends. He was a man in his dealings with men and with women, without fear and above reproach, a man take him for all in all, as a man, an actor, and a friend, whose like we will not soon look upon again. Who that has ever heard his full, rich, sympathetic voice, upon the stage and off, does not remember him as a perfect specimen of the traditional character of whom he sang so fondly, — "The Fine Old English Gentleman all of the Olden Time."

Although Mark Smith was not an Englishman, for he was an American of the Americans, and although hardly of the Olden Time, for he died comparatively a young man, he was nevertheless, always and under all circumstances, a gentleman in the best sense of that much abused term!

Like many other actors who have become successful in their profession, Mr. Smith came of theatrical people. His father, "Old Sol. Smith," as a representative of low comedy and "old-man" parts, enjoyed a great reputation in the cities of the South and West for many years. His brother, Sol. Smith, Jr., is still known favorably to our stage, a good general actor, inimitable as the *Apothecary* in "Romeo and Juliet." His wife, Mrs. Mark Smith, has been in past seasons a member of Burton's, Laura Keene's, and other New York companies; and his daughter, Miss Kate Smith, who has been studying under foreign masters, has lately made a successful *début* upon the operatic stage in Italy.

The part Mark Smith has played, if it has never been very important, has been at all events one always honorable and creditable to the actor and pleasant to his audiences. He first appeared here, we believe, at the Bowery Theatre in 1851, playing on the 11th of August of that year *Porthos* to the *Athos* of Eddy in the "Three Guardsmen." His reputation, however, has not been purely local; he has not belonged so particularly to us as do Wallack, Gilbert, and Fisher, and as did Burton, Blake, and Placide, to whose school of acting he belonged. He has played in almost every leading city in the United States, and was, at the time of his death, as sincerely mourned in Boston, St. Louis, and New Orleans as in New York.

Among our old play-bills, we find his name not so regularly or so often recurring as other honored names, but more than semi-occasionally figuring in important parts. His many friends may care perhaps to see and to have preserved for old times' sake, some record, even if disconnected, of his performances in New York, particularly during the last four or five years of his life.

We find him at Burton's Chambers Street House during the season of 1855–56, and at the opening of Burton's new theatre (the Metropolitan) in the fall of the next year, when on the first night, September 8th, 1856, he played *Sir Anthony Absolute* in the "Rivals," although not more than twenty-eight years of age. The cast was unusually strong. Burton was *Bob Acres*, Charles Fisher, *Captain Absolute;* D. Howard, *Sir Lucius;* Tom Placide, *David;* Mrs. Hughes, *Mrs. Malaprop;* Mrs. C. Howard (later Mrs. Harry Watkins), *Lydia Languish;* Fanny Brown, *Lucy.* Mr. Smith remained here until Mr. Burton retired from the management in 1859. On the evening of Monday, March 11th, 1862, he made his first appearance at Wallack's Theatre, in the "Love Chase," with a cast worthy of preservation as an historical record: —

"Love Chase."

Wildrake	Lester Wallack.
Sir Wm. Fondlove (his first appearance here) .	Mark Smith.
Master Waller	Charles Fisher.
Trueworth	Reynolds.
Humphries	Browne.
Constance	Mrs. Hoey.
Widow Green	Mary Gannon.
Lydia	Madeline Henriques.

During a revival of old comedies at this house, this season and later, Mr. Smith played — and excellently well — such parts as *Tom Coke*, in "Old Heads and Young Hearts;" *Russett*, in the "Jealous Wife;" *Dr. Pangloss*, in the "Heir at Law;" *Caustic*, in the "Way to get Married;" *Claude Plantagenet*, in "Love and Money," and *Colonel Damas*, in the "Lady of Lyons." How he won his audiences in these and in many other parts in which he played, those who saw him upon that stage must well remember. He was so hearty in everything he did, so whole-souled, gentle, kind, and good in his personal relations, so careful, natural, and yet so studied as an actor, that to know him was to love him, to see him upon the stage was to praise.

Our space will not permit of too detailed a narration of his professional career. We find him later at Booth's Theatre as stage manager, and playing in the opening piece, "Romeo and Juliet," February 3d, 1869. In October, 1870, he was supporting Mme. Janauscheck at the Academy of Music — her first appearance in English-speaking parts; the next month, November, he was at Niblo's supporting Mrs. Scott-Siddons. He went to Europe for a few months, but returned in time to play *Colonel Damas*, January 25th, 1871, at the French Theatre, Fourteenth Street, supporting Fechter and Miss Leclerq, for the benefit of the Holland Fund. We next find him playing *Autolycus*, in the "Winter's Tale," with Lawrence Barrett, at Booth's, in June, 1871. He sang the "Fine Old Gentleman" in his own fine, hearty way at the Matilda Heron Benefit, January 17th, 1872, and was the *Powhatan* in "Ye Gentle Savage," upon the return of Mrs. John Wood to the American stage, at Niblo's Garden, on the 4th of March of the same year. On the 6th of January, 1873, he appeared as *Farmer Grace*, at the Union Square Theatre, in John Brougham's "Atherly Court," and on the 29th of the same month, for the first time, as *Jacques Fauvel*, in "Le Centenaire."

The full cast of this drama we here preserve: —

Union Square Theatre, January 29, 1873, a drama, in five acts, adapted from the French, by Hart Jackson, Esq., and entitled, —

"100 YEARS OLD."

Jacques Fauvel { 100 years old, head of the house of Fauvel & Co. }	Mark Smith.
George Fauvel, his grandson	Welsh Edwards.
Martineau, a very rich poor man	F. F. Mackaye.
Rene d'Alby	Claude Burroughs.
Max de Maugars	George Parkes.
Bernard, a legal physician	H. Montgomery.
Camille, great grand-daughter of Jacques . . .	Clara Jennings.
Juliette, her married sister	Mary Griswold.
Madame Larocque	Imogene Fowler.

The piece ran for six weeks to full houses, and the character of the centenarian was generally considered to be one of Mr. Smith's best. He purchased the sole right to play it, went on a starring tour through the country, and, wherever he presented it, won high praise from press and public for his charming and touching rendering of the part.

Mr. Smith was to have played *Henry VIII.*, in Shakespeare's play of that name, to the *Queen Katherine* of Miss Cushman, at Booth's Theatre, in the fall of 1874; but, alas! instead of the bluff *King Hal*, a part in which we are sure he would have excelled, and which his *personelle* and hearty manner would so perfectly have enabled him to fill, he came back to us like the *Wolsey* in the play, only to lay his weary bones among us. The little earth we gave him was for love, not charity, and was heaped high with the laurels he had won. Like *Wolsey*, too, he gave his honors to the world again, his better part to heaven. May he sleep in peace!

Mr. Smith went to Europe early in the spring of 1874, to witness the *début* of his daughter. He seems to have failed rapidly in health after leaving home, although apparently well when he quitted our shores. Those who knew him well, and remember him as they saw him last in this city, only a few short months before his death, can form no idea of the great changes that had taken place in his appearance during that time. In person he was much emaciated, and the despondency from which he could not rouse himself, so unlike the genial, sunny character of the man, was the cause of more uneasiness to his friends than the physical illness from which he was suffering.

Although he did not speak of death, but often of what was before him professionally in the future, he seemed to feel that he was going into the valley of the shadow, and that the present parting from his wife and children was to be the last on earth. Always the most affectionate of men in his family, and the most demonstrative in his affection, he hardly dared trust himself to speak or to look his farewell that dismal afternoon when he left Milan to return to America. He drove from the door with the expression of a broken-hearted man, and with a deeper sigh than the jovial Mark Smith was ever known to have breathed before. His friends did not hear from him again until they learned that he lay dying in Paris. Falling speechless as he stepped from the railway station at the Lyons dépôt there, he was taken to the nearest hospital, that of St. Antoine, and information sent to the only address found upon his person, that of Mr. Chippendale, of the London Haymarket. Mr. Chippendale, unhappily, was filling at that time a professional engagement in Liverpool, and before the dispatch reached him, and he could in his turn send its contents to Italy, all was over. Mrs. Smith and the children did not reach Paris until he had breathed his last.

He died on the 11th of August, 1874. His remains were brought to this country in October, and on the 11th of that month funeral services, very largely attended, were held by Dr. Houghton at his Church of the Transfiguration on Twenty-ninth Street. He was buried by his father's side in the family plot in the Cemetery of St. Louis.

On the 11th of September a memorial meeting of Mr. Smith's many friends was held at Booth's Theatre, when resolutions were read, kindly and sorrowing words were spoken, and preparation made for benefit performances in aid of his family, which were given on the 8th of October, 1874, at Booth's and Wallack's theatres.

At Booth's Theatre, on this occasion, Miss Violetta Colville made her American *début;* Mr. J. L. Toole appeared in a specialty of his called "Off the Line;" and Mr. John T. Raymond, in "The Gilded Age" (one act), played his then popular, but comparatively new part of *Colonel Sellers.* At Wallack's, Mr. H. J. Montague played one act of "Partners for Life;" Mr. and Mrs. Barney Williams presented their "Customs of the Country;" Mr. Harry Beckett sang a song; and Mr. Daniel Bryant and his colored troupe performed the "Deluge."

The entertainments were largely attended, and were a pecuniary success, as indeed should have been any effort for the benefit of Mark Smith or his family. No man was ever more ready to respond to such a call than was Mark Smith himself; no man in his walk of life has done more for the benefit and assistance of other people; and no man, in any walk of life, ever bore more nobly, and with less abuse, the grand old name of Gentleman!

"CURTAIN!"

INDEX.

PERSONAL.

A.

B.

F.

G.

H.

T.

V.

W.

PLAYS.

E.

F.

G.

H.

I.

J.

K.

L.

M.

Y.

PLAY HOUSES.

www.ingramcontent.com/pod-product-compliance
Lightning Source LLC
LaVergne TN
LVHW010226110826
845151LV00004B/1203

9781425526092